D1554041

Marine Life

From Tropical Fish to Mighty Sharks

Marine Life

From Tropical Fish to Mighty Sharks

Michael Wright and Giles Sparrow

Reprinted 2020, 2022

Revised edition published in 2016

Copyright © 2003 Amber Books Ltd.

First published in 2003

All rights reserved. This publication may not be reproduced, stored in a retrieval system or transmitted in any form or by any means, electronic, mechanical, photocopying, recording or otherwise, without the prior permission of the Publishers.

Amber Books Ltd
United House
North Road
London N7 9DP
United Kingdom
www.amberbooks.co.uk
Instagram: amberbooksltd
Facebook: amberbooks
Twitter: @amberbooks

ISBN: 978-1-78274-445-0

Project Editor: James Bennett
Design: Neil Rigby at Stylus Design

Printed in China

PICTURE CREDITS:
David Shale/Naturepl.com: 7
Topham: 13

Artwork Credits:
All artwork © Istituto Geografico De Agostini, Novara SPA except the following:
Mike Langman: 9, 10, 11, 12, 16, 17, 18, 20, 26, 27, 28, 29, 30, 31, 32, 33, 101, 111, 121, 130, 136, 137, 143, 148, 149, 150, 151, 162, 172, 205.
Marshall Editions: 173, 174, 175, 193, 196, 201, 202, 203, 204, 206, 207, 212, 214, 216, 224, 225, 227, 228, 235, 239, 245, 246, 254, 269, 279, 280, 281, 283, 285, 298, 299, 300, 301, 302, 303, 304, 305, 306, 307, 308, 309, 310, 311

CONTENTS

Introduction

The world beneath the sea's surface is fascinating in its variety, but the difficulty of directly observing it without special skills or equipment means that most aspects of marine life remain hidden to most people. And even marine biologists have an enormous amount still to discover; the underwater world is without doubt the natural world's 'final frontier'. This book takes you under the waves and introduces you to the vast range of marine animals that live there. It visits the brilliant, jewel-like life of the tropical coral reef, teeming with fish and other organisms; it visits the eternal gloom of the deepest oceans, where bizarre creatures never see any light except perhaps the eerie glow produced by luminescent organs on their own or their fellow creatures' bodies; and it visits every part of the marine world in between, from the tropics to the poles.

It is, of course, impossible in a book of this size – or even in a much bigger one – to cover every known type of fish, crustacean, mollusc and the myriad other types of marine animal that are known to exist. They number many, many thousands – with undoubtedly many more thousands still to be discovered. (Remember that the seas make up about 70 per cent of the Earth's surface.) So we have selected 300 representatives that illustrate the great diversity and geographical range of marine life on our planet. They include examples from every type of marine habitat and, as explained below, examples of virtually every important major division of the animal kingdom.

They are not always the most familiar types. For one thing, what is familiar in one part of the world – a particular fish on sale in the market, for example – may never be seen in another (although even marine produce is today traded internationally). But this helps to emphasize the great diversity of life in the seas. They include examples of the smallest microscopic animals and of the biggest ones that have probably ever existed on Earth. They include favourite food items and deadly poisonous, venomous or aggressively predatory types. They include brilliantly coloured creatures that are favourite aquarium species and ones so ugly that fishmongers need to cut them into ready-to-cook fillets so that customers are not repelled! (One quick note about what this book does *not* cover: it excludes marine plants, birds, and creatures that live only in fresh water – inland rivers and lakes – although it does include a number that inhabit both fresh and salt water, either exclusively or at different stages of their life.)

The book is organized in approximate order of evolutionary complexity (*see below*), from the simplest to the most highly evolved organisms. Each main species (distinct kind of creature) covered is illustrated in colour, while the 'data' panel at the foot of each page summarizes the important facts about that species in a standard format. The general text in between focuses on various special aspects of the species or its life – and in some cases that of related species or the group as a whole to which it belongs – for every marine creature is unique and fascinating in its own special way. We very much hope you enjoy finding out about them.

Above: Many bizarre and fierce-looking fish species live in the ocean depths, but despite its fearsome appearance this fangtooth (Anoplogaster cornuta) *is only 15cm (6in) long. It is found worldwide down to about 5000m (16,500ft), and eats mainly small crustaceans and fish.*

THE MOST PRIMITIVE ANIMALS

It is not surprising that the seas contain examples of almost all of the major life forms that exist on Earth, since scientists believe that life itself first arose in the primaeval ocean thousands of millions of years ago, and a major part of its evolution took place there. Even in many of those groups – such as the reptiles and mammals – that evolved after life emerged onto dry land, some types returned to make the seas their home. As a result, today's seas contain direct descendants illustrating most of the stages in life's evolutionary history. The major exceptions are the insects and amphibians. Insect species make up three-quarters of the animal kingdom, with an estimated 2 million species. Of these, some 30,000 live in water at some stage of their life history, yet only around 300 normally come into contact with seawater and even fewer are truly marine. Those few live only on the sea surface, not in it. Nor are there any truly marine amphibians – sea-frogs or sea-toads – for these would lose water from their bodies into the salty seawater through their porous skin, and could not survive.

The first and simplest animals to evolve were the single-celled protozoans, and present-day marine examples include the beautiful radiolarians and the chalky-shelled foraminiferans (*see pp.14–15*). These make up a large part of the zooplankton – the tiny floating animals that form part of the bottom-most link in the marine food-chain. Not a great deal more complex, zoologically speaking, are the sponges (*see pp.16–17*). They have a non-living skeleton made of horny, chalky or glassy material within which the jelly-like living part of the sponge is found. This consists of many cells, but they are only loosely organised and do not have specialized functions; if a sponge is broken into parts, the separate sections can continue to live without permanent disruption.

The next stage of complexity is shown by the jellyfishes, anemones, corals and their relatives – the group known as cnidarians (*see pp.18–27*) – and the rather similar but distinct ctenophores (*see pp.28–29*), which include the comb jellies. In these creatures, different types of cells have specialized functions – stinging, movement, digestion and so on. In some cases such as the Portuguese man o'war (*see p.18*) separate types of polyps – in effect, separate individual creatures – have separate functions and work in cooperation with each other.

To most people, a worm is simply a worm, but in fact worms differ greatly in their level of complexity. Marine worms include examples ranging from the primitive flatworms (*see pp.30–31*) to the much more highly evolved segmented or annelid worms (*see pp.110–119*). Strange forms include the spoon worms (*see p.120*) and the deep-ocean rift worm (*see p.121*), which lives in extremely hot water at the edge of ocean-floor hot vents several thousand metres (more than a mile) below the surface.

ANIMALS WITH SHELLS

The most familiar marine invertebrates (animals without a backbone) belong to two major groups: the molluscs (*see pp.34–109*) and the crustaceans (*see pp.122–149*). Both generally have shells of one kind or another – although in some molluscs it is reduced to a small internal stiffening body called the pen (in the case of squids and cuttlefish) or is absent altogether (in the case of octopuses and some other species). In other molluscs the shell is very obvious, and hardly any of the soft, living part of the animal is ever seen – although, in the case of mussels, oysters, clams and their like, it is of course the part that is eaten. Oysters and mussels are examples of so-called bivalve molluscs; they have two hinged 'valves' or shells which can be held tightly closed when the creature is threatened or when it is uncovered by the falling tide.

MAIN EXTERNAL PARTS OF A SQUID

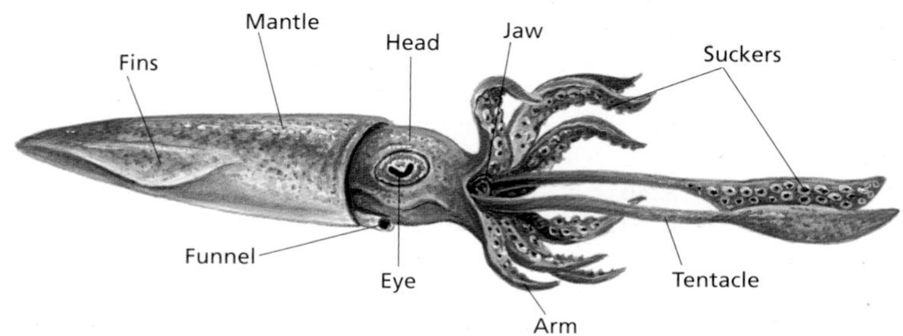

The shells of crustaceans – which include shrimps, lobsters and crabs – are jointed in a much more complex way than those of bivalve molluscs. The main part of their body is made of many jointed segments, while their legs – five walking legs on each side in the major group that includes lobsters and crabs – have seven segments each. In many species, the first pair of legs have large pincers that are used for fighting and capturing food; the other legs also end in much smaller pincers. Crustaceans have complex sensory organs, including compound eyes made up of as many as 10,000 individual elements, touch-sensitive palps and antennae, and bristles on the antennae and mouth parts that detect tastes or smells.

MAIN EXTERNAL PARTS OF A LOBSTER

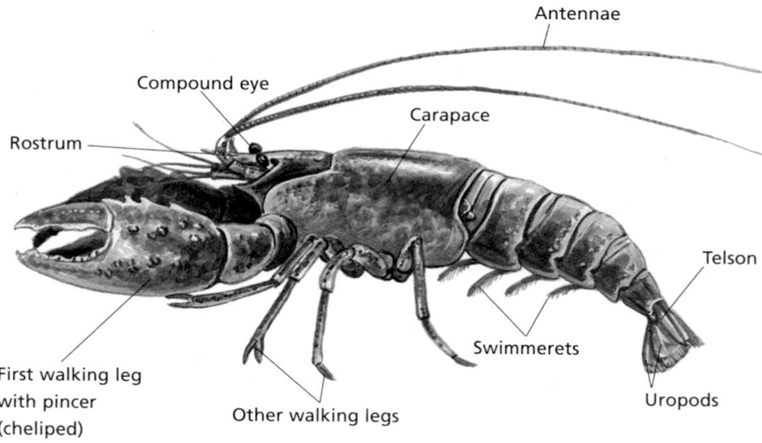

Not every sea creature that looks like a crustacean is one, however. The horseshoe crabs (*see p.150*) belong to a group known as chelicerates, which also includes the arachnids (scorpions and spiders). Most of the latter live on land, but there are also marine spiders, including some remarkably large specimens that live in the ocean depths (*see p.151*). The final major group of marine invertebrates is the echinoderms, whose name means 'spiny-skins' (*see pp.152–171*). They do not have a true shell, but have a spiny skeleton just below the skin; they include such well-known marine creatures as sea urchins and starfish.

FISHES AND OTHER VERTEBRATES

The peak of animal evolution is represented by creatures that have a backbone – the vertebrates, which in the sea include fishes (*see pp.173–277*), reptiles (see *pp.278–283*) and mammals (*see pp.284–313*). Vertebrates in fact form the great majority of a larger group called chordates; non-vertebrate chordates include the sea squirts (*see p.172*), whose life history gives an insight into how vertebrates evolved.

Of all the vertebrates, it is of course the fishes that are most completely adapted to a marine environment – 'of course' because they first evolved there several hundred million years ago, and because they are virtually confined to the water. (There are a few fishes that can also breathe air, such as the mudskippers [*see p.264*].) In fact, however, the bony fishes that are now the dominant group first evolved in fresh water and later returned to the sea, where at the time fishes with a skeleton of cartilage (like today's sharks and rays) were far more numerous. Fishes have evolved into an enormous variety of distinct forms – some 24,000 known species in fresh and salt water, far more than of any other vertebrate group – and they fill by far the biggest single section of this book.

MAIN EXTERNAL PARTS OF A FISH

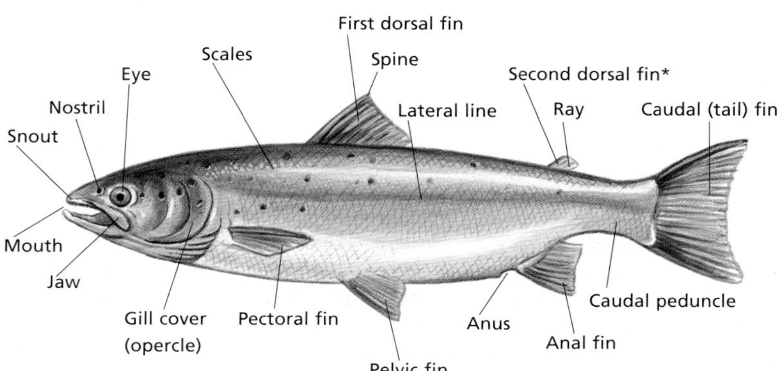

(*Many fish have only one dorsal fin)

In order to understand and explain the relationships between individual species of fishes (and of other creatures), ichthyologists (biologists who specialize in fishes) have organized them into various groupings. The basic category, already mentioned, is the *species*, which in some cases is subdivided into *subspecies* which show minor variations and often inhabit a certain part of the species's overall geographical range. A group of closely related species form a *genus* (plural *genera*), although sometimes a genus contains only one species. In the scientific (Latin) name, the genus name comes first, followed by the species name. For example, in the case of the cod, *Gadus morrhua*, *Gadus* is the genus name and *morrhua* the species name; you need to give both to be precise about which fish you are referring to. When an article refers to two or more species of the same genus, the genus name is abbreviated after the first mention.

MAIN INTERNAL PARTS OF A FISH

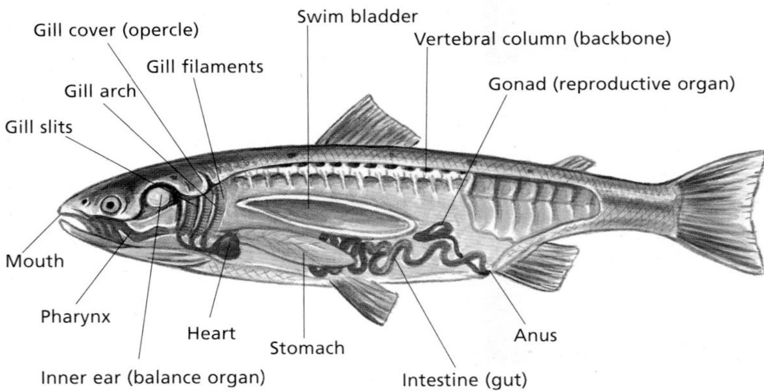

There are also bigger classifications. One, two or more genera may be grouped together as a *family*, whose name usually ends in '...idae'; for example, Gadidae is the cod family, which includes haddock, pollack and other related fishes. A number of families are grouped to form an *order*, whose name ends in '...iformes'. Sometimes, orders are split into suborders, and families into subfamilies. The classification of each species is given in the 'data' panel at the foot of the page. The even larger groupings – such as Osteichthyes (bony fishes) and Chondrichthyes (cartilaginous fishes) – appear as 'signposts' at the very top of each page, above the common (ordinary English) name of the creature.

Above: Coral reefs are among the richest environments on Earth in terms of numbers of individuals and species. Many of the fish species found there are brightly coloured and defend small territories, but reefs are under threat from global warming, from alien species such as the crown-of-thorns starfish (Acanthaster planci; see p.167), *and from illegal fishing with dynamite or cyanide.*

Foraminiferans

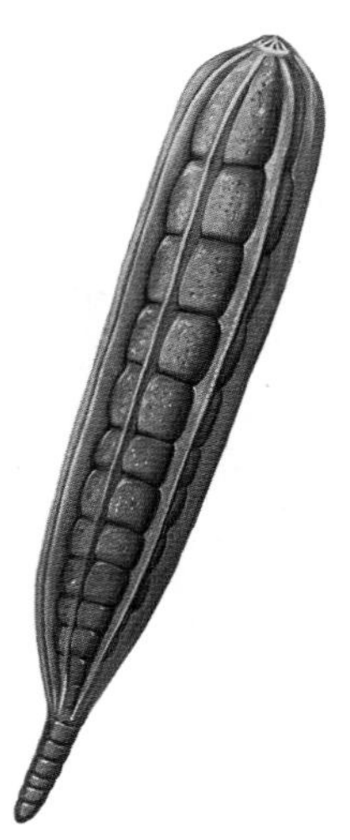

The simplest animals living in the sea are the protozoa – single-celled and usually microscopic animals that are nevertheless capable of feeding and reproducing. The most widespread of all protozoans are foraminiferans, which have developed a calcium-rich shell around their bodies. These tiny creatures feed with finger-like appendages called pseudopods (false feet) that emerge through pores in the shell, capturing bacteria, algae, and smaller protozoa. Mud made of foraminiferan bodies forms around one third of the global sea floor. When compressed over millions of years, these crushed foraminiferan shells can form limestone and chalk.

Scientific name	*Nodosaria raphanus*
Classification	Kingdom Protista; Phylum Sarcodina;
	Order Foraminifera; Class Rotaliina
Size	Microscopic
Distribution	Global
Habitat	Seafloor
Diet	Bacteria; algae; protozoa
Reproduction	Binary fission – one individual splits to produce two

Radiolarians

Radiolarians are related to foraminiferans, but have far more elaborate and complex glassy skeletons. These skeletons, called tests, are made of silicate minerals the radiolarian extracts from seawater, and are often spherically symmetrical. Radiolarians frequently live in symbiosis (a mutually beneficial relationship) with algae. The radiolarian produces waste that feeds the algae, while the algae provide oxygen and food for the radiolarian. These strange creatures mostly float free in the sea, migrating through the water column daily, though no one is sure how or why they do this.

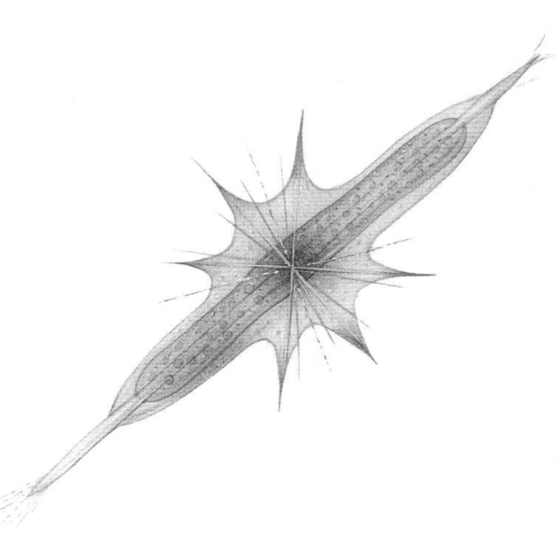

Scientific name	*Amphilonche elongata*
Classification	Kingdom Protista; Phylum Sarcodina; Superclass Actinopoda;
	Class Radiolaria; Order Entolithia; Family Acanthometrida
Size	Up to several millimetres (⅛–¼ inch)
Distribution	Global
Habitat	Free-floating
Diet	Algae; protozoa; copepods
Reproduction	Binary fission – one individual splits to produce two

Venus's flower-basket

Sponges are the simplest multicellular animals – loose collections of specialized cells combined to produce a more efficient feeding mechanism. They range from inconspicuous prickly layers growing on rocks to large, complex and beautiful structures like Venus's flower-basket. This conical 'glass sponge' is made of cells interlinked by six-rayed silicate spikes. Sponges feed by filtering water through large apertures called osculae, and into a network of internal passages, where feeding cells can filter out plankton and other food. Small prawns sometimes live inside Venus's flower-basket, unable to escape, but taking advantage of the regular food supply.

Scientific name	*Euplectella aspergillum*
Classification	Kingdom Metazoa; Phylum Porifera;
	Class Hexactinellida (glass sponges); Family Euplectellidae
Size	Up to 1.3m (4¼ft) high
Distribution	Japan; Philippines
Habitat	Deep seas
Diet	Plankton and organic debris
Reproduction	Probably hermaphroditic, distributing sperm on currents

Bath sponge

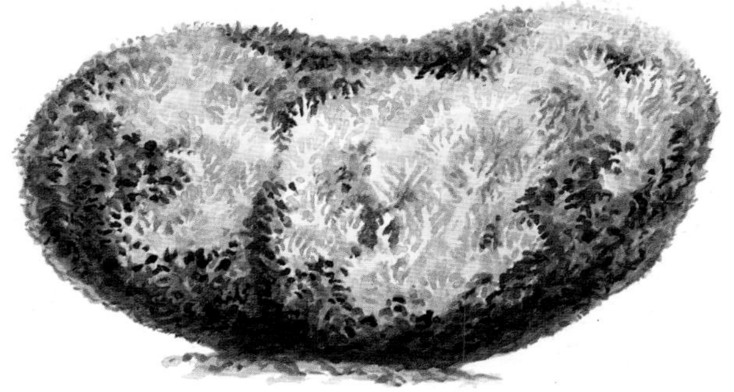

The largest and most widespread class of sponges are the horny sponges or demospongiae. They mostly build silica skeletons, but these lack the six-rayed symmetry of the glass sponges. Some, including the bath sponge, have frameworks built of spongin, a tough protein similar to those found in muscle tendons. Horny sponges include many encrusting sponges, but also larger, brightly coloured species. They often provide shelter for fish and other small sea creatures, but only a few animals will eat them, due to the arsenal of different toxins they have developed to defend themselves.

Scientific name	*Spongia officinalis*
Classification	Kingdom Metazoa; Phylum Porifera;
	Class Demospongiae (horny sponges)
Size	Up to 50cm (20in)
Distribution	Global
Habitat	Temperate and tropical waters
Diet	Plankton and organic matter
Reproduction	Can reproduce sexually or asexually depending on conditions

Portuguese man o'war

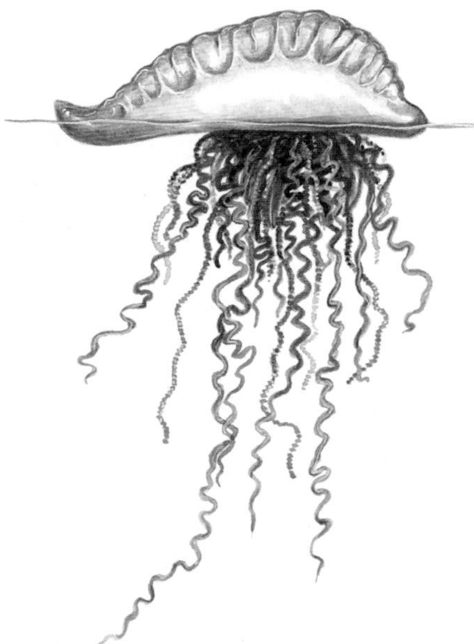

The Portuguese man o'war has a fearsome reputation as one of the most deadly creatures in the sea, though in fact its stings are rarely fatal to humans. Although it looks like a jellyfish, this strange creature is a colony of polyps closely working together. One of the polyps forms a large gas bladder that allows the colony to rise and sink in the waters. Others are specialized feeding cells, and stingers called nematocysts, forming long tendrils that spread out over a large area of water, stinging small fish that stray too close. This does not, however, prevent the small blue man o'war fish living among the tentacles for protection, or protect the man o'war from the sea turtles which like to eat it.

Scientific name	*Physalia physalis*
Classification	Phylum Cnidaria; Class Hydrozoa;
	Order Siphonophora; Family Physaliidae
Size	Tendrils stretch up to 20m (66ft) in all directions
Distribution	Worldwide in tropical and temperate waters
Habitat	Ocean surface and shallow waters
Diet	Small fish
Reproduction	Reproduces by 'budding' a group of cells to form a new colony

Purple jellyfish

Jellyfish are relatively simple animals with bodies that are more than 97 per cent water. They have no central nervous system and only rudimentary senses, but are nevertheless efficient hunters. The bell-like body of a jellyfish contains a substance called mesoglea, and it has a simple mouth on its underside, surrounded by 'arms' to grasp prey and trailing stingers to stun, paralyse, or even kill it outright. The purple jelly or purple stinger has a relatively small collection of tentacles, but makes up for it with stinging cells covering the surface of its bell. It sometimes glows at night, perhaps due to eating bioluminescent prey.

Scientific name	*Pelagia noctiluca*
Classification	Phylum Cnidaria; Class Scyphozoa;
	Order Semaeostomeae; Family Pelagiidae
Size	Bell up to 20cm (8in)
Distribution	Mediterranean and worldwide
Habitat	Warm temperate waters
Diet	Small fish; plankton
Reproduction	Adult jellyfish spawns polyps sexually, but polyps can split asexually

Sea wasp or Box jellyfish

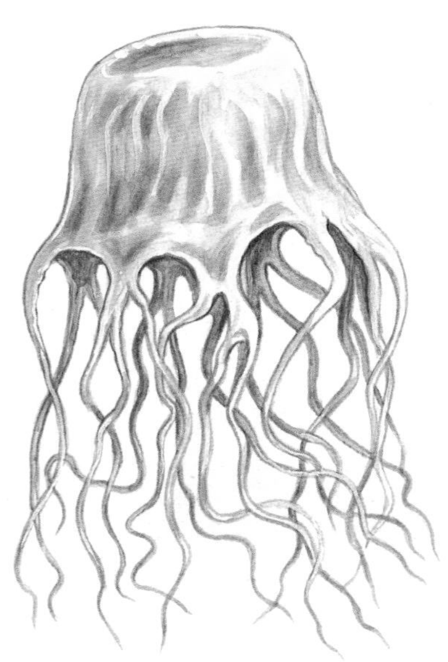

Infamous in Australian waters for their painful sting, box jellyfish have a unique shape that sets them apart from their relatives – their body is box-shaped, with tentacles spreading out from the corners. This feature may help to improve their swimming strength – unlike scyphozoans, which can only drift where the water takes them, cubozoans are strong swimmers. They also have unusually good eyesight for jellyfish, and pack some of the most vicious stings in the animal kingdom. All jellyfish have an unusual life-cycle. They mate with each other sexually to produce young called planulae. The planulae then settle on the sea bed and develop into polyps, which can in turn bud off new, free-swimming medusae.

Scientific name	*Chironex fleckeri*
Classification	Phylum Cnidaria; Class Cubozoa;
	Order Cubomedusae; Family Chirodropidae
Size	Body up to 20cm (8in), tentacles up to 3m (10ft)
Distribution	Australia; Indian Ocean
Habitat	Shallow coastal waters
Diet	Small fish, worms, and crustaceans
Reproduction	Sexual and asexual

Gem anemone

Sea anemones are cnidarians that have developed a generally stationary lifestyle – they attach themselves to rocks and use stinging tentacles to grab prey that passes too close, as well as waving to create currents that bring food to them. An anemone's body is called a polyp, and resembles the polyp form of a jellyfish. A muscular 'foot' on the base of the body, called the pedal disc, attaches to a suitable surface, and some anemones can even use this to move around, snail-fashion. Others relocate by simply inflating themselves and letting currents carry them to a new site.

Scientific name	*Bunodactis verrucosa*
Classification	Phylum Cnidaria; Class Anthozoap; Subclass Hexacorallia;
	Order Actinaria; Suborder Nyantheae; Family Actiniidae
Size	Up to 25cm (10in)
Distribution	Eastern Atlantic
Habitat	Rocky, battered coastlines
Diet	Small mussels
Reproduction	Apparently asexual, budding live young

Burrowing anemone

The tube or burrowing anemones are unusual because they create a hard tubular body case from sand particles mixed with their own mucus, and burrow backwards into soft sand and muddy sea floors. This means they look very like normal or 'true' anemones at first glance, but can have a hidden body up to a metre (40in) or more long. Normally, they lie on the sea floor with their tentacles outstretched, feeding on plankton and other small invertebrates. Many of the species have tentacles that are fluorescent, absorbing ultraviolet light and releasing it at visible wavelengths. The anemone can retreat into its tube if danger threatens.

Scientific name	*Cerianthus filiformis*
Classification	Phylum Cnidaria; Class Anthozoa; Subclass Hexacorallia;
	Order Ceriantharia; Suborder Spirularia; Family Cerianthidae
Size	Up to 25cm (10in) across
Distribution	Coasts of Japan
Habitat	Sand and mud on sea floor
Diet	Plankton; organic matter
Reproduction	Sexual and asexual

Sea fan

Despite their plant-like appearance, sea fans are in fact a form of soft coral or gorgonian (so-called because of their branching, snake-like appearance, similar to the hair of the gorgons in Greek myth). They are colonial animals made up of hundreds or even thousands of anemone-like creatures. These 'polyps' grow a broad, flat, semirigid skeleton from protein. Individual animals line the close-woven branches, with their tentacles spread out to catch passing plankton. Because they are filter-feeders, sea fans always keep their broad 'leaves' facing into the current. *Eunicella cavolinii* is the most common species in Mediterranean waters, found on steep rocky slopes.

Scientific name	*Eunicella cavolinii*
Classification	Phylum Cnidaria; Class Anthozoa; Subclass Octocorallia;
	Order Alcyonacea; Family Gorgoniidae
Size	20–50cm (8–20in)
Distribution	Mediterranean and North Atlantic
Habitat	Steep rock shelves at moderate depths
Diet	Plankton
Reproduction	Eggs and sperm released from colonies fertilize in open water

Sea pen

Named because of their resemblance to old-fashioned feather quill pens, sea pens are colonial animals made from a large number of polyps working together. One large 'axial polyp,' called the rachis, buries itself deep into the seabed, while other secondary or lateral polyps form chains growing out from the axis to either side. The secondary polyps are specialized to pump water through the sea pen's arms, and to capture food. In the case of the deep-red *Pennatula phosphorea*, the polyps form large triangular 'leaves.' This is one of several seapens known to bioluminesce, emitting brilliant flashes and pulses of light passing in waves through the colony – though no one understands why.

Scientific name	*Pennatula phosphorea*
Classification	Phylum Cnidaria; Class Anthozoa; Subclass Octocorallia;
	Order Pennatulacea; Family Pennatulidae
Size	Up to 40cm (16in) long (25cm [10in] visible)
Distribution	North Atlantic; North Sea; Mediterranean
Habitat	Sandy and muddy sea floors of moderate depth
Diet	Plankton and organic matter
Reproduction	Colonies of a single sex release eggs or sperm into water

Devonshire cup coral

Hard corals are similar to anemones, sea fans and sea pens in their basic form, but different because they all secrete a hard shell of limestone called a corallum around their bodies for protection. Also, nearly all species are colonial, forming vast undersea reefs that are some of the world's richest marine habitats. The Devonshire cup coral is one of the few non-colonial corals, found on rocky coasts around western Europe. It is found in a wide variety of colours, and has a large number of tentacles to capture food and transfer it to the mouth. Although not considered colonial, cup corals do sometimes grow in clusters on suitable surfaces.

Scientific name	*Caryophyllia smithii*
Classification	Phylum Cnidaria; Class Anthozoa; Subclass Hexacorallia;
	Order Madreporaria; Family Dendrophilliidae
Size	Up to 25mm (1in)
Distribution	North Atlantic; North Sea; Mediterranean
Habitat	Rocky coasts down to 100m (330ft)
Diet	Plankton; organic matter
Reproduction	Sexual – males release sperm; eggs develop inside females

Brain coral

Brain corals are so-called because of the lumps and folds that bear a startling resemblance to a human brain. Being among the bulkiest and most solid corals, they can survive storms that damage and even destroy their delicate neighbours. Typically brain corals live on plankton, and nutrients from the algae that grows in their folds and grooves. Their structure gives them a large surface area and many passages through which water can flow. In fact brain corals are not a taxonomic group – the name is given to a wide variety of similar-looking creatures that are not necessarily close relations, of which *Oulophyllia*, illustrated here, is one.

Scientific name	*Oulophyllia* species
Classification	Phylum Cnidaria; Class Anthozoa; Subclass Hexacorallia;
	Order Madreporaria; Family Faviidae
Size	Up to 1m (40in) across, weighing over a tonne
Distribution	Pacific Ocean
Habitat	Coral reefs
Diet	Algal nutrients and plankton
Reproduction	Sexual – sperm and eggs fertilize in open water

Staghorn coral

While brain corals survive in coral reefs by sheer bulk, staghorn corals hold on to their environmental niche by rapid growth – although the price for this is that they are fragile and easily damaged. They may grow at a relatively breakneck speed of 10cm (4in) per year in the race to grab the best niches and collect as much sunlight as possible from above. Staghorn is used as a general name for corals of the *Acropora* genus, but not all the species have the forked appearance of antlers. Some grow to look more like bushes, while others develop flat tops that act as platforms to collect light for the symbiotic algae growing on them. They can also develop many different bright colours.

Scientific name	*Acropora* species
Classification	Phylum Cnidaria; Class Anthozoa; Subclass Hexacorallia;
	Order Madreporaria; Family Acroporidae
Size	Up to 2m (6½ft) tall
Distribution	Global
Habitat	Coral reefs
Diet	Algal nutrients and plankton
Reproduction	Sexual – sperm and eggs fertilize in open water

Sea gooseberry

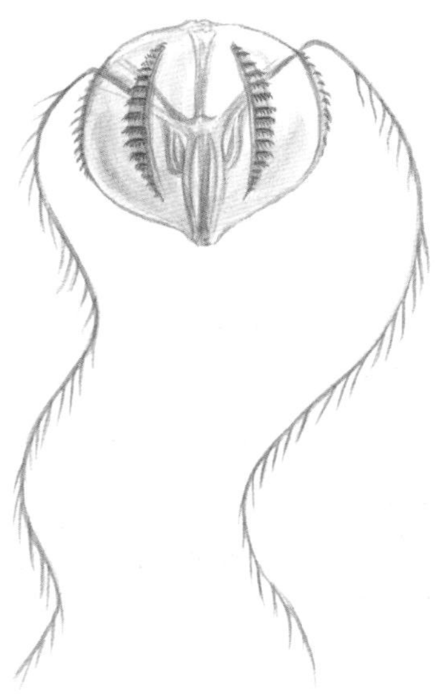

Looking superficially like a jellyfish, the sea gooseberry is in fact an animal from a completely different phylum – a comb jelly. The similarities are thought to be the result of similar adaptations to a floating lifestyle, but comb jellies lack the stinging nematocysts of jellyfish – instead they capture their food using specialized sticky cells called colloblasts. The comb jellies get their name from the eight rows of 'combs' along the sides of their bodies. In fact, these combs are fused plates called cilia which the jelly paddles back and forth to propel itself. Most comb jellies share the sea gooseberry's pair of long tentacles, which retract rapidly when stimulated.

Scientific name	*Pleurobrachia pileus*
Classification	Phylum Ctenophora; Class Tentaculata;
	Order Cydippida; Family Pleurobrachiidae
Size	Body up to 25mm (1in) across, tentacles up to 60cm (24in) long
Distribution	Atlantic Ocean; Mediterranean
Habitat	Open waters of varying depth
Diet	Plankton and organic matter
Reproduction	Animals are hermaphroditic, but release sperm and eggs into water

Venus's girdle

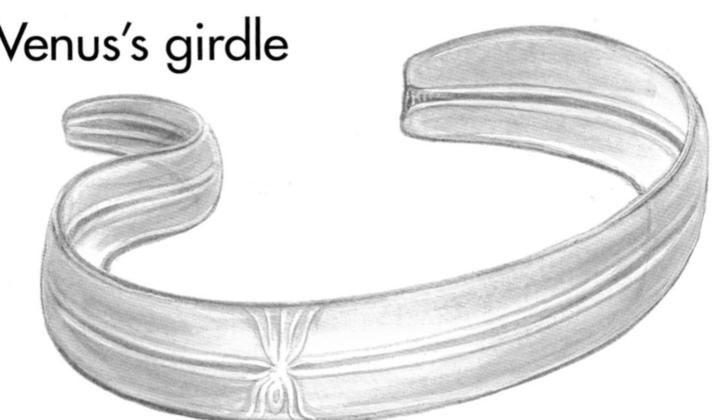

Although most comb jellies resemble the sea gooseberry, a couple of genera are startlingly different, with a long belt-like shape. The most beautiful of these is Venus's girdle, found around the world in tropical waters, and growing to 1m (40in) or more in length. In these animals the combs or cilia run along the edges of the body, allowing the animal to ripple through the water. Nearly all free-swimming comb jellies belong to the class Tentaculata – though in Venus's girdle the tentacles are not so obvious as in others. A second class of comb jellies, the Nuda, have no tentacles and generally dwell on the sea floor.

Scientific name	*Cestum veneris*
Classification	Phylum Ctenophora; Class Tentaculata;
	Order Cestida; Family Cestidae
Size	Up to 1m (40in) long
Distribution	Worldwide in tropical waters
Habitat	Open waters of varying depth
Diet	Plankton and organic matter
Reproduction	Hermaphroditic but gametes are released in water to mix with others

Polyclad flatworm

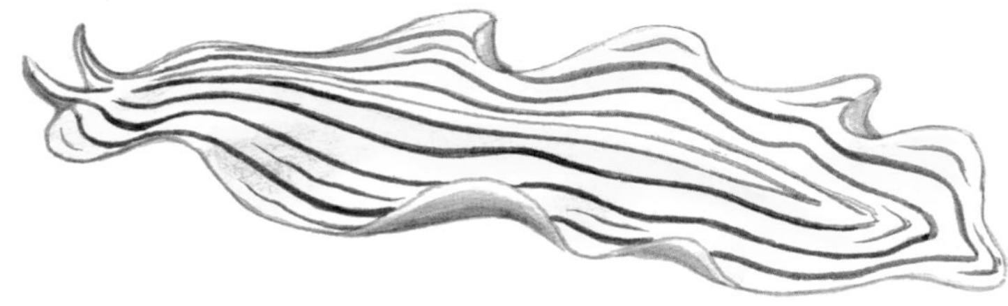

Flatworms are a simple type of worm with thin solid bodies and only a gut running down their centres. They have no blood and no lungs – instead they absorb oxygen directly from the waters around them through their paper-thin bodies. Many flatworms are parasitic, but turbellarians are mostly free-swimming predators. Many have brightly patterned skins and they move either by rippling through the water or by crawling like a land-based worm. Flatworms have a primitive head around which their sensory organs such as simple eyes and pseudotentacles (made from folds of the body wall) are clustered.

Scientific name	*Prostheceraeus vittatus*
Classification	Phylum Platyhelminthes; Class Turbellaria;
	Order Polycladida; Family Eryeptidae
Size	Up to 50mm (2in) long
Distribution	North Atlantic; North Sea
Habitat	Coastlines, generally below rocks
Diet	Plankton; smaller invertebrates
Reproduction	Hermaphrodites; also capable of asexual reproduction

Ribbon worm

Up to 1,200 species of ribbon worms exist worldwide, and they form a unique phylum of the animal kingdom. Most are marine, and many have extremely long bodies – the group includes the world's longest animals, which can grow up to 55m (180ft) long. Although they are often brightly coloured with rings around their bodies, they are actually unsegmented. Ribbon worms are predators, often living wrapped around corals and other undersea outcrops. They hunt with a unique proboscis, a long tube pushed out from the mouth by hydraulic pressure, frequently equipped with thorn-like barbs that inject poisons into their prey.

Scientific name	*Tubulanus annulatus*
Classification	Phylum Nemertini; Class Anopla;
	Subclass Palaeonemertini; Family Tubulanidae
Size	Up to 0.5m (20in)
Distribution	Eastern North Atlantic; Mediterranean
Habitat	Coral reefs; rock outcrops; pilings
Diet	Small invertebrates
Reproduction	Sexual – worms have one sex only

Sea moss

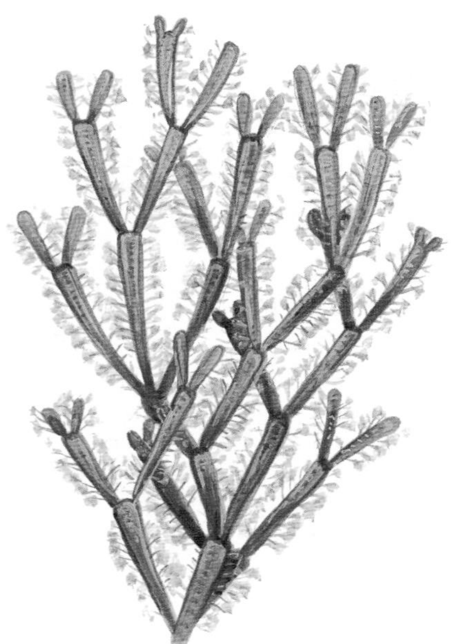

Bryozoans or moss animals look superficially plant-like, but are in fact colonial animals made of thousands of individual members called zooids. The zooids, less than 1mm (1/25in) long, each live inside a cubicle called a zooecium or house, which link together to form a leaf or mat-like structure depending on the species. They extend their tentacles to filter the water that flows around them for microscopic plankton. One species of bryozoan, *Bugula neritina*, produces a chemical called bryostatin that has proved to be a powerful anti-tumour agent, and is now being farmed off the coast of California.

Scientific name	*Bugula neritina*
Classification	Phylum Bryozoa; Class Gymnolaemata;
	Order Cheilostomata; Family Bugulidae
Size	25–50mm (1–2in)
Distribution	Temperate and tropical waters worldwide
Habitat	Sea floor, attached to rocks and other outcrops
Diet	Plankton
Reproduction	Asexual, producing larvae in ovicells on the corners of houses

Lamp shell

Lamp shells or brachiopods are externally similar to clams, living inside a bivalved shell with two halves, but they attach to a stable surface by a stalk called a pedicle (which either sticks to rock or burrows into sand). The animal inside the shell is also different, with small tentacles called lophophores filtering the water and supplying food to the mouth. Similarities to the tentacles of bryozoan zooids show that these two very different-looking groups of creatures are actually related. Brachiopods are very important in the fossil record, where they can help palaeontologists to date rock deposits, but only a few hundred species exist today.

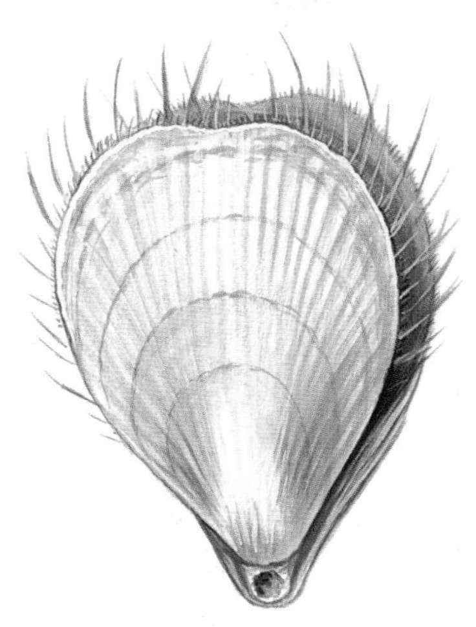

Scientific name	*Terebratulina retusa*
Classification	Phylum Brachiopoda; Class Articulata;
	Order Terebratulida
Size	Around 15mm (⅝in) across
Distribution	North Atlantic cold and temperate waters
Habitat	Sea floor to depths of 1500m (5000ft)
Diet	Plankton
Reproduction	Sexual – individuals of each sex release gametes into water

Abalone

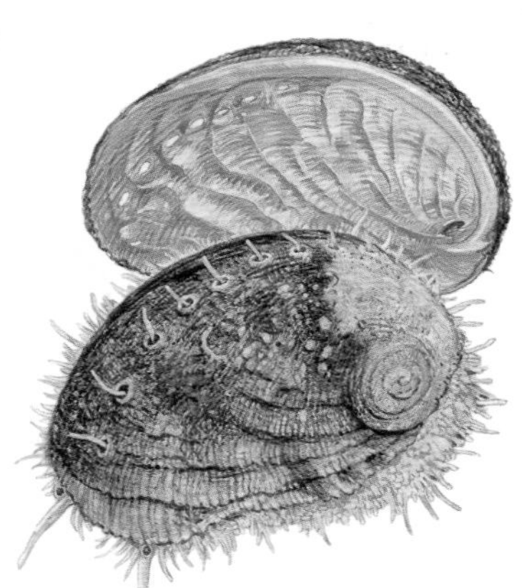

Abalones are snail-like gastropods that graze on the sea bed and are widely farmed both for food and for their decorative shells, the pearly interiors of which are used to make jewellery. They are molluscs, with a muscular foot on the bottom of the body which they use to move around and anchor themselves to rocks. The body is protected by a low, bumpy, and characteristically ear-like shell, with a series of small holes that allows water to reach the internal gill and provides the animal with oxygen. This shell is surrounded by a frilly margin and may be one of many different colours, depending on the individual's diet.

Scientific name	*Haliotis lamellosa*
Classification	Phylum Mollusca; Class Gastropoda;
	Order Archaeogastropoda; Family Haliotidae
Size	Up to 5cm (2in) long
Distribution	Mediterranean
Habitat	Shallow coastal waters with plentiful plants
Diet	Phytoplankton (microscopic plants)
Reproduction	Separate sexes release sperm and eggs into the water

Emperor slit shell

One of the major problems for early gastropods was how to expel waste from the body. The anus is on top of the body between the gills, so either its waste must pass down the sides of the shell past the gills, or down the front, past the mouth. The slit shells were a group of abalone-like gastropods that evolved a unique solution to the problem – a slit-shaped extra opening in the shell, allowing exhaled water from the gills to pass out and carry the waste with it. At first, these primitive gastropods were only known from fossils, but then the first living one was discovered, and today some 16 species are known.

Scientific name	*Perotruchus hirasei*
Classification	Phylum Mollusca; Class Gastropoda;
	Order Archaeogastropoda; Family Pleurotomariidae
Size	Up to 10cm (4in)
Distribution	Japanese coast
Habitat	Deep water
Diet	Phytoplankton (microscopic plants)
Reproduction	Separate sexes release sperm and eggs into the water

Keyhole limpet

Like many marine gastropods, keyhole limpets lead a grazing lifestyle, moving slowly around on the sea floor in shallow waters, in search of algae and organic detritus. Their muscular foot also allows them to anchor to rocks and withstand heavy waves. The distinctive hole in the keyhole limpet's shell is a vent where air passed through the gills, as well as the animal's waste, can be ejected cleanly. When alive, the limpet's internal body casing, called the mantle, spreads out from under the shell's edges to cover most of the shell. The hole in the top of the shell is just a hint that the keyhole limpet is a quite different animal from the true limpet.

Scientific name	*Megathura crenulata*
Classification	Phylum Mollusca; Class Gastropoda;
	Order Archaeogastropoda; Family Fissurellidae
Size	Up to 125mm (5in) long
Distribution	Californian coast
Habitat	Sea floor from intertidal zone to 33m (100ft)
Diet	Algae and tunicates
Reproduction	Separate sexes release sperm and eggs into the water

Painted topshell

Topshells are small, pretty, and widespread gastropods, with very attractive shells. The shells are conical with very straight sides and usually pink or purple patterning, while the exposed lip of the interior is covered in iridescent nacre (mother-of-pearl). A horny valve called the opercula can block the shell's opening if it is left stranded on the shore when the tide goes out. Topshells in general reproduce sexually by releasing eggs and sperm into the water, where they fertilize to form a larval stage. The painted topshell, however, has no larval stage – instead miniature versions of the adults are born directly onto the shore.

Scientific name	*Calliostoma zizyphinum*
Classification	Phylum Mollusca; Class Gastropoda;
	Order Archaeogastropoda; Family Trochidae
Size	Up to 3cm (1in) long
Distribution	Eastern North Atlantic; Mediterranean; North Sea
Habitat	Rocky shorelines from low water to 300m (1000ft) depth
Diet	Algae; organic detritus; corals
Reproduction	Sexual, through free-swimming gametes

Common periwinkle

Periwinkles are grazing gastropods with snail-like shells, often with bright colours. They are widespread on shores around the North Atlantic, and some have gills partly converted to lungs so they can venture far up the beach. Although periwinkles will venture onto sand, they spend most of their time attached to hard rock surfaces, where they can glue themselves down and survive harsh conditions such as the absence of water or even being frozen. In order to reproduce, the male creeps up alongside the female to insert a packet of sperm under her shell, and the female then produces a sac of larvae that develop in the sea.

Scientific name	*Littorina littorea*
Classification	Phylum Mollusca; Class Gastropoda;
	Order Mesogastropoda; Family Littorinidae
Size	Up to 50mm (2in) tall
Distribution	North Atlantic
Habitat	Rocky coasts and shorelines; estuaries
Diet	Algae and organic detritus
Reproduction	Sexual

Architectonica

The genus architectonica contains some of the most attractive of all shelled molluscs, with black, white, yellow, and brown concentric markings. Often these animals are called sundials, for obvious reasons. The conical shell is unusually flattened, and formed from a series of expanding whorls that leaves a large chamber, the umbilicus, open in the centre. The animal can close up this aperture with a button-shaped operculum. Sundial larvae can spend a very long time in their free-swimming 'veliger' stage, allowing them to cross large distances floating among the plankton, and giving them a wide distribution.

Scientific name	*Architectonica perspectiva*
Classification	Phylum Mollusca; Class Gastropoda;
	Order Heterogastropoda; Family Architectonicidae
Size	Up to 50mm (2in) across
Distribution	Indo-Pacific
Habitat	Shallow sandy sea beds
Diet	Small invertebrates
Reproduction	Sexual – larvae have a prolonged free-swimming stage

Turret shell

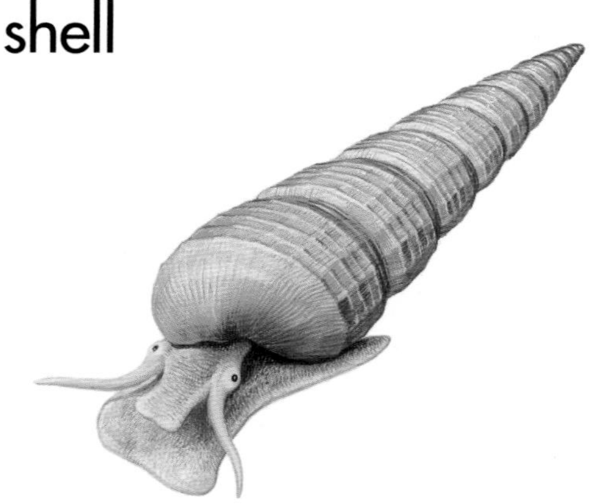

Although they look very different from the more snail-like gastropods, turret shells in fact follow the same basic pattern, simply stretched out into a long conical form. The animal can retreat far inside the shell when threatened, closing the door behind it with a horny flexible operculum that itself withdraws well inside the shell. Turritellidae burrow into the sand in search of organic particles, and they can also consume microscopic food from the water by passing it through their gills. The Turritellidae, also called deep sea augers, look superficially very similar to another group called 'auger shells,' the Terebridae.

Scientific name	*Turritella communis*
Classification	Phylum Mollusca; Class Gastropoda;
	Order Mesogastropoda; Family Turritellidae
Size	Up to 50mm (2in) long
Distribution	Mediterranean
Habitat	Sandy sea beds
Diet	Algae
Reproduction	Sexual – free-swimming sperm released by male are taken in by female

Worm shell

Perhaps the most distorted forms of gastropod shell are found in the worm shells or Vermetidae. These animals begin life with a tightly wound but elongated shell resembling a turret shell, but their conical structure gradually 'unwinds' as the mollusc grows older. In extreme cases, the shell completely loses any resemblance to a normal gastropod, as the animal inside changes the direction in which it builds new chambers. The worm shells also have an unusual method of feeding, using secretions from the muscular foot to produce a web-like mucous filter that is held up by tentacles on the feet to trap small planktonic animals.

Scientific name	*Vermetus* species
Classification	Phylum Mollusca; Class Gastropoda;
	Order Mesogastropoda; Family Vermetidae
Size	Up to 40cm (16in) long
Distribution	Tropical waters
Habitat	Below shoreline, frequently inside sponges
Diet	Plankton
Reproduction	Sexual – male produces free-floating sperm packet

Violet sea snail

One of the most unusual marine gastropods, the violet sea snail floats near the surface of tropical waters. In order to do this, it secretes a 'raft' of mucus from its foot, which traps air bubbles and allows the snail to stay buoyant. In order to reduce its weight, the snail only has a papery shell, and it is also blind. With few natural defences, these sea snails rely on camouflage to protect them from predators – their shells are shaded so they are difficult to see from above or below. However, because it has evolved to be permanently in the water, the snail lacks an operculum to close its shell, and dries out rapidly if washed up on land.

Scientific name	*Janthina janthina*
Classification	Phylum Mollusca; Class Gastropoda;
	Order Mesogastropoda; Family Janthinidae
Size	Up to 2cm (⅘in)
Distribution	Cosmopolitan
Habitat	Ocean surface in tropical waters
Diet	Floating hydrozoan colonies
Reproduction	Sexual

Precious wentletrap

The precious wentletrap gets its unusual name from the Dutch word for a spiral staircase, on account of its complex geometrical shape. Its porcelain-like shell has made it a favourite with shell collectors ever since its discovery in the seventeenth century – at first it was such a rarity that shells frequently sold for small fortunes. Some Chinese craftsmen even constructed fakes from a paste made with rice. Today the habits of the wentletrap are better known – it feeds on anemones, often inserting a proboscis into their bodies and feeding on them for hours at a time – and so it is easily found by fishermen.

Scientific name	*Epitonium scalare*
Classification	Phylum Mollusca; Class Gastropoda;
	Order Heterogastropoda; Family Epitoniidae
Size	5–6cm (2–2½in)
Distribution	Japan; South Pacific
Habitat	Sea floors at 20–50m (65–165ft)
Diet	Anemones
Reproduction	Sexual, by copulation

Pelican's foot shell

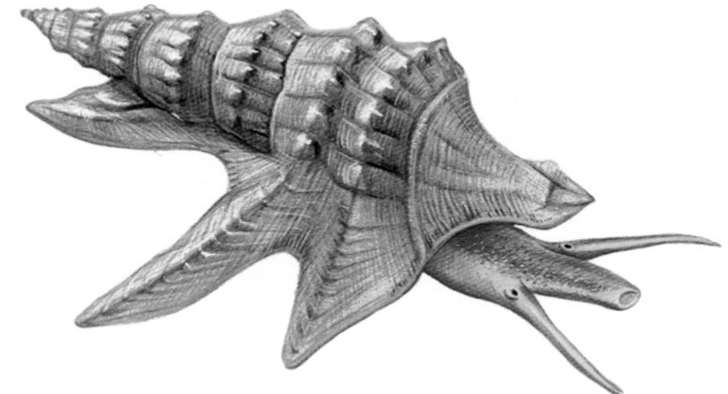

The pelican's foot shell is so-called after the shape formed by the distinctive outer lip of its shell. Only seven species are known from around the world, living at medium depths on the sea floor. The lip only develops in mature adults, and acts as a shield for the animal's head as it crawls around on sandy and muddy sea floors, digging out its prey using a specially strengthened and lengthened operculum (shell door). The muscular foot is also particularly powerful and active, allowing the animal an unusual method of movement – the body rears up off the ground and the heavy shell falls forward, so the mollusc takes 'steps' along the seabed.

Scientific name	*Aporrhais pespelecani*
Classification	Phylum Mollusca; Class Gastropoda;
	Order Caenogastropoda; Family Aporrhaidae
Size	Up to 50mm (2in)
Distribution	North Atlantic and Mediterranean
Habitat	Sandy sea floors down to around 200m (660ft)
Diet	Small invertebrates
Reproduction	Sexual; eggs develop to larvae inside female's shell, then float free

Spider shell

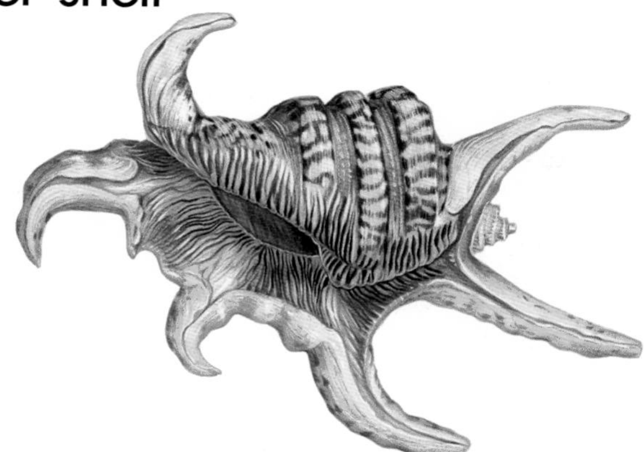

The spider shells are representatives of the strombid family of gastropods, which include conches and tibias. These molluscs all have highly developed eyes on the end of their front tentacles, which emerge through a special notch in the front of the shell. They are active animals, with a unique way of moving, hopping across the seabed by rapidly flipping their operculum (the horny 'doorway' to the shell) open and closed. Spider shells, also sometimes called scorpion shells, have developed their characteristic spines to help anchor them on sandy and muddy sea floors, and as a defence against predators.

Scientific name	*Lambis chiragra*
Classification	Phylum Mollusca; Class Gastropoda;
	Order Mesogastropoda; Family Strombidae
Size	Around 15cm (6in) long
Distribution	Indo-Pacific
Habitat	Sandy sea floors at moderate depths
Diet	Algae and organic debris
Reproduction	Sexual; internal fertilization; eggs laid in long strands

Rooster-tail conch

Conches have some of the most attractive shells found in nature, and have been prized for many centuries across their home territory of the Caribbean. They have been used in art and decoration, as musical instruments, and as food. Unfortunately this means they are overfished and are already a protected species in US waters. The name conch (pronounced 'konk') comes from the Greek for shell, and they have lent it to the entire hobby of shell-collecting: conchology. Conches are sea floor grazers, feeding on algae and organic debris. They live for several years, and during the breeding season lay huge strings of eggs up to 20m (66ft) long.

Scientific name	*Strombus gallus*
Classification	Phylum Mollusca; Class Gastropoda;
	Order Mesogastropoda; Family Strombidae
Size	10–15cm (4–6in)
Distribution	Caribbean
Habitat	Sea floor at moderate depths; coral reefs
Diet	Algae; organic debris
Reproduction	Sexual; female fertilized internally by male

Tibia

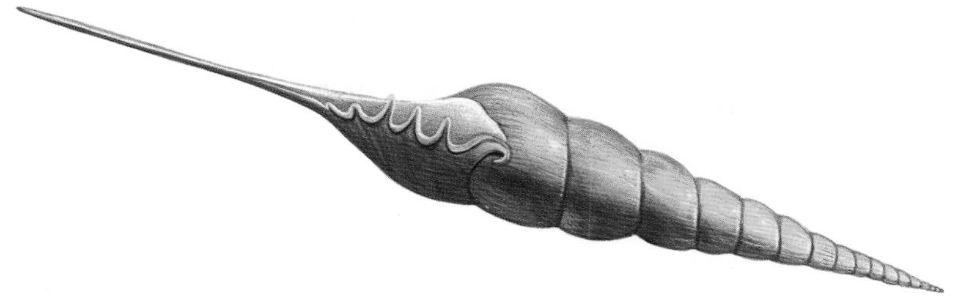

Although they look very different from other strombidae shells, tibias (also known as spindle shells) are members of the same group, and share the unique trait of hopping along with powerful flicks of their operculum. Like all strombids, they also have highly developed eyes – the best of any gastropod. *Tibia fusus*, from the Indo-Pacific, has a particularly long and fragile 'spike' – in fact a channel along which the animal can extend its siphon, the chemical-detecting equivalent of a 'nose'. It has a lustrous brown coloration, and five small 'fingers' along the outer lip of the shell opening.

Scientific name	*Tibia fusus*
Classification	Phylum Mollusca; Class Gastropoda;
	Order Mesogastropoda; Family Strombidae
Size	Up to 30cm (12in) long
Distribution	Indo-Pacific
Habitat	Sandy and muddy sea floors, down to 60m (200ft) depth
Diet	Algae and small invertebrates
Reproduction	Sexual, by copulation

Carrier shell

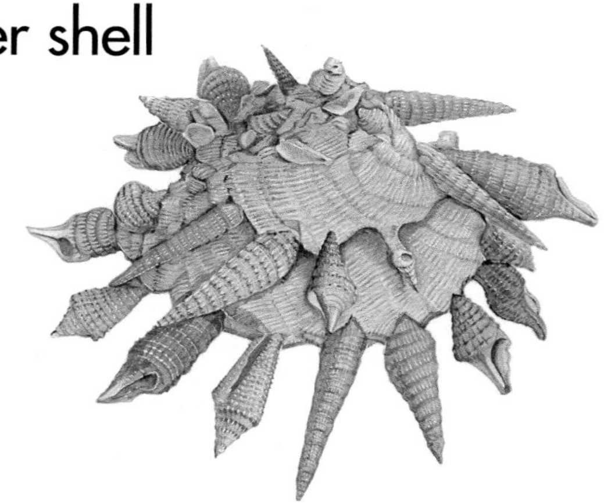

The strange-looking carrier shells are a type of mollusc that has developed unique behaviour – though no one is quite sure why! The xenophora (the name means 'bearers of foreigners') collect the shells of other dead molluscs and carefully cement them to their own shell. This laborious process may take several hours for each shell. The most likely explanation is that they do this as a form of camouflage, but several carrier shells live in the deep sea where no light penetrates. Alternatively they might be strengthening their own shells. *Xenophora pallidula* is even more of a puzzle, since it usually has a sponge attached to the apex of its shell.

Scientific name	*Xenophora pallidula*
Classification	Phylum Mollusca; Class Gastropoda;
	Order Caenogastropoda; Family Xenophoridae
Size	Around 8cm (3⅛in)
Distribution	Indo-Pacific; South Africa
Habitat	Muddy sea floor
Diet	Possibly algae and organic debris
Reproduction	Sexual

Carinaria

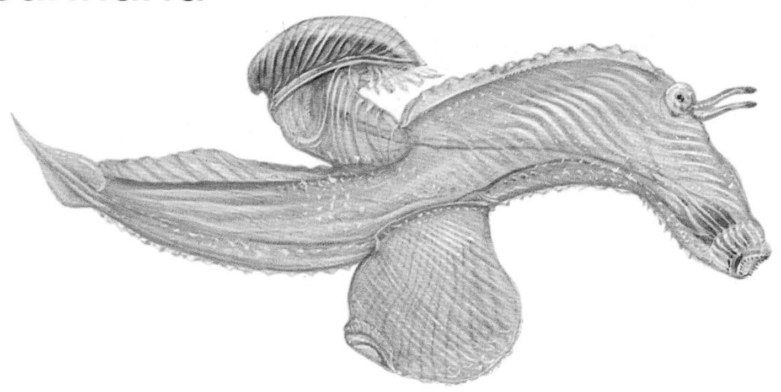

Two different groups of gastropods have developed independently towards a free-floating lifestyle away from the ocean floor. One is the pteropods or 'wing-feet,' while the other is the heteropods or 'different feet'. The common name 'sea butterflies' is often applied to both. Heteropods such as *Carinaria mediterranea* are related to the violet sea snail. They have reduced their shells to a minimum and in some cases lost them completely, while the foot has become a modified fin, held upright in the water. *Carinaria* holds its body rigid with a dorsal crest, and swims with an undulating movement through the water.

Scientific name	*Carinaria mediterranea*
Classification	Phylum Mollusca; Class Gastropoda;
	Order Caenogastropoda; Family Carinariidae
Size	20–40mm (⅘–1⅔in)
Distribution	Atlantic; Mediterranean
Habitat	Free-swimming at a range of depths
Diet	Larvae; plankton
Reproduction	Sexual; young are all born male, but some turn female

Cowrie

Cowries have beautiful glossy shells, covered with pebble-like patterns that make them highly prized among collectors. In life, though, the patterns on the shell are usually covered by two flaps of the mantle (the mollusc's body case) that wrap around it. These flaps are sometimes dull in colour, but in the case of the sieve cowry (*Cypraea cribraria*), the mantle is bright red, while the shell has distinctive white spots and a white rim around its edge. Cowrie shells have a long, narrow opening in their shells, folded in on itself along the shell's underside and with serrated edges. Thus the animal inside can retreat a long way if threatened.

Scientific name	*Cypraea cribraria*
Classification	Phylum Mollusca; Class Gastropoda;
	Order Mesogastropoda; Family Cyrpraeidae
Size	Around 25mm (1in)
Distribution	Indo-Pacific
Habitat	Coral reefs
Diet	Algae; organic matter; sponges
Reproduction	Sexual; internal fertilization; female guards eggs after laying them

Warted egg cowry

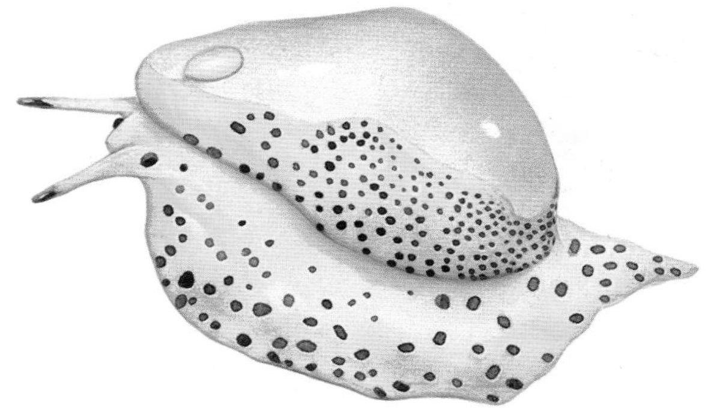

The egg cowries or ovulidae are closely related to the true cowries, and come in an equally wide variety of shapes and colorations, some of which are highly specialized. The warted egg cowry inhabits coral reefs in the Indian Ocean and West Pacific, where it wanders over the surfaces of mushroom leather corals, feeding on polyps. Its spotted mantle blends perfectly with the coral skeleton when the polyps are retracted, and as an additional defence, this cowry tastes extremely unpleasant to predators. Beneath the mantle, the shell is smooth and white, kept shiny by the constant back-and-forth motion of the mantle.

Scientific name	*Calpurnus verrucosa*
Classification	Phylum Mollusca; Class Gastropoda;
	Order Mesogastropoda; Family Ovulidae
Size	Up to 4cm (1⅝in)
Distribution	Indo-Pacific
Habitat	Shallow coral reefs
Diet	Coral polyps
Reproduction	Sexual; internal fertilization

Shuttlecock volva

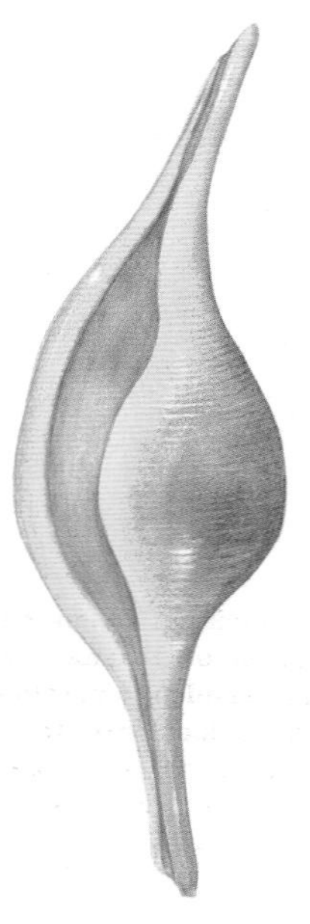

Some egg cowries have unusually extended ends to their shells, giving them a spindle-like appearance. However, the main distinction between egg cowries and true cowries is that the inward curling edge of the shell is not serrated. The shuttlecock volva is one example. Like all egg cowries it feeds on corals, and its carnivorous habit gives a pink or pale purple colouring to its shell. In life, the shuttlecock volva's body is covered by a mottled brown and white mantle that confuses potential predators. Volvas live buried in the sea floor or hidden among the soft corals on which they feed.

Scientific name	*Volva volva*
Classification	Phylum Mollusca; Class Gastropoda;
	Order Mesogastropoda; Family Ovulidae
Size	Up to 135mm (5⅜in) long
Distribution	Indo-Pacific
Habitat	Sandy seabeds; coral reefs
Diet	Coral polyps
Reproduction	Sexual; internal fertilization

Naticaria

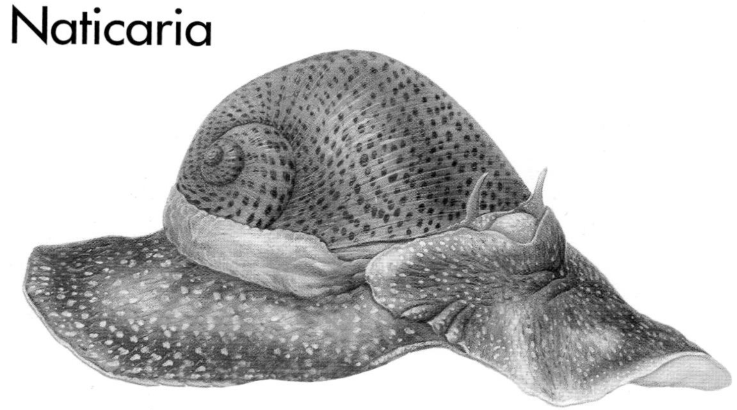

The Naticidae or moon shells get their name from their half-moon-shaped shell aperture. They are highly evolved burrowing predators that move along the sea floor ploughing into the surface layers with their powerful muscular foot. When they find a suitable victim (often a bivalve mollusc), the foot clasps the shell while the mollusc's toothed radula saws a neat hole through it and shreds the creature inside. Some species have pores in the foot which allow water to pump in and out, expanding and contracting the foot to increase its efficiency as a plough. *Naticarius millepunctatus* is a Mediterranean example.

Scientific name	*Naticarius millepunctatus*
Classification	Phylum Mollusca; Class Gastropoda;
	Order Mesogastropoda; Family Naticaridae
Size	Around 40mm (1⅗in) tall
Distribution	Mediterranean and Eastern North Atlantic
Habitat	Sandy seabeds
Diet	Bivalve molluscs
Reproduction	Sexual, by copulation

Fig shell

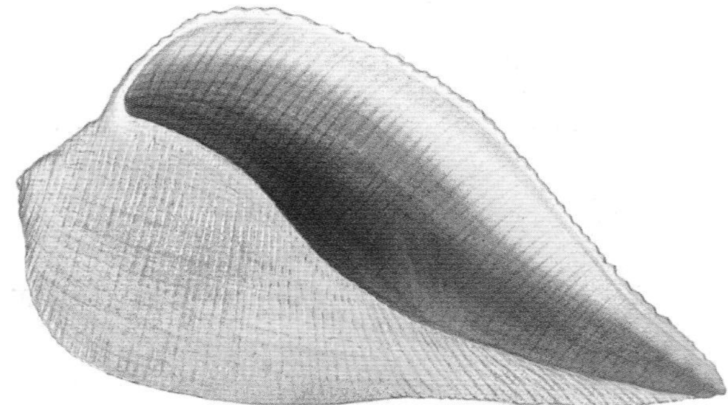

The delicate shells of the family ficidae have a bulging body and a flattened top that gives them their resemblance to figs. They were once known as pear shells or pyrulae, and live on sandy seabeds in tropical regions. The gastropod that lives inside has a large and distinctive head which it sticks out through the end of the shell, sniffing around with its siphon in search of organic detritus and small prey. Its most remarkable feature, though, is its large foot, which is truncated across the front, giving it a triangular shape. Ficus shells are thin and delicate – they rarely survive being washed up on the shore.

Scientific name	*Ficus filosa*
Classification	Phylum Mollusca; Class Gastropoda;
	Order Caenogastropoda; Family Ficidae
Size	Up to 100mm (4in)
Distribution	Indo-Pacific
Habitat	Sandy seabeds, 100–200m (330–660ft)
Diet	Detritus and small invertebrates
Reproduction	Sexual

Helmet shell

The cassidae or helmet shell family include some of the largest of all molluscs, and are named from their supposed resemblance to the helmets of Roman gladiators. They inhabit tropical warm waters, where they feed on other molluscs and poisonous sea urchins, pouncing on them by rearing up and then abruptly dropping and engulfing the prey, whose shell is then dissolved by secretions of strong sulphuric acid. *Cypraecassis rufa*, the bullmouth helmet, was much prized for its decorative value in Roman times, and was used by craftsmen for carving cameos. Julius Caesar is said to have given one as a gift to Queen Cleopatra of Egypt.

Scientific name	*Cypraecassis rufa*
Classification	Phylum Mollusca; Class Gastropoda;
	Order Caenogastropoda; Family Cassidae
Size	Around 16cm (6⅓in)
Distribution	Indo-Pacific
Habitat	Sandy seabeds; coral reefs
Diet	Molluscs; sea urchins
Reproduction	Sexual, through copulation

Tun shell

Tun shells are named from an old word for a cask or barrel. These molluscs have large but relatively thin shells, often surrounded by spiral ribs that resemble the metal bands around an old wooden barrel. They have huge ranges because their larval stages can float among the plankton for months at a time before settling to the seabed. *Tonna galea*, the giant tun, spends most of the day in the sands off coral reefs and islands, emerging at night to hunt crustaceans, small fish, and sea urchins, whose poison it counters with a paralysing chemical of its own. The females lay thousands of eggs in a ribbon-like mat on the seabed.

Scientific name	*Tonna galea*
Classification	Phylum Mollusca; Class Gastropoda;
	Order Caenogastropoda; Family Tonnidae
Size	Up to 25cm (10in)
Distribution	Atlantic; Mediterranean; Indo-Pacific
Habitat	Sandy seabeds, down to 40m (130ft)
Diet	Crustaceans; sea urchins; small fish
Reproduction	Sexual, through copulation

Triton

Tritons are found throughout the world in tropical and warm temperate waters – there are some 150 different species, and the shells of many have been used for centuries as trumpets. The shells frequently have strong ridges and bumps, but when alive, the triton extends its mantle over the outside, and many species have extensions called papillae which give them a 'hairy' appearance. Most species live on shallow sandy sea floors, hunting invertebrates with a similar technique to the helmet shells – but some live at great depths. Tritons produce a paralysing anaesthetic which stops their prey struggling as it is swallowed whole.

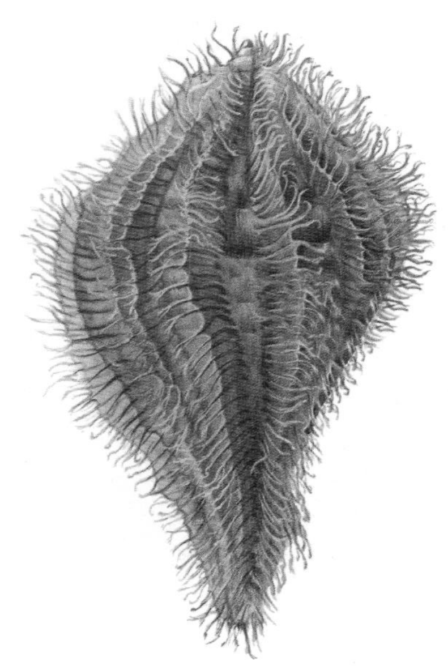

Scientific name	*Cymatium parthenopaeum*
Classification	Phylum Mollusca; Class Gastropoda;
	Caenogastropoda; Family Cymatiidae
Size	Around 80mm (3⅛in)
Distribution	Worldwide in tropical waters
Habitat	Sandy sea floors
Diet	Molluscs, worms, sea cucumbers and other invertebrates
Reproduction	Sexual, through copulation

Spiny murex

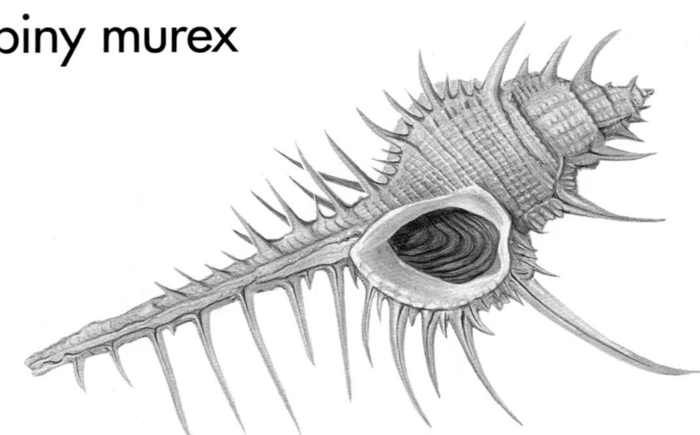

The murexes are neogastropods – the most highly evolved type of marine snails. They are voracious predators with a unique method of feeding, drilling holes into the shells of bivalves and other creatures by a variety of chemical and mechanical means. Once it has penetrated the shell, the murex consumes the flesh of the animal inside with its toothed tongue, the radula. Murexes are widely distributed around the world – this spiny variety is found around Micronesia. Other murexes from around the Mediterranean were used in ancient times to make a dye called Tyrian purple.

Scientific name	*Murex troscheli*
Classification	Phylum Mollusca; Class Gastropoda;
	Order Neogastropoda; Family Muricidae
Size	Up to 150mm (6in) long
Distribution	Indo-Pacific
Habitat	Sandy seabeds
Diet	Other molluscs; barnacles
Reproduction	Sexual

Baler shell

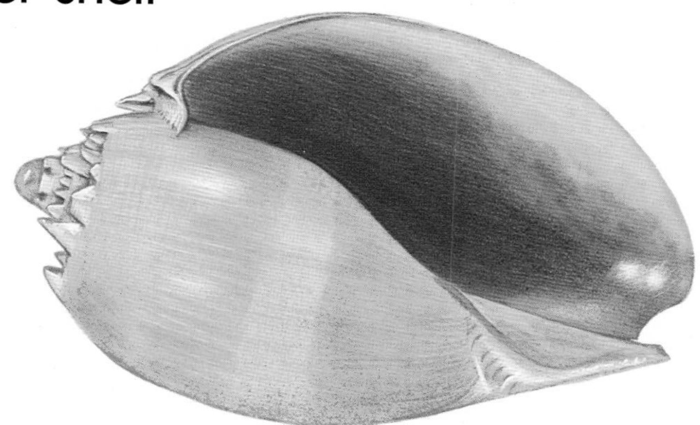

Balers have some of the largest shells of any gastropods, growing up to 45cm (18in) long. Found around Australian coasts, they were used by fishermen as useful buckets to bale out their canoes. The baler lays very few eggs for a gastropod – typically just a few dozen – because it makes a large investment in them. Each egg is wrapped into a gelatinous sac before birth, and the whole mass is glued down to a rock or other hard surface. The eggs are glued together in a spiral stack, which can take several weeks to build, and the young develop inside the egg mass until they are strong enough to break free.

Scientific name	*Melo amphora*
Classification	Phylum Mollusca; Class Gastropoda;
	Order Neogastropoda; Family Volutidae
Size	Around 45cm (18in) long
Distribution	Australian coastal waters
Habitat	Sandy sea floors
Diet	Other molluscs and invertebrates
Reproduction	Sexual; small number of eggs laid in egg mass

Olive shell

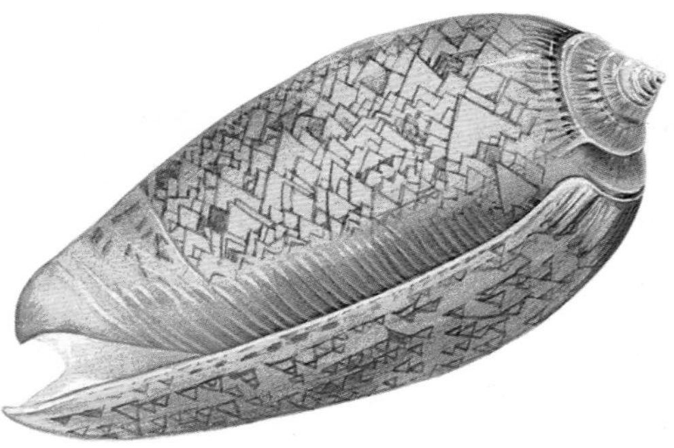

The olive shells are widespread in tropical seas. They exhibit some of the most complex patterning in nature – overlapping zigzags and v-shapes that confuse predators and prey alike – and no two shells are identical. For this reason, they have been treasured as ornaments and jewellery for centuries. Inside the shell lives a large mollusc, and the shell is usually covered by the animal's mantle. They spend most of the day buried in the sand, emerging at night to hunt on smaller molluscs, crustaceans and worms, which they hold down with their large foot. They are among the fastest-moving gastropods.

Scientific name	*Olivia porphyria*
Classification	Phylum Mollusca; Class Gastropoda;
	Order Neogastropoda; Family Olividae
Size	Around 35mm (1⅜in)
Distribution	Tropical Atlantic
Habitat	Sandy seabeds at moderate depths
Diet	Small invertebrates
Reproduction	Sexual, mating throughout the year

Harp shell

The harp shells or harpidae are close relatives of the olividae, but their shells have strong ribs that resemble a harp. These molluscs are shoreline predators, spending the time while the tide is out buried in the sand to preserve moisture, since they have no operculum to close their shells. The animal inside is quite oversized for its shell, and has an enormous foot that extends when it is on the hunt, trapping unwary invertebrates in the same way as the olive shells. If a predator attempts to grab the rear portion of the foot, the harp shell can simply shed it and retreat into its shell, rather as some lizards drop their tails when cornered.

Scientific name	*Harpa amouretta*
Classification	Phylum Mollusca; Class Gastropoda;
	Order Neogastropoda; Family Harpidae
Size	Up to 60mm (2⅖in)
Distribution	Indo-Pacific
Habitat	Sandy shores, burrowing up to 3m (10ft) down
Diet	Small invertebrates
Reproduction	Sexual, mating throughout the year

Mitre shell

Although their shell looks more like a bullet than anything, mitre shells are named from their supposed resemblance to a bishop's ceremonial hat. There are over 500 species known, and most are found around the world buried in offshore sand and mud. Mitres stay on the sea floor in the day, sheltering beneath rocks and coral. At night they burrow into the sand to hunt other invertebrates, such as clams and worms, but unusually they kill their prey before eating it. They can do this because they have specially evolved glands in the radula that inject poison.

Scientific name	*Mitra zonata*
Classification	Phylum Mollusca; Class Gastropoda;
	Order Neogastropoda; Family Mitridae
Size	Around 50mm (2in)
Distribution	Mediterranean; Eastern North Atlantic
Habitat	Sandy offshore seabeds at depths 30–150m (100–500ft)
Diet	Other invertebrates
Reproduction	Sexual, through copulation

Cone shell

The cone shells are an extremely widespread family, found around the world in tropical waters with a wide variety of variations on the basic design. They are prized by collectors, but trying to catch live ones can be a risky business because they have a highly venomous bite. The cone shell 'sniffs out' prey with an organ called the siphon, then spears it with harpoon-like teeth and injects a paralysing poison. It then swallows the unfortunate animal whole and digests it within its distended stomach. Cone shell venom has been known to kill humans, but it is now attracting the attention of medical researchers investigating painkillers.

Scientific name	*Conus marmoreus*
Classification	Phylum Mollusca; Class Gastropoda;
	Order Neogastropoda; Family Conidae
Size	Around 100mm (4in)
Distribution	Indo-Pacific
Habitat	Sandy shorelines down to depths of 30m (100ft)
Diet	Small fish; molluscs
Reproduction	Sexual; several hundred eggs laid in a capsule

Actaeon

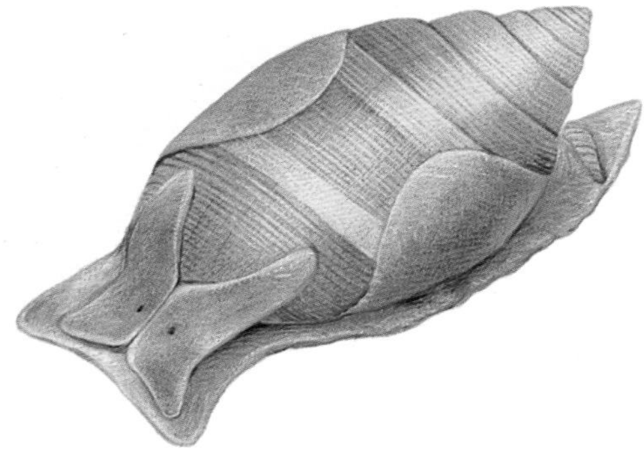

Most gastropods have a body that has been modified in order to fit it into the shell – the organs have been twisted and rearranged and it is said to be 'in torsion'. However, one group, called the opisthobranchiae, show evolution towards escaping their shells – they have less twisted body plans and some have reduced or even absent shells. The actaeonidae show the first step on this path – the shell is still large, usually with a pinkish coloration and three white bands around it, but the animal has a spade-like head specially adapted for burrowing, and the internal body plan is less distorted than usual.

Scientific name	*Actaeon tornatilis*
Classification	Phylum Mollusca; Class Gastropoda;
	Order Cephalaspidea; Family Actaeonidae
Size	Up to 25mm (1in)
Distribution	Eastern North Atlantic; Mediterranean
Habitat	Sandy shorelines below low-tide mark
Diet	Algae and organic debris
Reproduction	Sexual

Sea hare

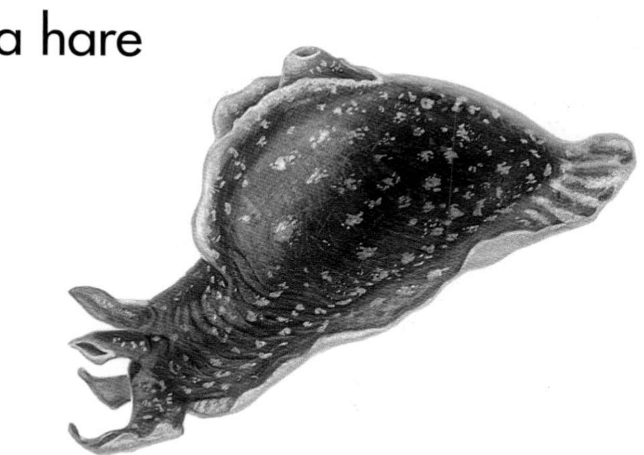

Sea hares are gastropods in which the shell has become less important – evolutionarily they are midway between marine snails and sea slugs. Their name comes from the two ear-like erect tentacles on the front of the head, and they appear to have lost their shells. But although the shell is not obvious from the outside, it is still present inside the animal's body. Sea hares have also developed limb-like folds in their bodies, called parapodia, which enable them to swim around in the seaweed beds where they feed on algae. When threatened, they can squirt a purple ink to confuse predators and cover their escape.

Scientific name	*Aplysia punctata*
Classification	Phylum Mollusca; Class Gastropoda;
	Order Anaspidea; Family Aplysiidae
Size	Up to 30cm (12in)
Distribution	Eastern North Atlantic and Mediterranean
Habitat	Offshore seabeds with rich vegetation
Diet	Algae
Reproduction	Individuals are hermaphrodites, but form chains to mate

Sea butterfly

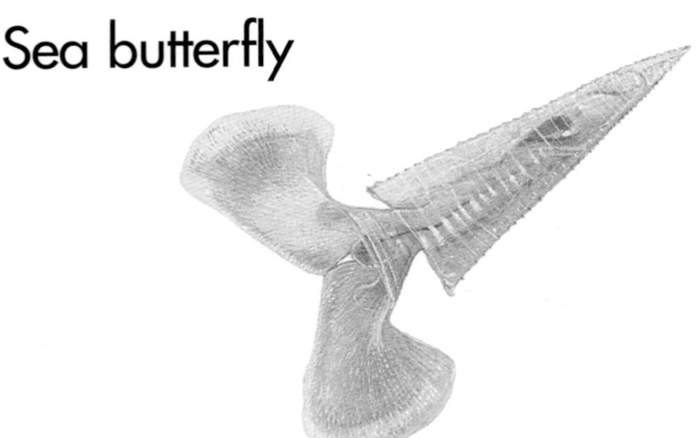

The pteropods are a group of opisthobranchs that have developed a free-floating lifestyle, but have taken a different evolutionary pathway from the undulating heteropods. These molluscs have a reduced shell and an extended foot, spreading out and forming two wing-like lobes, which they flap back and forth in order to 'fly' through the water. The scientific name for these animals, pteropods, means wing-feet, appropriately enough. *Hyalocylis striata* belongs to a group called the Thecosomata, which are plant-eaters, floating in the water and feeding on minute algae and organic particles they find there.

Scientific name	*Hyalocylis striata*
Classification	Phylum Mollusca; Class Gastropoda;
	Order Thecosomata; Family Cavolinidae
Size	Up to around 8mm (⅜in)
Distribution	Atlantic and Caribbean
Habitat	Free-swimming at 100–300m (330–1000ft)
Diet	Algae and organic particles
Reproduction	Sexual

Naked sea butterfly

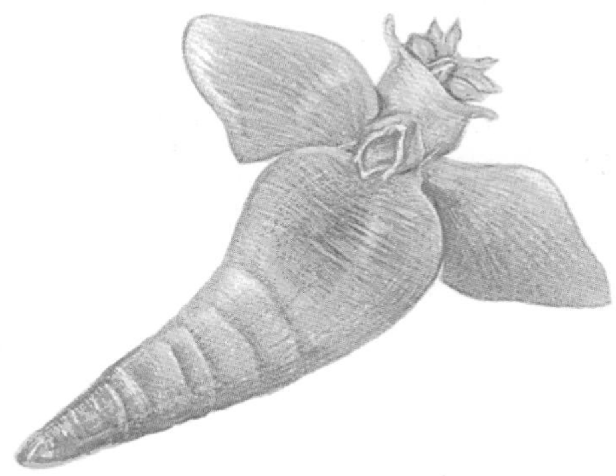

Some pteropods have lost their shells completely, transforming into plankton-like predators. *Clione limacina* has a small shell as a larva, but loses this by the time it reaches adulthood. It mostly hunts shelled, plant-eating pelagic snails. When it finds a victim it grips the shell with a set of specially adapted tentacles, turning it until the shell's opening faces its mouth. It then extends large hooks that dig into the shell and evict the occupant, which the clione swallows whole. Most species of clione flourish in cold waters, and can happily survive among pack-ice – hence one nickname for them is 'the angel of the ice floes.'

Scientific name	*Clione limacina*
Classification	Phylum Mollusca; Class Gastropoda;
	Order Gymnosomata; Family Clionidae
Size	Up to 40mm (1⅗in)
Distribution	Worldwide in polar and cold temperate seas
Habitat	Free-swimming at a range of depths
Diet	Plankton, other marine snails
Reproduction	Sexual

Hypselodoris

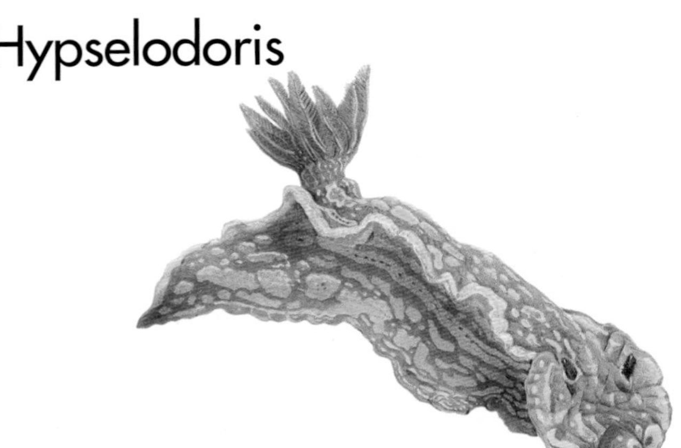

Nudibranchs are marine gastropods that have completely shed their shells and roam the seabed looking like larger versions of their terrestrial cousins, the slugs. They carry a flower-like secondary set of gills on their backs, and two sense organs called rhinophores on their heads, which can retract into sheaths when threatened. These rhinophores act as the nudibranch's nose, detecting chemical changes in the water. *Hypselodoris picta*, from the Mediterranean and Atlantic, comes in a variety of colours, but all have bright yellow marking to indicate that they are poisonous to predators.

Scientific name	*Hypselodoris picta*
Classification	Phylum Mollusca; Class Gastropoda;
	Order Nudibranchia; Family Chromodorididae
Size	Up to 20cm (8in)
Distribution	Mediterranean; Eastern North Atlantic
Habitat	Rocky seabeds in warm, shallow seas
Diet	Sponges
Reproduction	Sexual, through copulation

Chromodoris

One of the most brilliantly coloured of all ocean animals is *Chromodoris quadricolor* (its very name means four-coloured). It is just one of more than 150 brightly coloured species that make up the genus Chromodoris, and always has the same pattern – orange rhinophores, gills, and mantle edge, blue and black stripes along the back, and a thin white band around the inner edge of the mantle. Without protective shells, many nudibranchs have evolved bright or complex colours, either to warn off predators or to camouflage themselves. Their eyesight is so poor that these colours cannot be for communication between nudibranchs.

Scientific name	*Chromodoris quadricolor*
Classification	Phylum Mollusca; Class Gastropoda;
	Order Nudibranchia; Family Chromodorididae
Size	Up to 30mm (1⅛in)
Distribution	Red Sea, Western Indian Ocean
Habitat	Rocky sea floors
Diet	Sponges
Reproduction	Sexual, through copulation

Dendronotus

Several different animals took different evolutionary pathways to end up as sea slugs, so there is a lot of variety in their appearance. As well as the flat Chromodorididae, there are more slender forms with multiple gill attachments called cerata on their backs. Dendronotids are one of these forms – they have evolved branched cerata along their backs which give them a strong resemblance to floating seaweed. In *Dendronotus arborescens*, the rhinophores are also placed on long stalks and surrounded by further bushy growths called papillae, adding to the camouflage. The animal may be found in a number of colour variations.

Scientific name	*Dendronotus frondosus*
Classification	Phylum Mollusca; Class Gastropoda;
	Order Nudibranchia; Family Dendronotinae
Size	Up to 100mm (4in)
Distribution	North Atlantic; North Pacific; Arctic
Habitat	Coastal waters with plentiful plant life
Diet	Sea anemones; corals
Reproduction	Sexual

Flabellina

Flabellina is a member of the Aeolidiidae, a group of sea slugs with a more slender plan from the flat Chromodorididae. They are distinguished by longer rhinophores on their heads, tentacles beneath their mouths, and multiple gills (cerata) on their backs. The cerata do not attach directly to the animal's back, but instead emerge from 'trunks' that sprout from the back. *Flabellina affinis* (the name means 'fan-like') is a small but distinctive purple sea slug that is common throughout the Mediterranean. It specializes in feeding on colonies of a bushy polyp called eudendrium.

Scientific name	*Flabellina affinis*
Classification	Phylum Mollusca; Class Gastropoda;
	Order Nudibranchia; Family Flabellinidae
Size	Up to 50mm (2in)
Distribution	Eastern North Atlantic; Mediterranean
Habitat	Coastal waters with plentiful plant life
Diet	Sea anemones; corals
Reproduction	Sexual

Coryphella

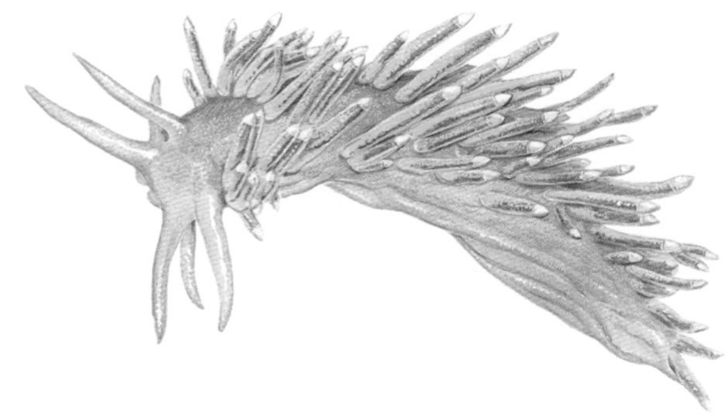

Yet another animal known as a 'sea butterfly,' *Coryphella verrucosa* is a distinctive and attractive nudibranch, related to Flabellina and found throughout the North Atlantic and its neighbouring seas. Its body has a translucent white colour offset by large numbers of tube-shaped red, brown, or black cerata with white tips. It shows a great deal of variation in colour, partly because the pigmentation of its cerata depends on diet (its favourite food is a hydroid called *Tubularia*). Coryphella females lay their eggs in a very distinctive way, producing a spiral thread on the seabed.

Scientific name	*Coryphella verrucosa*
Classification	Phylum Mollusca; Class Gastropoda;
	Order Nudibranchia; Family Flabellinidae
Size	Around 25mm (1in)
Distribution	Eastern North Atlantic; Baltic; Mediterranean
Habitat	Shallow offshore waters
Diet	Hydroids
Reproduction	Sexual

Grey sea slug

The grey sea slug is a large example of the aeolid group, with a flattened body covered with thick, dense cerata that give it a furry appearance. Although grey is the most common colour, these nudibranchs can vary from purple to pale orange, usually with an inverted white V-shaped marking on the head. Grey sea slugs roam the coastal sea floor hunting for a wide range of sea anemones. They release a variety of secretions that cause the anemone's stinging cells to fire prematurely, neutralizing it so that the oral tentacles beneath the slug's mouth can grab hold of the prey safely.

Scientific name	*Aeolidia papillosa*
Classification	Phylum Mollusca; Class Gastropoda;
	Order Nudibranchia; Family Aeolidiidae
Size	Up to 12cm (4⅔in)
Distribution	Worldwide in temperate waters
Habitat	Offshore seabeds down to 800m (2600ft)
Diet	Sea anemones
Reproduction	Sexual

Nut shell

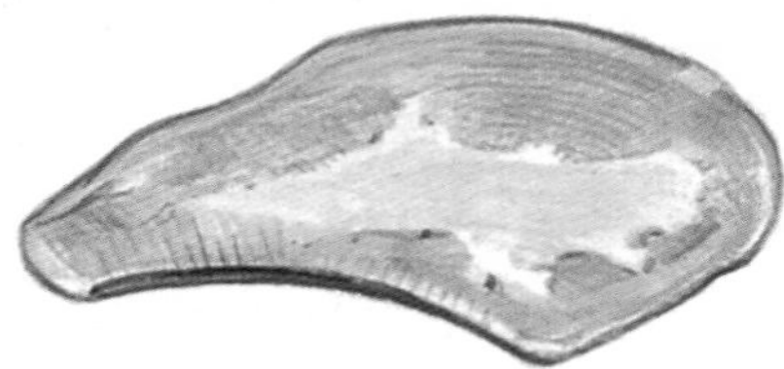

The nut shells or Nuculanidae are simple bivalves – that is, they live inside a pair of shells, hinged together on one side by a powerful muscle. In more advanced bivalves, the gills are used to filter food from the water and pass it to the gut, but in nut shells they are simply for extracting oxygen from the water. This mollusc lives buried in the sandy or muddy sea floor, using its muscular foot for burrowing. Tentacles collect food particles such as algae that have collected on the sand around it, and pass them to a pair of sense organs called the labial palps which sort food from waste and pass the former to the mouth.

Scientific name	*Nuculana acinacea*
Classification	Phylum Mollusca; Class Bivalvia;
	Order Nuculoida; Family Nuculanidae
Size	Around 10mm (⅜in)
Distribution	Indo-Pacific
Habitat	Sandy shallow seabeds
Diet	Algae and organic debris
Reproduction	Sexual, with external fertilization

Zebra ark shell

The ark shells are roughly square or rectangular in shape, with radial ribs running across their surface. When the animal is alive, the exterior of the shell is covered by velvety tissue called a periostracum. Pigments in this tissue help the shell blend with its surroundings, making it look like a stone. The zebra ark gets its name from its striped shell, and is also known as the turkey wing, which it resembles when splayed out. It secures itself to rocks and other hard substances by means of a byssus – a cluster of strong filaments produced from secretions in a special gland of the body.

Scientific name	*Arca zebra*
Classification	Phylum Mollusca; Class Bivalvia;
	Order Arcoida; Family Arcidae
Size	Up to 10cm (4in)
Distribution	Western Atlantic
Habitat	Shallow seabeds
Diet	Algae and organic debris
Reproduction	Sexual, with external fertilization

Horse mussel

Mussels are pear-shaped bivalves that form large colonies. Some attach themselves to rocks while others bury themselves in sand by means of their byssus filaments. Both types rely on strong flows of water to bring them food, which they filter out with their gills, so they are usually found at or just below the surface on wave-beaten shores. Horse mussels are not edible, but other types are a major food source and edible mussels are farmed widely. However, their feeding method means that toxins can become highly concentrated in them – algal blooms can sometimes render whole populations poisonous.

Scientific name	*Modiolus difficilis*
Classification	Phylum Mollusca; Class Bivalvia;
	Order Mytiloida; Family Mytilidae
Size	Up to 20cm (8in)
Distribution	Indo-Pacific
Habitat	Sandy seabeds in shallow waters
Diet	Algae and organic debris
Reproduction	Sexual, with external fertilization

Pearl oyster

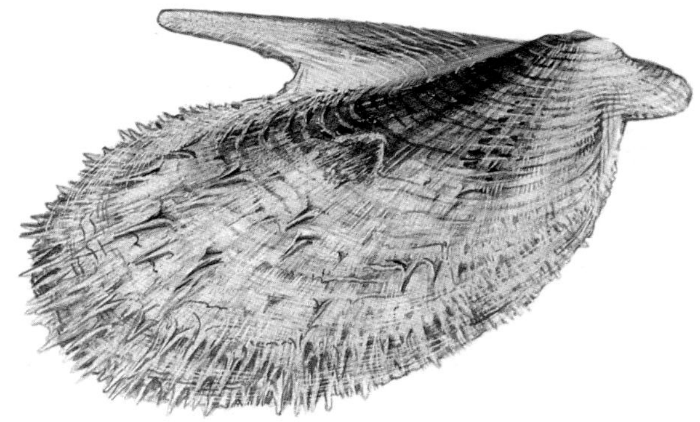

Oysters are bivalves that usually lay flat on rocks and have therefore evolved one flat shell and one convex one. However, they still retain their byssus gland, which allows them to attach to corals, rocks, or anything handy. The family Pteriidae are famous as the oysters that form pearls. They are easily distinguished by the long straight extension of the hinge, giving the shell a wing-like shape. This is particularly pronounced in *Pteria hirundo*, the Mediterranean pearl oyster. Pearls form when a piece of grit lodges in the oyster – the oyster secretes layers of nacre (the substance with which its inner shell is coated) onto the grit to neutralize it.

Scientific name	*Pteria hirundo*
Classification	Phylum Mollusca; Class Bivalvia;
	Order Pterioida; Family Pteriidae
Size	Around 11cm (4⅜in)
Distribution	Mediterranean; Eastern North Atlantic
Habitat	Sandy seabed just offshore
Diet	Floating detritus and algae
Reproduction	Sexual, with external fertilization

Hammer oyster

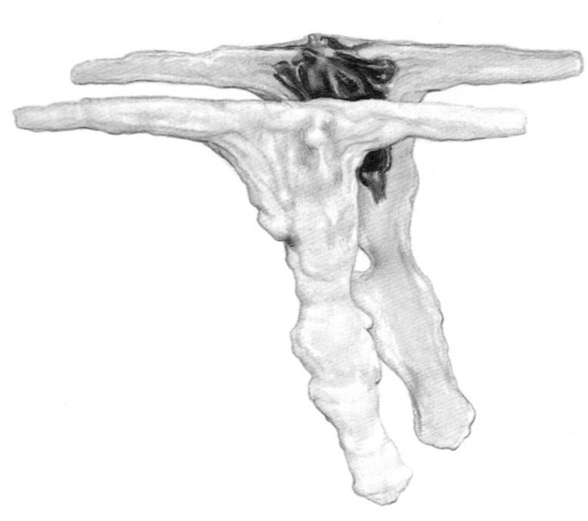

Since oysters have evolved to attach themselves to rocks by one valve, the foot of these molluscs has fallen out of use and become vestigial, while the shape of the shell has become elongated, especially in more advanced oysters. Perhaps the ultimate example are the hammer oysters, which have evolved into a long T-shape, with the crossbar of the T forming the hinge, and the downstroke enclosing the main body of the animal. *Malleus malleus,* from the Indo-Pacific, lives around coral reefs and has a white shell with a pearly blue lining near the hinge, where the mollusc itself lives.

Scientific name	*Malleus malleus*
Classification	Phylum Mollusca; Class Bivalvia;
	Order Pterioida; Family Malleidae
Size	Up to 17cm (6⅔in)
Distribution	Indo-Pacific
Habitat	Shallow waters around coral reefs
Diet	Algae and organic debris
Reproduction	Sexual, with external fertilization

Pen or ear shell

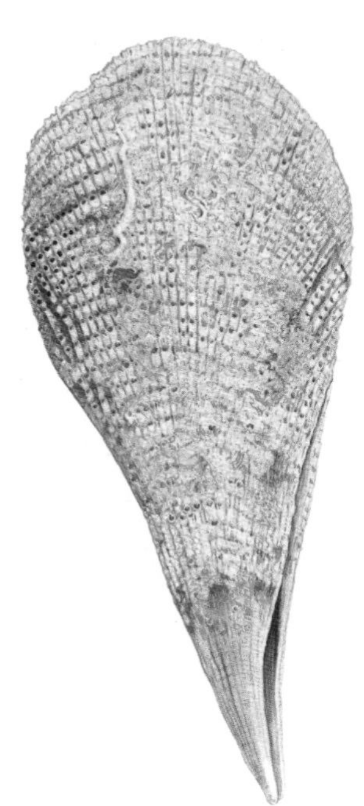

One of the largest bivalves in the world, *Pinna nobilis* is found across the Mediterranean. Typically it grows to around 30–50cm (12–20in), but it continues to grow throughout its life and specimens have been found as large as 1.2m (48in) long. The shell grows with up to one third of its body buried beneath the sand, in coastal waters overgrown with plants. It attaches itself to the sea floor by a byssus of long, fine threads – the Romans used threads from this creature to weave light and transparent textiles. The shell frequently becomes overgrown with smaller organisms, and two small crab species have evolved to live in symbiosis with it.

Scientific name	*Pinna nobilis*
Classification	Phylum Mollusca; Class Bivalvia;
	Order Pterioida; Family Pinnidae
Size	Typically around 30–50cm (12–20in)
Distribution	Mediterranean
Habitat	Coastal waters with plant life, down to 30m (100ft)
Diet	Algae and organic debris
Reproduction	Hermaphroditic, alternating sexes; external fertilization

Regal thorny oyster

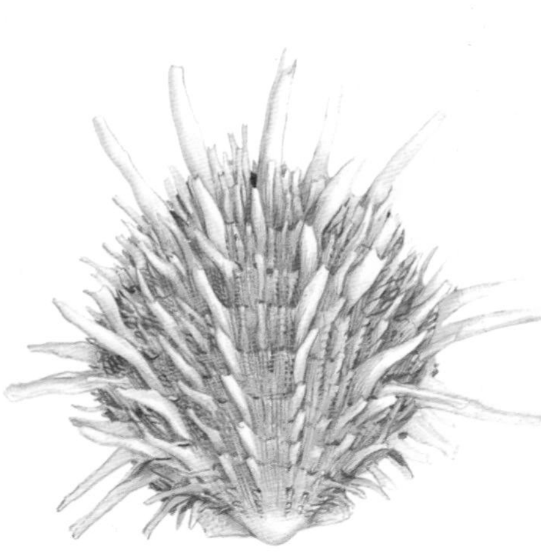

Despite their common name, thorny oysters are not oysters at all – they are a type of scallop. Important differences include the nature of their hinge – while oysters (and most bivalves) have a relatively simple toothed hinge held together by muscle, the thorny oysters have a more complex ball-and-socket arrangement. Like scallops, they also have a more complex nervous system, with eyes on the end of tentacles peering out from the shell in all directions, and sending information back to a simple brain. Thorny oysters seem to have developed their thorns for camouflage – they encourage the growth of other marine creatures on them.

Scientific name	*Spondylus regius*
Classification	Phylum Mollusca; Class Bivalvia;
	Order Pterioida; Family Spondylidae
Size	Around 150mm (6in)
Distribution	Indo-Pacific
Habitat	Coral reefs
Diet	Algae and organic debris
Reproduction	Sexual, with external fertilization

Queen scallop

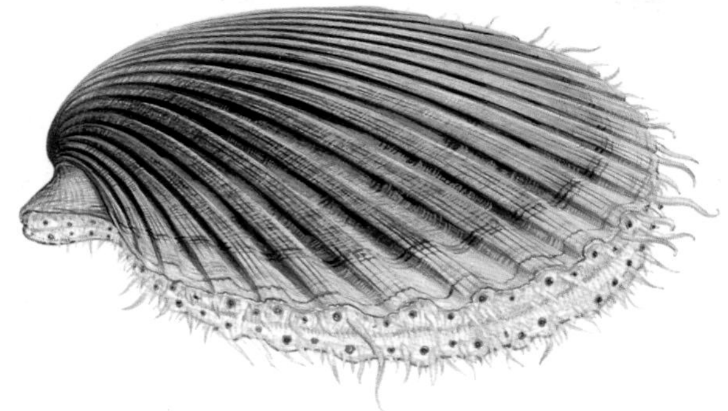

With their attractive fan-shaped shells, scallops have been a motif of art around the world for centuries, in everything from Boticelli's 'Birth of Venus' to oil company logos. But these molluscs fully deserve the attention – they are highly evolved with several unique features. Eyes on tentacles around the edge of the creature's mantle allow it to sense light and dark, and probably more complex patterns. They are also fast movers – by rapid opening and closing of their shells, they can pump water in and out of siphons near the hinge, allowing them to make a jet-propelled escape from predators.

Scientific name	*Chlamys opercularis*
Classification	Phylum Mollusca, Class Bivalvia,
	Order Pterioida, Family Pectinidae
Size	Up to around 9cm (3⅝in)
Distribution	North Atlantic
Habitat	Rocky offshore waters
Diet	Algae and organic debris
Reproduction	Sexual, with external fertilization

Oyster

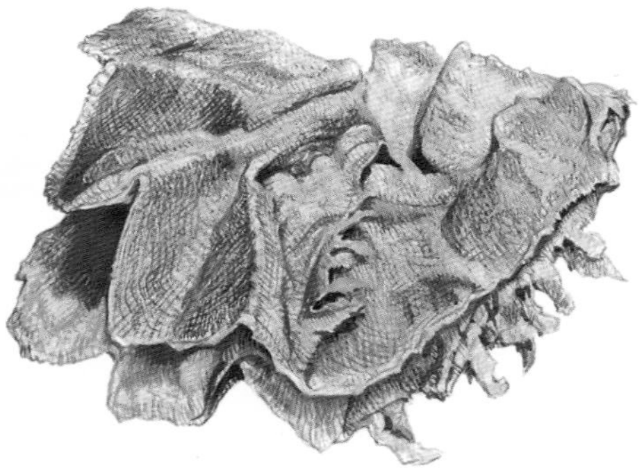

The edible oysters of the family Ostreidae are found around the world and widely used as a source of food. They are designed for an adult life permanently fixed to a single rock, typically in estuaries and shallow coastal waters, and can be readily farmed if suitable conditions can be produced. *Ostrea edulis* is the common European species, and has been introduced to oyster farms around the world, but is threatened in some of its native habitats by the faster-growing Pacific oyster. *O. cristagalli* from the Pacific is a more unusual species, with several large folds in its valves and special anchoring spines to secure itself to rocks.

Scientific name	*Ostrea cristagalli*
Classification	Phylum Mollusca; Class Bivalvia;
	Order Ostreoida; Family Ostreidae
Size	Up to around 9cm (3⅔in)
Distribution	Indo-Pacific
Habitat	Coral reefs
Diet	Algae and organic debris
Reproduction	Sexual, with external fertilization

Oxheart cockle

Cockles are bivalves whose two shells are identical and symmetrical. They live buried half-in and half-out of sandy seabeds, and their shells are rigid and hard enough to resist most predators. The valves frequently have strong well-defined ridges across them. *Glossus humanus*, the ox-heart cockle, covers its shell with a red periostracum when alive. It is distinctive because of the two curved 'umbones' at the back of the shell by the hinge. Interestingly, many shallow-water species of bivalve are thought to have triangular shells because it aids them in re-embedding if they are torn loose from the seabed by storms.

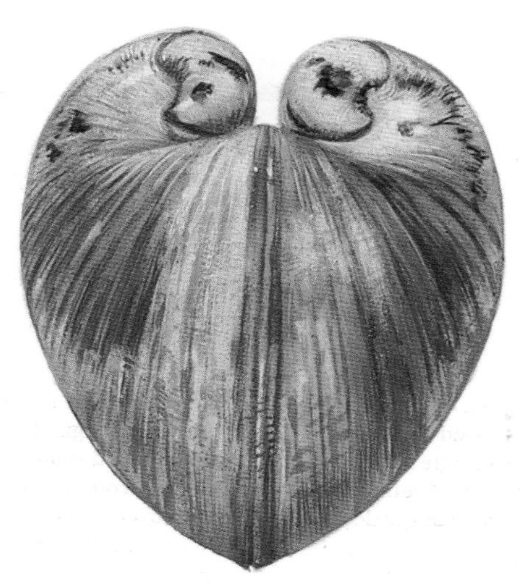

Scientific name	*Glossus humanus*
Classification	Phylum Mollusca; Class Bivalvia;
	Order Glossoidea; Family Glossidae
Size	Typically around 7cm (2¾in), but up to 12cm (4¾in)
Distribution	Eastern North Atlantic and Mediterranean
Habitat	Sandy off shore seabeds
Diet	Algae and organic debris
Reproduction	Sexual, with external fertilization

Spiny cockle

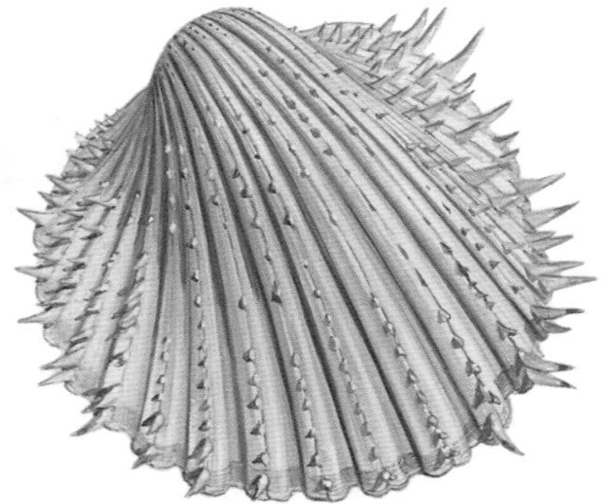

The European spiny cockle, *Acanthocardia aculeata*, is common in waters off Europe and West Africa. Its strong radial ridges are marked with rows of thorn-like spines, and separated by wide channels. The shell itself is relatively thin, and because the thorns are relatively fragile, they rarely survive intact when the shell is washed ashore. However, the live animal, which roots itself to sandy seabeds at depths down to around 100m (330ft), typically has many ranks of evenly arranged spines. Spiny cockles are popular edible shellfish around the Mediterranean, and are now being harvested in Scandinavia too.

Scientific name	*Acanthocardia aculeata*
Classification	Phylum Mollusca; Class Bivalvia;
	Order Heterodonta; Family Cardiidae
Size	Typically 6–7cm (2⅖–2⅘in), up to 10cm (4in)
Distribution	Eastern North Atlantic; Mediterranean
Habitat	Sandy seabeds down to 100m (330ft)
Diet	Algae and organic debris
Reproduction	Sexual, with external fertilization

Giant clam

Giant clams are the largest and most impressive bivalves, growing to more than a metre (40in) across, and weighting up to 270 kilos (600lb). But although they may look fearsome, and have a reputation from numerous horror stories, giant clams are far too slow-moving to attack divers, or even fish. They dwell on coral reefs, and feed off organic nutrients produced by the algae colonies that grow on their mantle. During the day, the mollusc extends its mantle out over the lips of its shell to absorb sunlight that allows the algae to flourish. The algae in turn flourish on the clam's waste products.

Scientific name	*Tridacna gigas*
Classification	Phylum Mollusca; Class Bivalvia;
	Order Heterodonta; Family Tridacnae
Size	Up to 1m (40in) across
Distribution	Indo-Pacific
Habitat	Coral reefs
Diet	Nutrients from algae, some filter-feeding in harsh conditions
Reproduction	Sexual, with external fertilization

Venus clam

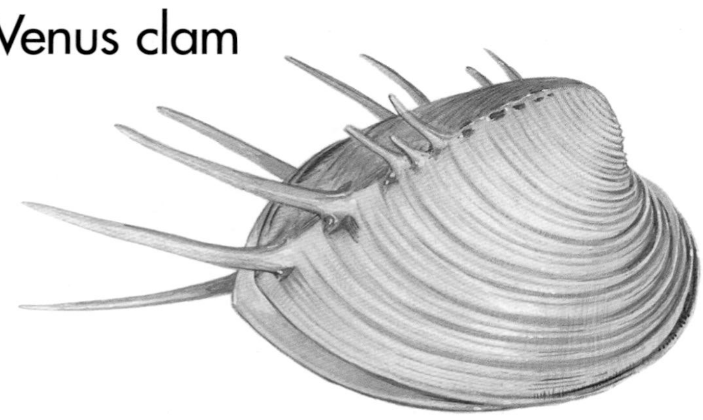

The Venus clams are the largest family of bivalves, and generally live buried in sandy seabeds at a wide variety of depths. They have a hard porcelain-like shell, and show a wide variety of variations in both the sculpture and the coloration of their shells. However, as rules of thumb they usually have a polished surface and often have rounded, concentric ribs. They also have an inward curve near the rear of the shell, called a pallial sinus. This curve, present on both valves, creates an opening for an organ called the siphon, which pumps water down through the sand. Spiny forms such as *Pitar lupanaria* are relatively rare.

Scientific name	*Pitar lupanaria*
Classification	Phylum Mollusca; Class Bivalvia;
	Order Veneroida; Family Veneridae
Size	Up to 6cm (2⅜in)
Distribution	Eastern Pacific
Habitat	Sandy offshore seabeds
Diet	Algae and organic debris
Reproduction	Sexual, with external fertilization

Wedding-cake Venus shell

Venus shells often exhibit elaborate patterns, as shown by the many-tiered appearance of the wedding-cake Venus shell, *Bassina disjecta*. The individual layers of the mollusc's shell, called lamellae, form a typical pattern of concentric but irregularly shaped rings, and extend outward in fragile, thin frills that may provide some form of defence. The wedding-cake Venus can grow up to 65mm (2½in) long, and is found in waters around southern Australia and Tasmania. It is typically a pale pinkish-white colour, and lives buried in shallow muddy sands just offshore, filtering water and food through its gills via its siphon.

Scientific name	*Bassina disjecta*
Classification	Phylum Mollusca; Class Bivalvia;
	Order Veneroida; Family Veneridae
Size	Around 40mm (1⅗in)
Distribution	Australia
Habitat	Sandy coastal seabeds
Diet	Algae and organic debris
Reproduction	Sexual, with external fertilization

Common razor shell

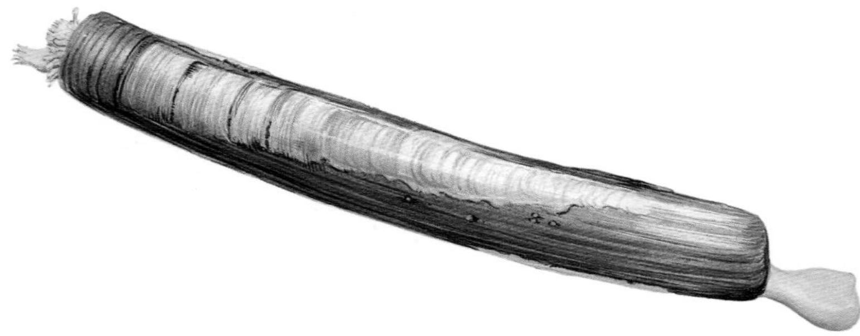

Razor shells are unusual bivalves that have evolved a tube-like shape. The two valves fit together with a gap at both ends, and the animals bury themselves upright in the sand, with either the tip of one end or just the breathing and feeding siphons sticking up through the seabed. Razor shells leave a distinctive keyhole-shaped hole in the sand when they withdraw their siphons, which can reveal their presence. If threatened, the razor shell can dig down through the sand at high speed, expanding and contracting its foot rapidly to push sand out of the way. When it settles, the foot extends from the bottom of the shell and forms an anchor.

Scientific name	*Ensis ensis*
Classification	Phylum Mollusca; Class Bivalvia;
	Order Veneroida; Family Pharidae
Size	Up to 20cm (8in)
Distribution	Eastern North Atlantic; Mediterranean
Habitat	Sandy shores just below low-water mark
Diet	Algae and organic debris
Reproduction	Sexual, with external fertilization

Otter shell

Otter shells are large bivalves found around most European and North African coasts. They can grow up to 12cm (4¾in) across, and their shells are stretched into a long elliptical shape with only shallow sculpting on the surface. The shell itself is a creamy white colour, and in life is covered with a brownish periostracum. The otter shells' stretched shape is an adaptation to a deep burrowing lifestyle – they bury themselves up to 25cm (10in) deep in the sand and feed and breathe through a long siphon. Other members of their family, the Mactridae, are even capable of burrowing into rock.

Scientific name	*Lutraria lutraria*
Classification	Phylum Mollusca, Class Bivalvia,
	Order Veneroida, Family Mactridae
Size	Typically around 10cm (4in), up to 12.5cm (5in)
Distribution	Eastern North Atlantic, Mediterranean
Habitat	Sandy seabeds just offshore
Diet	Algae and organic debris
Reproduction	Sexual, with external fertilization

Ship worm

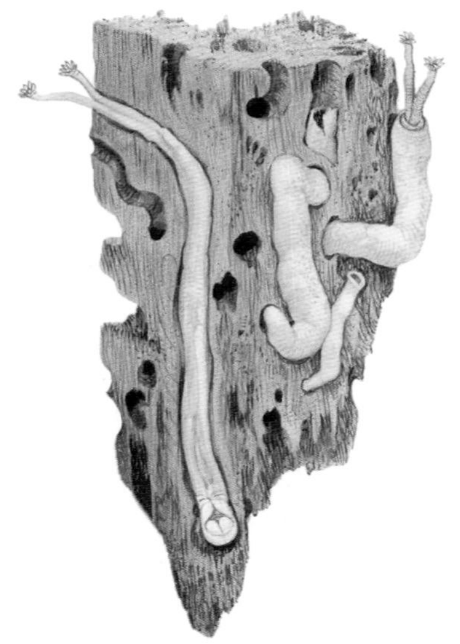

Shipworms have evolved for a highly specialized lifestyle, boring into driftwood and, in more modern times, ships' hulls and shipwrecks. They are sometimes referred to as marine woodworm, but are in fact unusual bivalves. They penetrate wood when they are still larvae, and as they grow they bore holes through the wood simply by rocking their abrasive shell back and forth. As they move through the wood, they line their tunnel with a white chalky deposit. Since the signs of entry are microscopic, timbers can frequently be riddled with shipworm before the first signs of damage are noticed.

Scientific name	*Teredo navalis*
Classification	Phylum Mollusca; Class Bivalvia;
	Order Myoida; Family Teredinidae
Size	Up to 20cm (8in) long
Distribution	Eastern North Atlantic
Habitat	Waterlogged wood
Diet	Wood, algae and organic debris through filter-feeding
Reproduction	Hermaphroditic, alternating sexes; fertilization takes place in water

Giant watering-pot shell

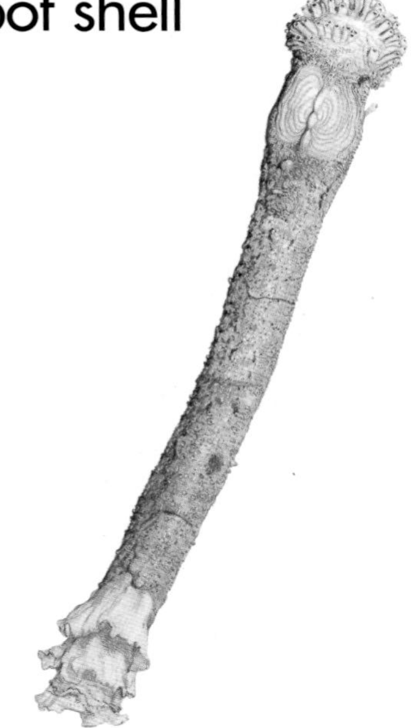

The Clavagellidae are bizarre bivalves that have long-outgrown their original shells, and all but abandoned them in favour of life in a chalky tube somewhat similar to those formed by shipworms. *Penicillus giganteus*, known as the giant watering-pot shell, has tiny vestigial valves at the bottom end of an upright tube that it builds from its own calcium-rich secretions. The tube sticks up through shallow, sandy seabeds in the Indian and Pacific oceans, and allows the animal to filter-feed on algae and organic particles. Clavagellidae are just one family within the Pholadomyoida, which frequently show unusual adaptations.

Scientific name	*Penicillus giganteus*
Classification	Phylum Mollusca; Class Bivalvia;
	Order Pholadomyoida; Family Clavagellidae
Size	Up to 20cm (8in) long
Distribution	Indo-Pacific
Habitat	Sandy shallow seabeds
Diet	Algae and organic debris
Reproduction	Sexual, with external fertilization

Angelwing clam

Angelwing clams have some of the most attractive shells of all bivalves. They are members of the family Pholadidae, the piddocks, and are specialized burrowers. Piddock shells do not actually join up to enclose the animal itself – rather they are attached to either side and are slowly rotated to grind through sand, wood, or even rock. The shells themselves are sturdy and have blunt forward-facing spikes to increase their grinding ability. Young angelwings bury themselves as much as 90cm (3ft) into sand or mud. They grow rapidly, feeding through a long siphon to the seabed, and are unable to rebury themselves if disturbed as adults.

Scientific name	*Cyrtopleura costata*
Classification	Phylum Mollusca; Class Bivalvia;
	Order Myoida; Family Pholadidae
Size	Up to 20cm (8in)
Distribution	Western Atlantic
Habitat	Sandy shores in intertidal zone, or just below low-tide mark
Diet	Algae and organic debris
Reproduction	Sexual, with external fertilization

Pearly nautilus

The bizarre, prehistoric-looking nautilus is a cephalopod (from the Greek for 'head-foot'), like squids and octopuses. It is the most primitive member of the class still surviving, with a strong resemblance to the famous fossil ammonites. Nautiluses have ninety tentacles on their heads, rather than the eight or ten in other living cephalopods, and they are also the only cephalopods with shells. However, their shells are very different from those of other molluscs – they consist of a number of chambers, and the animal itself lives in the outermost one. By pumping gas in or out of the inner chambers, the nautilus can rise or sink like a submarine.

Scientific name	*Nautilus pompilius*
Classification	Phylum Mollusca; Class Cephalopoda;
	Order; Family Nautilidae
Size	Up to 20cm (8in) diameter
Distribution	Western Pacific
Habitat	Free-swimming at depths to 500m (1600ft)
Diet	Crustaceans; small fish
Reproduction	Sexual, through copulation

Spirula

The curious cephalopod spirula seems to be a half way stage between nautiloids and cuttlefish and squid proper. It has a curling, horn-shaped spiral shell within its body, with similar 'buoyancy tanks' to those found in the nautilus, allowing it to rise and sink in the water column. However, it has eight short arms and two longer tentacles, plus a pair of tiny fins to help it swim. The animal lives in the outermost chamber of its shell, and can withdraw completely when threatened, closing the shell up with its mantle flaps. It has also abandoned any shell structures that would help it to remain 'horizontal', and is quite content to hang head-down in the water.

Scientific name	*Spirula spirula*
Classification	Phylum Mollusca; Class Cephalopoda;
	Order Sepioidea; Family Spirulidae
Size	1.5–5cm (⅔in–2in)
Distribution	Worldwide
Habitat	Free-swimming at depths from 100–1000m (330–3300ft)
Diet	Plankton
Reproduction	Sexual, through transfer of sperm

Common cuttlefish

Cuttlefish are remarkably complex cephalopods, commonly found in shallow offshore waters. Their bodies are built around a curved internal 'bone' (in fact the remnant of their ancestors' shells). They have well-developed eyes and brains, and move around by a form of 'jet propulsion' – pumping water through their siphons at high speed. One of their most impressive features is their ability to rapidly alter their skin pigmentation – for courtship, camouflage, help in hunting, or even, it seems, purely depending on their mood. They catch their prey by ambush, suddenly unleashing their two long tentacles to grab unwary fish and crustaceans.

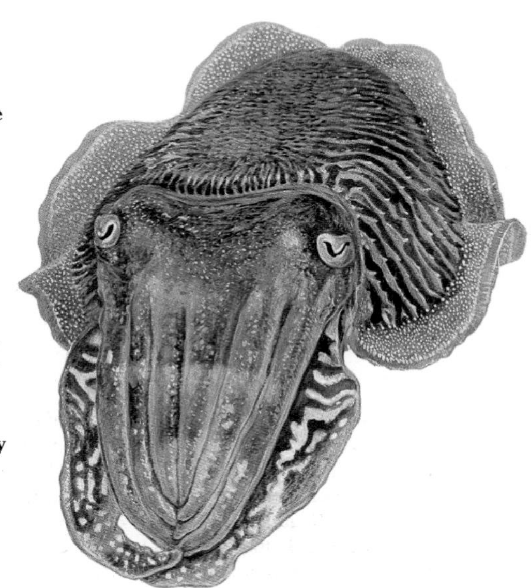

Scientific name	*Sepia officinalis*
Classification	Phylum Mollusca; Class Cephalopoda;
	Order Sepiida; Family Sepiidae
Size	Body up to 40cm (16in)
Distribution	Eastern North Atlantic, Mediterranean
Habitat	Shallow offshore waters
Diet	Small fish; molluscs; crustaceans; other cuttlefish
Reproduction	Sexual, through transfer of sperm

Lycoteuthis

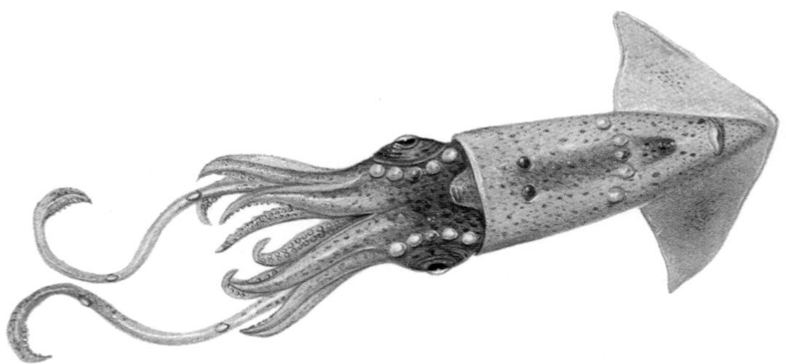

The small deep-sea squid *Lycoteuthis diadema* has all the typical features of a squid – eight arms and two longer tentacles, large eyes, muscular mouthparts with a horny beak for tearing prey, a bullet-shaped body with fins and a shield-like blade called the pen (the remnant of the shell) to which muscles attach. What makes *L. diadema* unusual, though, is the bioluminescent patches or photophores that dot the bodies of both males and females. The two sexes have distinctly different patterns and colours, and scientists think they must indulge in elaborate mating rituals, although these have never been observed.

Scientific name	*Lycoteuthis diadema*
Classification	Phylum Mollusca; Class Cephalopoda;
	Order Teuthida; Family Lycoteuthidae
Size	Body up to 15cm (6in)
Distribution	Pacific
Habitat	Free-swimming in deep seas, migrating upwards at night
Diet	Crustaceans; small fish
Reproduction	Sexual, through transfer of sperm

Common squid

The common squids of the genus *Loligo* are widespread around the world, and are fished for food in many countries. They are long and slender, with broad fins at the rear creating a diamond-shape. Like all squids, they hunt with their tentacles, which have clubs on the end and are covered with grasping suckers. Once captured, prey is pulled towards the mouth, where the shorter arms help manoeuvre it into the mouth, and the beak and radula (a tooth-lined tongue), help shred it into digestible chunks. Another common feature shared by all advanced cephalopods is the ability to squirt ink when threatened to cover their escape.

Scientific name	*Loligo vulgaris*
Classification	Phylum Mollusca; Class Cephalopoda;
	Order Teuthida; Family Loliginidae
Size	Body up to 55cm (22in) long
Distribution	Eastern North Atlantic; Mediterranean
Habitat	Shallow coastal waters
Diet	Small fish; crustaceans
Reproduction	Sexual, through transfer of sperm

Histioteuthis

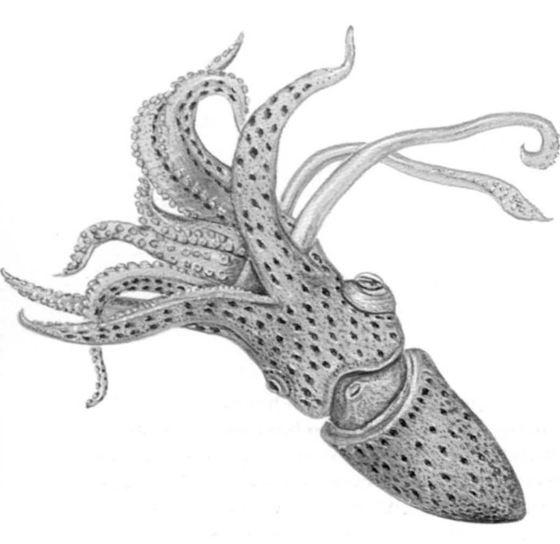

Squids of the Histioteuthidae family are distinguished in various ways – their arms are long and thick compared to those of most squids, and can be folded back over the head for protection, while their bodies are short, with only small fins. However, the strangest feature of this family by far is their unequal eyes. The left eye is much larger than the right, and angled upward to look for the silhouettes of animals against the weak light from the surface. It even incorporates a filter that is thought to help it spot creatures using bioluminescence to disguise themselves. The right eye, by comparison, is normal-sized and often ringed by bioluminescent spots.

Scientific name	*Histioteuthis reversa*
Classification	Phylum Mollusca; Class Cephalopoda;
	Order Teuthida; Family Histioteuthidae
Size	Body up to 33cm (13in)
Distribution	North Atlantic; Mediterranean; Eastern South Atlantic
Habitat	Free-swimming at moderate depths
Diet	Small fish; crustaceans
Reproduction	Sexual, through transfer of sperm

Sandalops

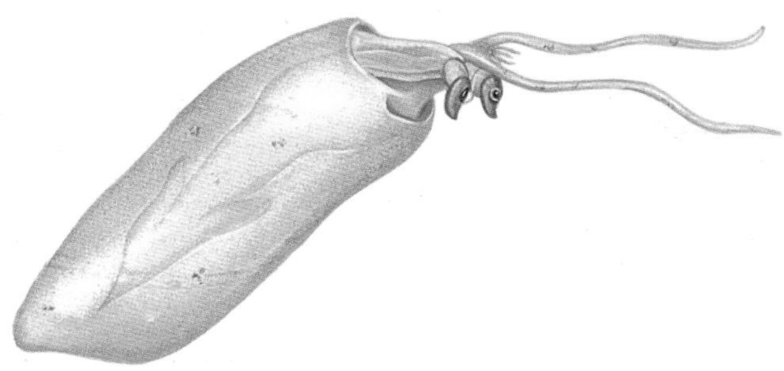

The Cranchiidae family of squids have an unusually enlarged buoyancy chamber, which tends to give them a bloated appearance. They also have shorter arms than some other squids, which they sometimes fold back over their heads in a little-understood 'cockatoo posture'. Many cranchiids are transparent – probably because they spend the early part of their lives near the sunlit top of the water column. As they grow older and larger, they also sink downwards, and some species undergo distinct biological changes – for example, the eyes of *Sandalops melancholicus* change radically to adapt to the lower light levels.

Scientific name	*Sandalops melancholicus*
Classification	Phylum Mollusca, Class Cephalopoda,
	Order Teuthida, Family Cranchiidae
Size	Up to 12cm (4¾in)
Distribution	Worldwide in tropical waters
Habitat	Free-swimming in mid-ocean depths
Diet	Plankton, small crustaceans
Reproduction	Sexual, through transfer of sperm

Chiroteuthis

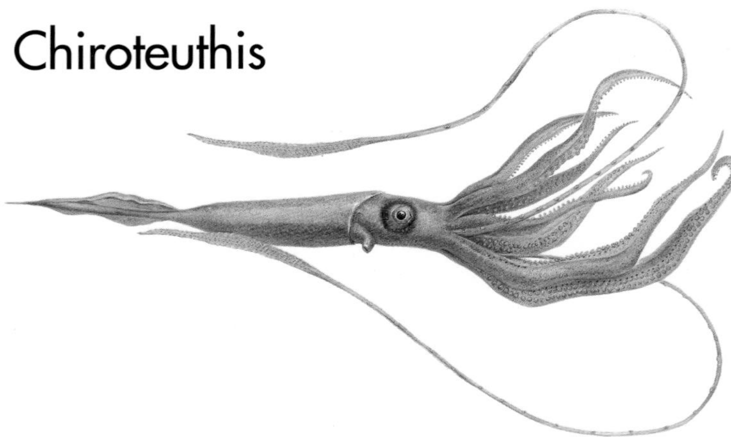

The chiroteuthids are medium-sized deep-sea squids with a very long and slender body pattern. They have long arms, and very long tentacles that can retract completely into a sheath. All chiroteuthids pass through a larval form called the doratopsis stage, which has an extremely long and highly complex tail. The adult squids are frequently semi-transparent, with complex light-producing photophores lining the arms and parts of the body. In order to function well in deep seas, they have 'flotation chambers' filled with ammonium chloride. This fluid is lighter than water, and balances the weight of the squid's other tissues, giving it neutral buoyancy.

Scientific name	*Chiroteuthis picteti*
Classification	Phylum Mollusca; Class Cephalopoda;
	Order Teuthida; Family Chiroteuthidae
Size	Body up to 40cm (16in) long
Distribution	Indo-Pacific
Habitat	Free-swimming in deep seas
Diet	Small fish; crustaceans
Reproduction	Sexual, through transfer of sperm

Giant squid

The giant squid is a living legend, a beast from sailor's stories that turned out to be real – but it is only known from dead specimens washed ashore, dredged up, or found in the stomachs of stranded sperm whales . It has never been seen alive. However, the animal is truly impressive – the largest invertebrate that has ever lived, with a body length of up to 5 metres (16ft), and total length up to 18m (60ft) – and the largest specimens may still not have been found! Despite their size, Architeuthids have relatively small fins. However, they have the largest eyes in the animal kingdom, some 25cm (10in) across, adapted to work in the inky deep seas.

Scientific name	*Architeuthis dux*
Classification	Phylum Mollusca; Class Cephalopoda;
	Order Teuthida; Family Architeuthidae
Size	Up to 18m (60ft) in known specimens
Distribution	Worldwide
Habitat	Free-swimming at depths of 200–1000m (660–3300ft)
Diet	Fish, other squid
Reproduction	Sexual – females lay up to a million eggs

Vampire squid

Looking like something from a nightmare, *Vampyroteuthis infernalis*, 'the vampire squid from hell' is not quite so fearsome as its name suggests, but it is fascinating nonetheless. A small and usually black gelatinous creature with the consistency of a jellyfish and a large collection of photophores, it actually lies in an order of its own, between squids and octopuses. *Vampyroteuthis* has eight arms almost completely joined by webbing, but also two long sensory filaments that it extends into the water. When a prey animal disturbs the filaments, *Vampyroteuthis* pounces, using its large fins to 'fly' through the water.

Scientific name	*Vampyroteuthis infernalis*
Classification	Phylum Mollusca; Class Cephalopoda;
	Order Vampyromorphida; Family Vampiroteuthidae
Size	Body up to 18cm (6in) long
Distribution	Worldwide in tropical and temperate seas
Habitat	Free-swimming at around 400–1000m (1300–3300 ft)
Diet	Small fish; crustaceans
Reproduction	Sexual, details unknown

Opisthoteuthis

The comical-looking octopus *Opisthoteuthis extensa* and its relatives are sometimes called 'flapjack devilfish' on account of their extremely flattened appearance. Like all octopuses, they have eight arms, but in this case the arms are engulfed and disguised by a broad web. Opisthoteuthids are also unusual in that their internal vestigial shell is quite large and well developed. They spend most of their time scuttling along the sea floor or swimming just above it by contractions of the web. The radula (toothed tongue) is nearly useless, which means they have to swallow prey whole.

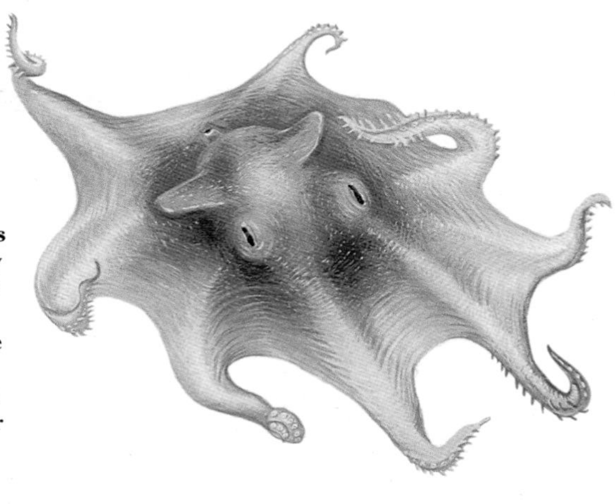

Scientific name	*Opisthoteuthis extensa*
Classification	Phylum Mollusca; Class Cephalopoda;
	Order Octopoda; Family Opisthoteuthidae
Size	Up to 1.5m (5ft) total length
Distribution	Eastern Pacific
Habitat	Sea floors at depths of 800–1500m (2700–5000ft)
Diet	Small fish; crustaceans
Reproduction	Sexual, through transfer of sperm

Bolitaena

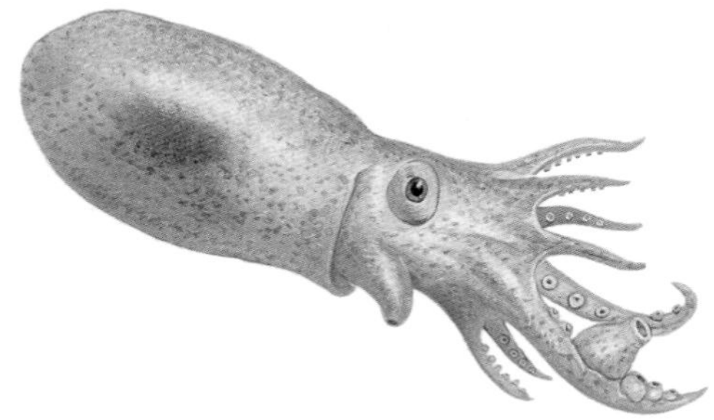

Bolitaenids are small octopuses found around the world in deep warm seas. They are semitransparent, with relatively short arms, each lined with a single row of suckers. Like most octopods, they are incirrate – they have lost their fins – and uniquely for this group they are bioluminescent. The females develop a large glowing ring around the mouth when they reach sexual maturity, which gives off a yellow-green light of a very specific wavelength that is difficult for predators to see. Presumably they use this to attract males, while the males have an enlarged saliva gland that may produce pheromones to attract the females.

Scientific name	*Bolitaena pygmaea*
Classification	Phylum Mollusca; Class Cephalopoda;
	Order Octopoda; Family Bolitaenidae
Size	Body around 25mm long
Distribution	Worldwide in tropical and subtropical seas
Habitat	Free-swimming at 800–1400m (2700–4600ft)
Diet	Plankton
Reproduction	Sexual, through transfer of sperm

Amphitretus

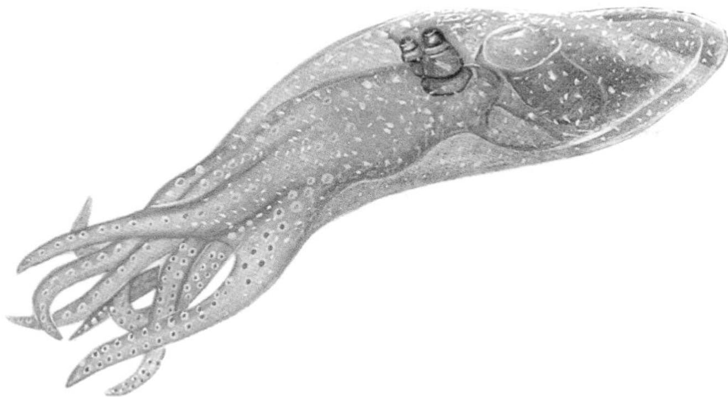

The small and almost transparent octopuses of the genus *Amphitretus* are thought to inhabit the mid-depths of all the world's tropical oceans. Floating in dark waters, they look more like plankton than advanced cephalopods. They have a single row of suckers along each tentacle, doubling near the tip. As with most cephalopods, one arm in the males is specially adapted to form a hectocotylus – a special organ used in conveying a packet of sperm from the male into the female's body. Another unusual feature of this *Amphitretus* are its eyes – simple cylindrical organs far removed from those of other cephalopods.

Scientific name	*Amphitretus pelagicus*
Classification	Phylum Mollusca; Class Cephalopoda;
	Order Octopoda; Family Opisthoteuthidae
Size	Body around 9cm (3⅝in)
Distribution	Worldwide in tropical and subtropical waters
Habitat	Free-swimming in moderate to deep seas
Diet	Plankton
Reproduction	Sexual, through transfer of sperm

Blue-ringed octopus

Small but fearsome predators, the blue-ringed octopuses live in Indo-Pacific waters and especially around Australia. Normally they are an undistinguished brown colour, but when threatened, they flush cream with blue rings or stripes (depending on species). This is a warning to predators that the octopus has a fearsome defence, usually used in hunting crustaceans and molluscs. After piercing skin or shell with its beak, it can spit a paralysing poison from modified saliva glands into its prey's bloodstream. This poison has been known to kill unwary people on Australian beaches by inhibiting respiration and suffocating the victim.

Scientific name	*Hapalochlaena maculosa*
Classification	Phylum Mollusca; Class Cephalopoda;
	Order Octopoda; Family Octopodidae
Size	Around 10cm (4in)
Distribution	Australia
Habitat	Seashores and offshore reefs to 40m (130ft)
Diet	Crustaceans; molluscs
Reproduction	Sexual, through transfer of sperm

Common octopus

The common octopus is a remarkable and highly successful creature. It is found all around the world, favouring sandy seabeds where it can dig itself a burrow and disguise itself when not feeding or breeding. Octopuses feed on a variety of creatures, including crustaceans and molluscs, and stockpile food supplies. When threatened, they can rapidly change their body shape or colour, or squirt ink to cover a rapid, jet-propelled escape. Fascinatingly, octopuses are highly intelligent – laboratory experiments have shown that they are skilled problem-solvers and good at remembering the solutions to previous problems when presented with new ones.

Scientific name	*Octopus vulgaris*
Classification	Phylum Mollusca; Class Cephalopoda;
	Order Octopoda; Family Octopodidae
Size	Up to around 90cm (36in) long
Distribution	Worldwide in tropical and temperate seas
Habitat	Shallow coastal waters, preferring sandy seabeds
Diet	Molluscs; crustaceans; fish
Reproduction	Sexual – females lay up to a quarter of a million eggs

Giant Pacific octopus

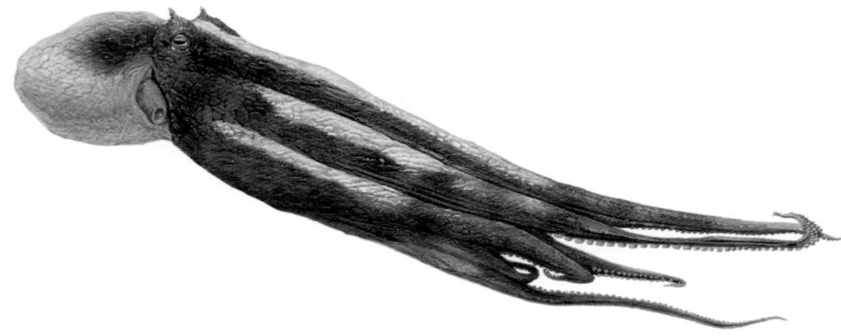

One of the largest and without doubt the heaviest of all cephalopods, the giant Pacific octopus is a creature of myth and legend. However, true giants are rare – these creatures reach sexual maturity at a weight of only 15 kilos (33lb), and have short lifespans, usually around five years. Females brood their huge clutches of eggs and die as the eggs begin to hatch. In many respects, giant octopus behaviour is similar to that of the common octopus – they hunt similar prey and make use of burrows for protection and brooding. Nevertheless, some truly monstrous examples have been found, with weights up to 270kg (600lb) and arms over 9m (30ft) across.

Scientific name	*Enteroctopus dofleini*
Classification	Phylum Mollusca; Class Cephalopoda;
	Order Octopoda; Family Octopodidae
Size	Typically around 2m (80in) across, up to 9m (30ft)
Distribution	Pacific Ocean
Habitat	Coastal seabeds from low tide to 750m (2500ft)
Diet	Molluscs; crustaceans; fish
Reproduction	Sexual, through transfer of sperm

Paper argonaut

The paper argonaut, also known as the paper nautilus, is in fact an unusual form of octopus. Females are typically 20cm (8in) across, and wrap themselves in a thin shell secreted by a special web between two of their arms. This shell acts as a brooding pouch for the female's eggs, and larvae only emerge once hatched. The males are equally unusual – they are typically just a fraction of the size of the female, and have a sperm-handling third arm (hectocotylus) that breaks off during breeding and wriggles into the female's mantle to fertilize the eggs. Thus, unusually for cephalopods, females can reproduce many times while males only breed once.

Scientific name	*Argonauta argo*
Classification	Phylum Mollusca; Class Cephalopoda;
	Order Octopoda; Family Octopodidae
Size	Females around 20cm (8in), males around 2cm (⅘in)
Distribution	Global in tropical and subtropical waters
Habitat	Free-swimming at moderate depths
Diet	Plankton – sometimes parasitize jellyfish
Reproduction	Sexual, through transfer of sperm

Errant polychaete, or scaleworm

Polychaetes are primitive segmented worms – creatures whose bodies are divided into a number of segments called metameres. The front segment forms the head, while the rearmost contains the anus, and the ones in between are usually identical. Polychaetes are divided into Errantia and Sedentaria – names suggested by their different lifestyles. Errantia are mobile, using appendages called parapodia, formed by folds in the body wall, for propulsion. They are also covered in irritating and sometimes poisonous spines. The heads of Errantia also have well-developed eyes and sensory tentacles for finding their way along the seabed.

Scientific name	*Hermione hystrix*
Classification	Phylum Annelida; Class Polychaeta (Polychaete worms);
	Subclass Errantia
Size	Up to around 25cm (10in) long
Distribution	Eastern North Atlantic; Mediterranean
Habitat	Rocky seabeds and shores
Diet	Predatory on small invertebrates
Reproduction	Sexual, by external fertilization

Sea mouse

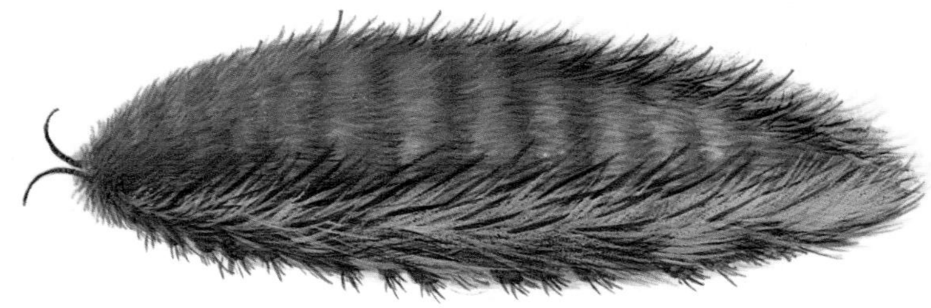

The sea mouse, so called because of its furry appearance, is a bottom-dwelling polychaete worm that normally lies buried head-first in the sand. Yet this unassuming creature has one unique feature – the iridescent threads or setae that emerge from its scaled back. Normally, these have a red sheen, warning off predators, but when light shines on them perpendicularly, they flush green and blue. The setae are made of millions of submicroscopic crystals that reflect and filter the faint light of the ocean depths – physicists hope that something similar might one day be used in light-based optical computers.

Scientific name	*Aphrodite aculeata*
Classification	Phylum Annelida, Class Polychaeta (Polychaete worms),
	Subclass Errantia, Family Aphroditae
Size	Up to 15–20cm (6–8in)
Distribution	Eastern North Atlantic, Mediterranean
Habitat	Muddy sea floors down to around 2000m (6600ft)
Diet	Predatory on small invertebrates
Reproduction	Sexual

Palolo worm

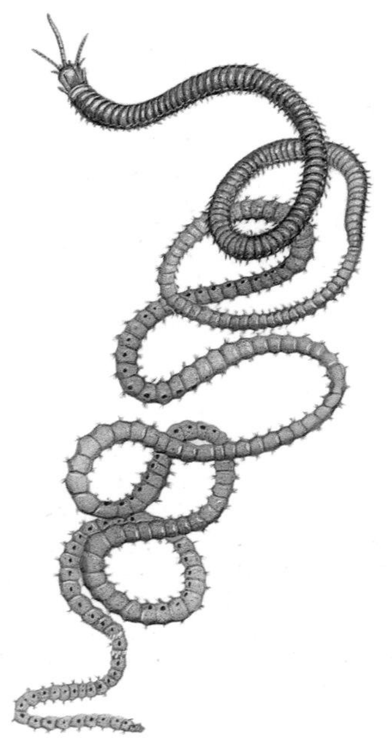

Palolo worms have one of the most unique reproduction methods in all of nature. Normally they live burrowed into shallow-water coral reefs, and are considered a delicacy by the natives of the Polynesian islands. However, on a couple of nights each year, tied precisely to the phase of the moon, the worms detach their rear segments, called gametophores. These swim to the surface and form a huge swarm, releasing eggs and sperm which fertilize to form larvae. After a few days floating on the surface, the surviving larvae swim down to the reefs below. The adults, meanwhile, continue feeding as normal, and regenerate a new gametophore so they can repeat the cycle next year.

Scientific name	*Eunice viridis*
Classification	Phylum Annelida; Class Polychaeta (Polychaete worms);
	Subclass Errantia; Family Eunicidae
Size	Around 40cm (16in) long
Distribution	South Pacific
Habitat	Coral reefs
Diet	Corals
Reproduction	Sexual with external fertilization by separate gametophores

Fireworm

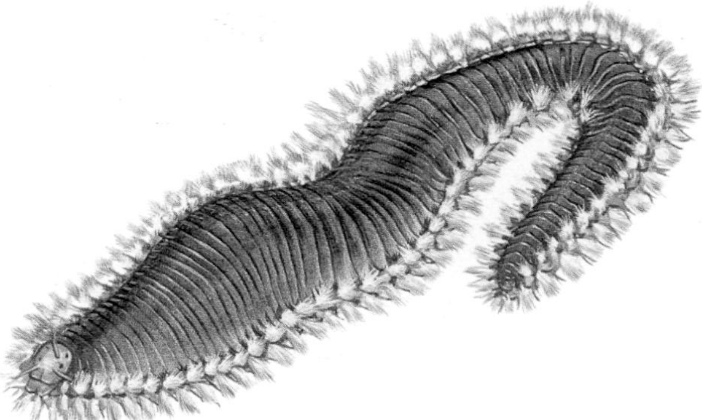

Coloured bright red or brown as a warning to other animals, fireworms are not to be trifled with – their bristles or setae are hollow and contain powerful venom. In fact, the name fireworm is a general term for a variety of venomous polychaetes. The most dangerous and voracious of these are the Amphinomidae, which live on reefs and feed on the coral by engulfing its tips and digesting the living tissue off the skeleton. These fireworms have setae designed to break off and embed themselves in a predator. The fibres are extremely brittle and difficult to remove, and humans who have touched them have sometimes lost fingers as a result.

Scientific name	*Hermodice Carunculata*
Classification	Phylum Annelida; Class Polychaeta (Polychaete worms);
	Subclass Errantia; Family Amphinomidae
Size	Up to 30cm (12in)
Distribution	Mediterranean; Caribbean
Habitat	Coral reefs
Diet	Corals
Reproduction	Sexual, with external fertilization

Myrianida

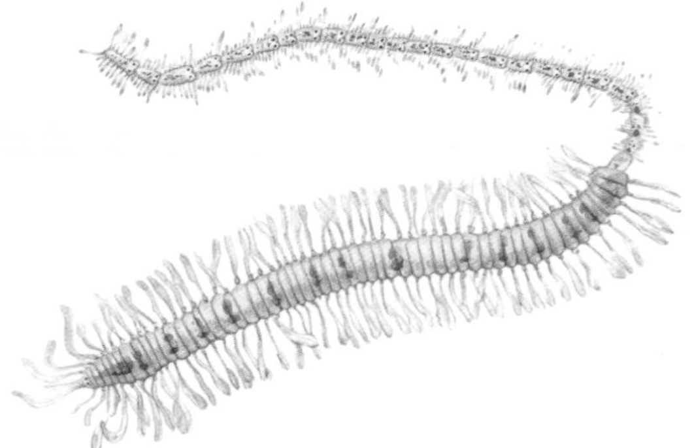

Myrianida is another errant polychaete with a bizarre reproductive system. Like several others, it practises 'schizogamy' for reproduction – an organism that separates from the main body of the worm is responsible for breeding. In Myrianida's case, each worm produces a series of sexual 'buds' from the penultimate (preanal) segment, which later release sperm and eggs. Myrianida normally dwells on the sea floor, rising to the surface to reproduce. Some species have developed into ectoparasites – for example *Myrianida pinnigera* fastens onto sea squirts and feeds off their bodily fluids.

Scientific name	*Myrianida sp.*
Classification	Phylum Annelida; Class Polychaeta (Polychaete worms);
	Subclass Errantia; Family Syllidae
Size	Variable
Distribution	Eastern North Atlantic; Mediterranean
Habitat	Sea floor at varying depths
Diet	Corals and other small invertebrates; some species parasitic
Reproduction	Schizogamy and reproduction by sexual buds

Fan worm

Sedentary polychaetes, as their name suggests, remain in one location throughout their lives. Typically they live either buried in the sand or hidden in tubes of their own construction. Fan worms occupy papery tubes made of their own solidified secretions, anchored either in the sand or preferably on rocks or shells. Their parapodia (rudimentary appendages) are underdeveloped or absent, but they have a spiral-shaped fan of brightly coloured tentacles around their head that are used to capture plankton, and retract instantly on contact or when the light is blocked by a shadow. *Spirographis* is a very successful colonist, having invaded Australian coastal waters attached to the hulls of ships.

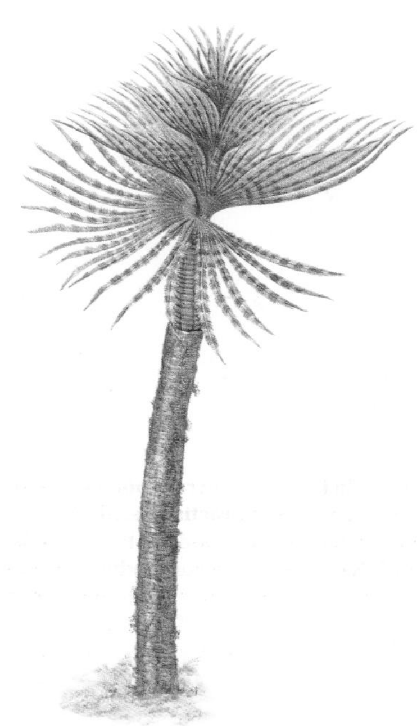

Scientific name	*Spirographis spallanzani*
Classification	Phylum Annelida; Class Polychaeta (Polychaete worms);
	Subclass Sedentaria; Family Sabellidae
Size	Tube up to 50cm (20in) long; fan up to 20cm (8in) radius
Distribution	Mediterranean; Australia
Habitat	Shallow subtidal waters and deep sheltered waters
Diet	Floating organic matter
Reproduction	Sexual, with external fertilization

Peacock worm

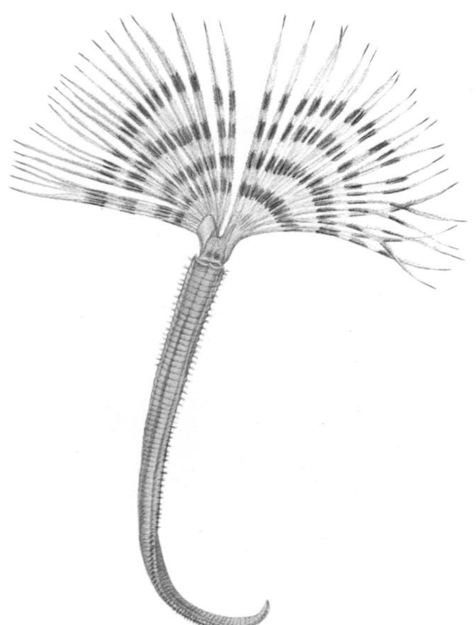

The peacock worm is one of the most beautiful fan worms, with striped feathery tentacles that give it its name. The worm itself lives buried in the sand, protected by a hardened tube of sand particles cemented with its own mucus. Only the top few centimetres protrude from the sand, along with the tentacles which spread out and act like gills to absorb oxygen. They also capture particles of organic and inorganic matter. Inorganic grains are used to repair and extend the protective tube, while organic ones are transported to the worm's mouth along grooves in the tentacles, each of which is lined with tiny hairlike cilia that wave back and forth to move the food downward.

Scientific name	*Sabella pavonina*
Classification	Phylum Annelida; Class Polychaeta (Polychaete worms);
	Subclass Sedentaria; Family Sabellidae
Size	Up to 40cm (16in) long
Distribution	Eastern North Atlantic; Mediterranean
Habitat	Shallow and tidal waters, including some freshwaters
Diet	Plankton, suspended organic particles
Reproduction	Sexual, with external fertilization

Encrusting polychaete

Some sedentary worms secrete harder materials to form pinkish-white calcareous (limestone) tubes. Some species even build a trapdoor (operculum) in the mouth of the tube for protection. Their trumpet-shaped tubes form reefs on solid rock outcrops or shells embedded in the seabed, which can act as habitats for other creatures. The worm that lives within the tube has red tentacles and a funnel-shaped head. Unlike other worms which are entirely passive feeders, these ones gently stir their tentacles to generate a current and bring food to them, allowing them to live in becalmed waters where other species could not survive.

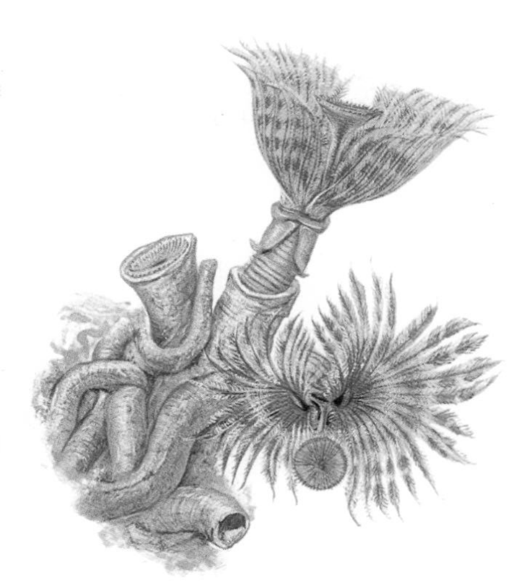

Scientific name	*Serpula vermicularis*
Classification	Phylum Annelida, Class Polychaeta (Polychaete worms)
	Subclass Sedentaria, Family Sabellidae
Size	Up to 7cm (2⅘in) long
Distribution	Eastern North Atlantic, Mediterranean
Habitat	Extreme low tide down to 250m (800ft)
Diet	Floating organic matter
Reproduction	Sexual, with external fertilization

Lugworm

The lugworm is best known as the favourite bait of many fishermen, and as the creature responsible for leaving casts on the sand as the tide goes out. Lugworms are a form of sedentary polychaete that burrow up to 60cm (24in) into the sand for protection, only emerging to feed on decayed organic matter that has fallen to the seabed. Because they gulp down food and sand together, they must excrete large amounts of waste in the form of casts. Lugworms are hermaphrodites, with the reproductive parts of both sexes. However, they do not reproduce on their own – their eggs must still be fertilized by another worm's sperm, and vice versa.

Scientific name	*Arenicola Marina*
Classification	Phylum Annelida; Class Polychaeta (Polychaete worms);
	Subclass Sedentaria; Family Arenicolidae
Size	Up to about 25cm (10in)
Distribution	North Atlantic and surrounding waters
Habitat	Tidal sands
Diet	Organic debris
Reproduction	Sexual; hermaphroditic but still require external fertilization

Chaetopterus

Also known as parchment worms, polychaetes of the genus Chaetopterus live in tough, U-shaped tubes of papery material they secrete themselves. Both ends of the tube taper, so the stout worm is permanently trapped inside. It feeds by using specially adapted parapodia (body folds) that wave back and forth and pump water and food particles through the tube. Among the most successful species is *Chaetopterus variopedatus*, which has two unique features – it can glow in the dark by bioluminescence, and more remarkably it can regenerate itself completely from even a single segment.

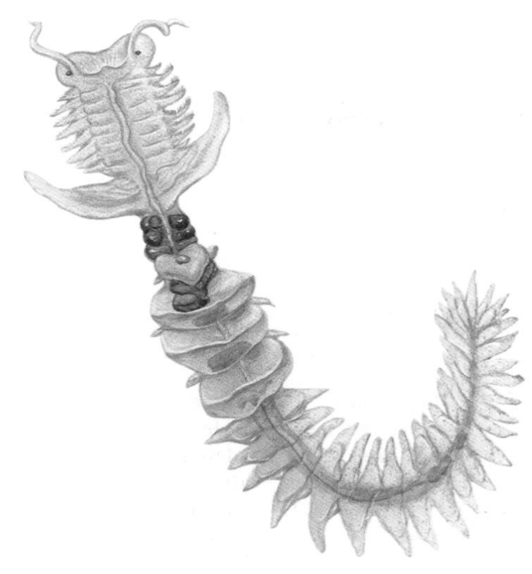

Scientific name	*Chaetopterus variopedatus*
Classification	Phylum Annelida; Class Polychaeta (Polychaete worms);
	Subclass Sedentaria; Family Chaetopteridae
Size	Up to 25cm (10in) long
Distribution	North Atlantic; North Pacific
Habitat	Sandy and rocky seabeds and rock outcrops to middle depths
Diet	Plankton
Reproduction	Sexual, with external fertilization

Spoon worm

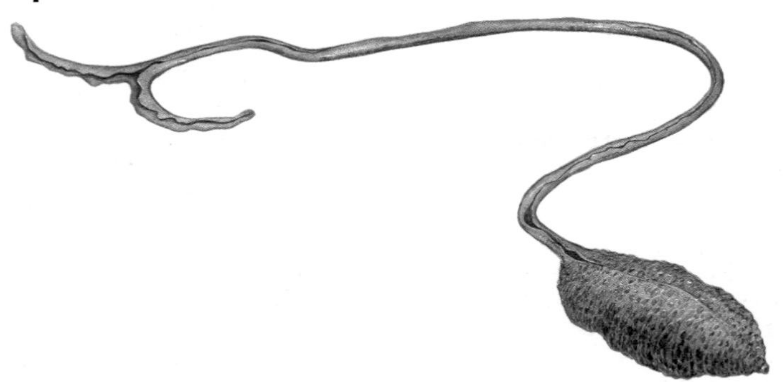

The spoon worms or Echiuridae are a group closely related to annelids, but which are only segmented as larvae – their segments disappear when they reach the adult stage. For this reason they are considered a separate phylum, but grouped with annelids and other close relatives in a larger group, the Trochozoa. *Bonellia viridis* has a bizarre reproduction method – the female is large and round, with a long proboscis. The male is tiny and lives permanently inside the female. Another unusual spoon worm is the innkeeper worm *Urechis caupo*, which lives in a U-shaped burrow and 'trawls' the water with a net of mucus.

Scientific name	*Bonellia viridis*
Classification	Group Trochozoa, Phylum Echiura
	Family Bonellidae
Size	Female up to 1m (40in) including proboscis; male about 2mm (⅛in)
Distribution	North Atlantic; Mediterranean; Red Sea
Habitat	Rocky seabeds
Diet	Plankton
Reproduction	Male lives permanently inside female

Giant rift worm

Growing taller than a man, and unknown to science until the 1970s, giant rift worms are among the strangest creatures of the deep ocean floor. They live in huge colonies around undersea thermal vents, where molten lava wells up from inside the earth and heats the waters. Rift worms look like giant tube worms, but grow from both ends, and have a segmented front and an unsegmented rear from which the tentacles burrow into the sand. Strangest of all, the worms have no digestive system – their food is provided by a colony of bacteria living within them, and the worms have developed to deliver oxygen and sulphur-rich compounds to these bacteria, allowing them to do their work.

Scientific name	*Vestimentefera sp.*
Classification	Group Trochozoa; Phylum Pogonophora;
	Class Vestimentifera or Phylum Vestimentifera (still disputed)
Size	Up to 3m (10ft) long
Distribution	Global mid-ocean trenches
Habitat	Deep sea thermal vents
Diet	Carbon compounds produced by internal bacteria
Reproduction	Larvae drift between thermal vents on deep-ocean currents

Ostracods

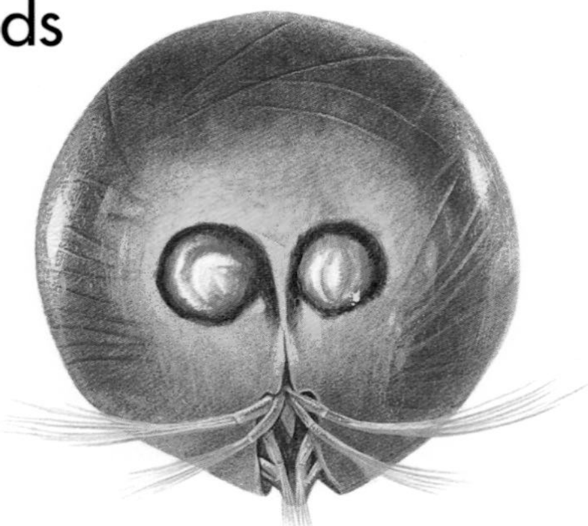

The seed shrimps or ostracods are a group of simple crustaceans that live in hinged spherical shells. They can retreat into these shells for protection with only their feathery antennae sticking out to find food. The antennae also propel the shrimp about by 'rowing' through the water. Over 12,000 species of these minute creatures are known – most dwelling on the sea floor but many floating freely in the oceans. Some species can cope with extremes of temperature and salinity, while others signal to each other in flashes of light. The largest of all, *Gigantocypris agassizi*, is a deep-ocean dweller with the most sensitive eyes in all of nature.

Scientific name	*Gigantocypris agassizi*
Classification	Phylum Crustacea; Class Ostracoda;
	Order Myodocopina; Family Cypridinidae
Size	Up to 3cm (1¼in)
Distribution	Cosmopolitan
Habitat	Deep oceans at 1000–3000m (3300–10,000ft)
Diet	Copepods and small fish
Reproduction	Sexual, through copulation

Copepods

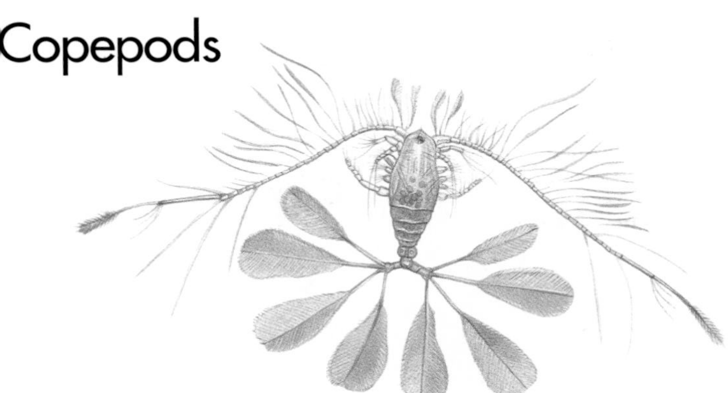

Copepods are often called the insects of the sea, because their 12,000 species are incredibly widespread and constitute the majority of the ocean's living mass. They form the basis of the marine food chain in many parts of the world, and occupy every available niche from the deep-ocean floor to freshwater rivers and lakes. About a third of known species are parasitic. Free-swimming copepods are called calanoids – they have long and elaborate feathery antennae ideal for swimming, despite their tiny size (most are just a couple of millimetres long). Many migrate to the surface waters at night, and sink back to the depths in daylight.

Scientific name	*Calocalanus pavo*
Classification	Phylum Crustacea; Class Copepoda;
	Order Calanoida; Family Paracalanidae
Size	A few millimetres across
Distribution	Cosmopolitan
Habitat	Free-swimming in the water column
Diet	Free-floating algae
Reproduction	Male mates by attaching a sperm package to the female

Goose barnacle

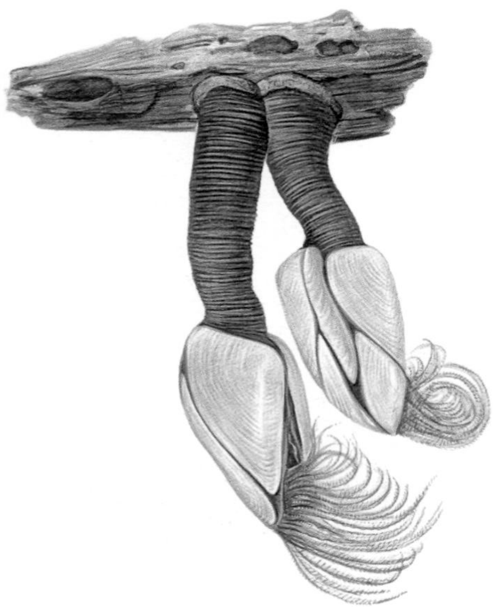

The goose barnacle is a member of the cirripedia – a specialized group of crustaceans that live all their adult lives without moving. Goose barnacles attach themselves to rocks and other hard surfaces by a stalk called a peduncle, that can grow up to 90cm (36in) long. Their main body consists of two plates that open to allow their six pairs of legs to emerge, and these legs act as a net, filtering the waters for food particles. Barnacle young swim freely until they attach themselves to a suitable surface, which may include floating debris, larger animals, and ships – a buildup of barnacles on a ship's hull can reduce its speed by up to 30%.

Scientific name	*Lepas anatifera*
Classification	Phylum Crustacea; Class Cirripedia;
	Order Thoracica; Family Lepadidae
Size	Up to 10cm (4in) long
Distribution	Worldwide in warm and temperate waters
Habitat	Intertidal zone
Diet	Plankton
Reproduction	Sexual, through copulation

Common barnacle

There are at least 800 known species of barnacle around the world, occupying a wide range of habitats from tidal shores down to the deep seas. Common barnacles, also called acorn barnacles, attach themselves directly to a hard surface and grow a cone of fixed limestone plates from which a pair of flexible opening plates emerges. They filter the water for food with their legs, in the same way as goose barnacles. Some barnacles are parasitic, burrowing into corals, other crustaceans, or the shells of molluscs. Others, while not parasitic, have evolved to live on larger animals such as whales.

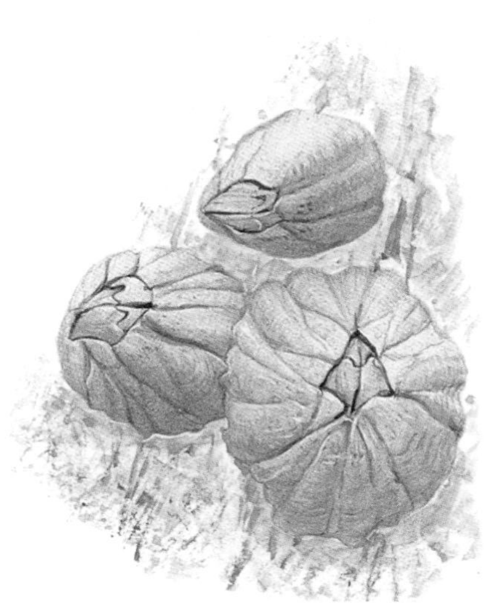

Scientific name	*Balanus crenatus*
Classification	Phylum Crustacea; Class Cirripedia;
	Order Thoracica; Family Balanidae
Size	Up to 25mm (1in) across
Distribution	Cosmopolitan
Habitat	Intertidal zone to deep sea
Diet	Plankton
Reproduction	Sexual, through copulation

Nebalia

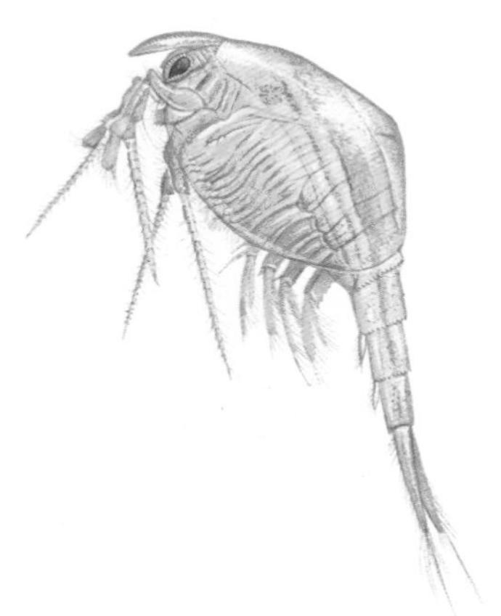

The Malacostraca are the crustacean group that contains most of the familiar crustaceans – shrimps, prawns, lobsters, and crabs. The most primitive members of this group are the Leptostraca, of which Nebalia are the most successful genus. Malacostrans are usually distinguished by a body with 20 segments (six fused ones forming the head, eight the thorax, and six the abdomen). The Nebaliidae are unusual because they have an extra segment in their abdomen. They also have a large transparent carapace in two parts – the rear section encloses and protects most of their body, while the smaller front section forms a visor to protect the head.

Scientific name	*Nebalia bipes*
Classification	Phylum Crustacea; Class Malacostraca;
	Order Leptostraca; Family Nebaliidae
Size	A few millimetres
Distribution	Northeast US coast; Europe
Habitat	Coastal waters, particularly with vegetation
Diet	Organic waste and vegetation
Reproduction	Sexual, through copulation

Mantis shrimp

The mantis shrimp's name is doubly misleading – it is unrelated to preying mantises, and is also not a shrimp. Mantis shrimps are fearsome hunters, capable of attacking prey much larger than themselves. They bear either vicious spines or heavily calcified clubs on their forelimbs, and these limbs are capable of lightning quick movements, lashing out faster than 10m/s (30ft/s) to spear or club passing prey. The largest 'smasher' mantis shrimps pack a punch equivalent to that of a 0.22 calibre bullet. The mantises also have the natural world's most complex eyes, with no less than 16 different types of photoreceptors for detecting light.

Scientific name	*Squilla empusa*
Classification	Phylum Crustacea; Class Malacostraca;
	Order Stomatopoda; Family Squillidae
Size	Up to 30cm (12in)
Distribution	Gulf of Mexico and surrounding waters
Habitat	Offshore seabeds down to 150m (500ft)
Diet	Small fish, crustaceans, and other invertebrates
Reproduction	Sexual, through copulation, with a complex mating ritual

Opossum shrimp

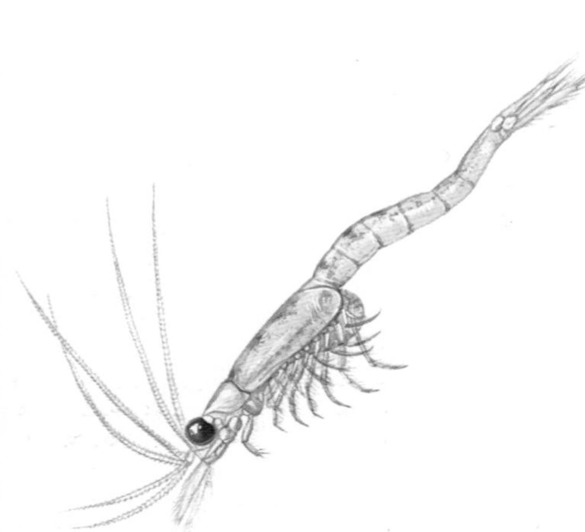

The opposum shrimps, or Mysidacea, are so-called because they carry their eggs and young in a pouch, like marsupial mammals. They are largely filter-feeders, swimming in huge swarms just above the sea floor and filtering plankton from the water. Sometimes they will also scavenge on dead animals and even hunt animals smaller than they are. Opposum shrimps are almost entirely transparent, except for their black compound eyes, making them difficult for predators to see. They propel themselves using a fan on the end of their tail. The tail also has a pair of statocysts – cavities containing a particle floating in fluid, which act as balance sensors.

Scientific name	*Mysis relicta*
Classification	Phylum Crustacea; Class Malacostraca;
	Order Mysidacea; Family Mysidae
Size	Up to 1.6cm (⅔in)
Distribution	Europe, Asia, North America
Habitat	Shallow seafloor and cold freshwater lakes
Diet	Plankton; carrion
Reproduction	Young brooded in a pouch

Diastylis

The cumaceans are a group of crustaceans that live on the sea floor, burrowing into mud (frequently backwards), in search of particles of organic matter. Areas of the sea floor with rich pickings are often densely colonized by cumaceans. They have five pairs of legs and three pairs of feeding appendages around their mouths, emerging from a large protective carapace that is often highly ornamented. Because the carapace is hard, juvenile cumaceans must shed it several times as they grow. In the case of *Diastylis rathkei*, all the juveniles moult at the same time, resulting in huge swarms coming to the surface at once.

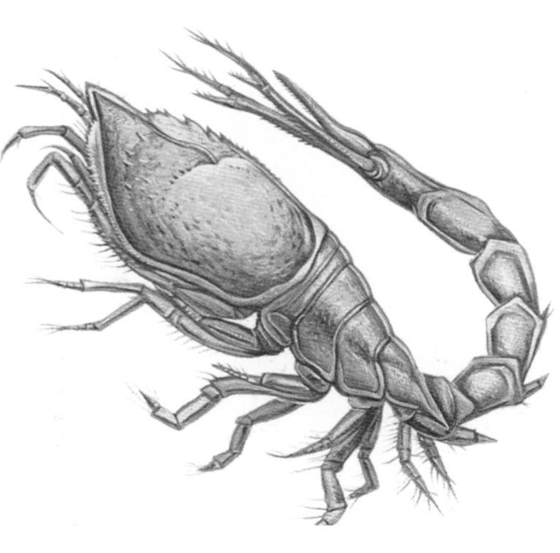

Scientific name	*Diastylis rathkei*
Classification	Phylum Crustacea; Class Malacostraca;
	Order Cumacea; Family Diastylidae
Size	Up to 2cm (¾in)
Distribution	Arctic waters
Habitat	Ocean floor at depths less than 200m (660ft)
Diet	Organic matter on sand grains; plankton
Reproduction	Probably mate while swimming freely at night

Sea slater

Sea slaters, also called sea cockroaches, are in fact shoreline animals – malacostracans who have shed their carapace, and whose gills have adapted to a terrestrial lifestyle. They are fast-moving scavengers with an obvious resemblance to woodlice, to which they are related. Other adaptations include sessile eyes (in other words, eyes on the exterior of the head, and not on stalks), and simple thoracic legs without pincers. Isopods form swarms of large numbers and only venture below the tidemark when the waters are out. They brood about 80 young in a pouch on the thorax, and release them as miniature versions of the adult.

Scientific name	*Ligia oceanica*
Classification	Phylum Crustacea; Class Malacostraca;
	Order Isopoda; Family Ligiidae
Size	Up to 3cm (1¼in)
Distribution	Coasts worldwide
Habitat	Rocky seashores
Diet	Organic detritus
Reproduction	Male fertilizes female using specialized spike on abdominal legs

Amphipod

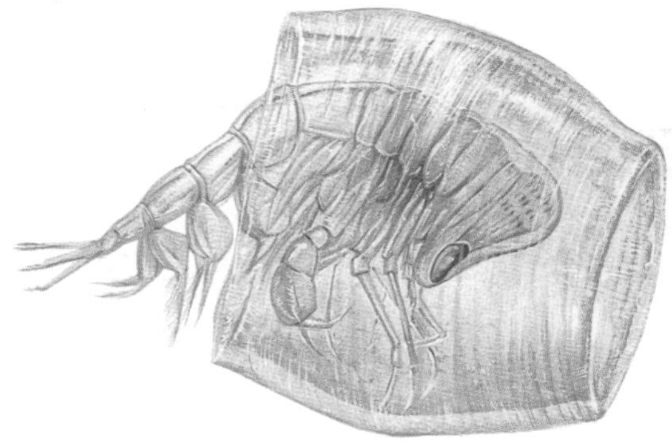

Like the sea slaters, amphipods are specially adapted malacostracans which have shed their carapaces. Their bodies have become flattened from side to side, and they are curved into a C-shape, which their long antennae continues. Their 4,000 species include the widespread sand hoppers and the skeleton shrimps, and are found in a variety of habitats around the world, ranging from the shorelines to the deep seas. *Phronima sedentaria* is a member of the family Hyperiidae, and like many of its relatives, it is parasitic, living, feeding, and bearing live young inside jellyfish and tunicates such as sea squirts and salps.

Scientific name	*Phronima sedentaria*
Classification	Phylum Crustacea; Class Malacostraca;
	Order Amphipoda; Family Hyperiidae
Size	A few millimetres
Distribution	Mid-ocean waters
Habitat	Living within gelatinous zooplankton
Diet	Internal tissues of hosts
Reproduction	Bears live young which can swim away to a new host

Skeleton shrimp

Skeleton shrimps are amphipods with slender, elongated bodies, a long thorax and a very short abdomen. They resemble a cross between a shrimp and a praying mantis and are equipped with fearsome-looking pincers on their front limbs. The shrimps do not swim, but instead climb around on sponges and seaweeds, scraping algae and polyps from the surface. They can also anchor themselves with their hind legs, reaching out to grab passing plankton with their foreclaws. Like opposum shrimps, they brood their young in a pouch. Several hundred species of skeleton shrimp are known, and close relatives live a similar lifestyle on the skins of whales and dolphins.

Scientific name	*Caprella linearis*
Classification	Phylum Crustacea; Class Malacostraca;
	Order Amphipoda; Family Caprellidae
Size	Up to 2cm (¾in)
Distribution	Eastern North Atlantic and surrounding waters
Habitat	Seaweeds and sponges at depths of up to 4m (13ft)
Diet	Algae; polyps; plankton
Reproduction	Females brood young in a pouch

Krill

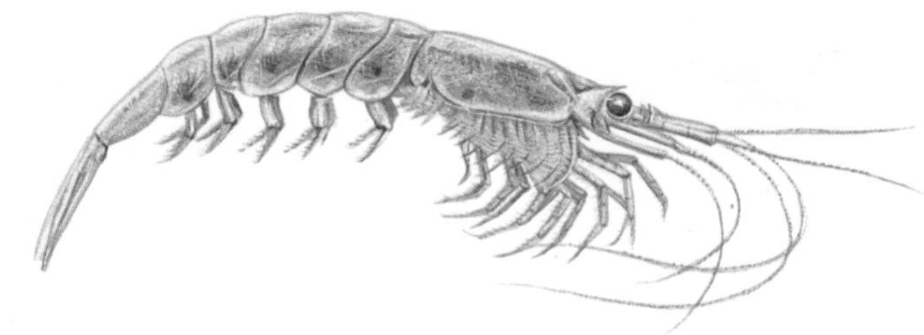

One of the most important species on the planet, the shrimp-like krill form the base of many food chains around the world. These small transparent, bioluminescent creatures form huge swarms in the cold waters around both poles. In the Southern Ocean particularly, Antarctic krill replace small fish as a major food supply for larger animals. Nordic krill (as illustrated) feed on copepods, giving them a distinctive red gut, while their larger southern cousins feed on phytoplankton floating at the water's surface. Krill migrate daily, spending the daylight hours in deep waters and coming to the surface to feed and lay eggs at night.

Scientific name	*Meganyctiphanes norvegica*
Classification	Phylum Crustacea; Class Malacostraca;
	Order Eucarida; Family Euphausiacea
Size	Up to 3cm (1¼in)
Distribution	Cold northern waters
Habitat	Free-swimming; sheltering among ice floes
Diet	Copepods
Reproduction	Eggs are laid at surface, but sink to deep waters

Penaeus prawn

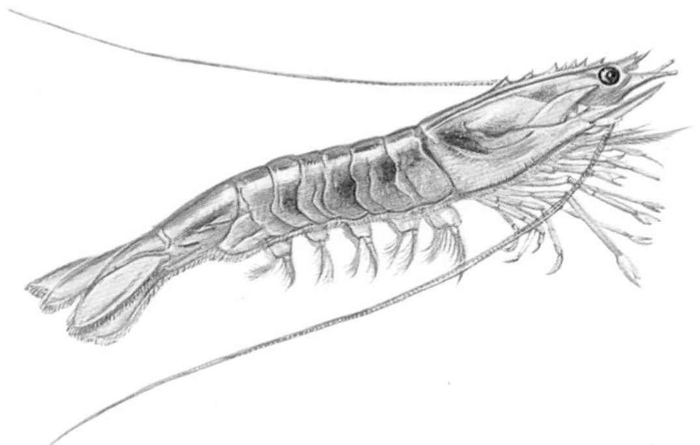

Prawns or shrimps of the genus *Penaeus* are among the most widely harvested – they include the large tiger prawns that are eaten throughout Asia, and the pink 'shrimp' from the western Atlantic. Pink shrimps spend the day burrowed into the seabed, emerging on the darkest nights to hunt and scavenge. They mate throughout the year, with the eggs hatching in the water and the young migrating to shallow inshore 'nursery grounds' rich in vegetation. As shrimps grow, they must cast off their old shells, leaving their soft bodies exposed until a new larger shell hardens around them. This is the time at which females lay their eggs.

Scientific name	*Penaeus duorarum*
Classification	Phylum Crustacea; Class Malacostraca;
	Order Decapoda; Family Penaeidae
Size	Around 17.5cm (7in) long – females larger than males
Distribution	Western Pacific, Carolina to Uruguay
Habitat	Sandy shallow seabeds down to 100m (330ft)
Diet	Algae; organic particles; plankton
Reproduction	Sexual, through copulation; breeds throughout the year

Common prawn

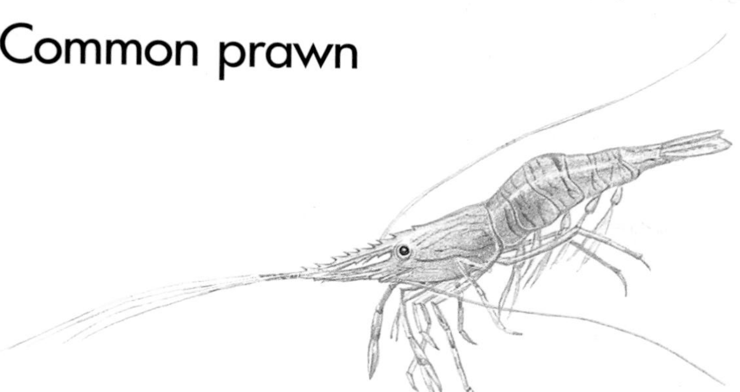

The common prawn, *Palaemon serratus*, is found throughout the eastern North Atlantic, Mediterranean, and surrounding seas, where it is harvested in large amounts for food. It has a semitransparent carapace, extending forward above the eyes to form a head-shield or rostrum. The head turns upwards and has several indentations, and the rostrum splits in two at the end. The common prawn also has extremely long antennae, up to one and a half times its body length, which it uses to sense danger. Like most prawns and shrimps, its preferred habitat is a shallow seabed where it can hide among rocks and seaweed.

Scientific name	*Palaemon serratus*
Classification	Phylum Crustacea; Class Malacostraca;
	Order Decapoda; Family Palaemonidae
Size	Up to around 10cm (4in)
Distribution	Eastern North Atlantic; Mediterranean
Habitat	Shallow rocky seabeds with plentiful seaweed
Diet	Plankton; organic debris
Reproduction	Sexual, through copulation; breeds throughout the year

Common shrimp

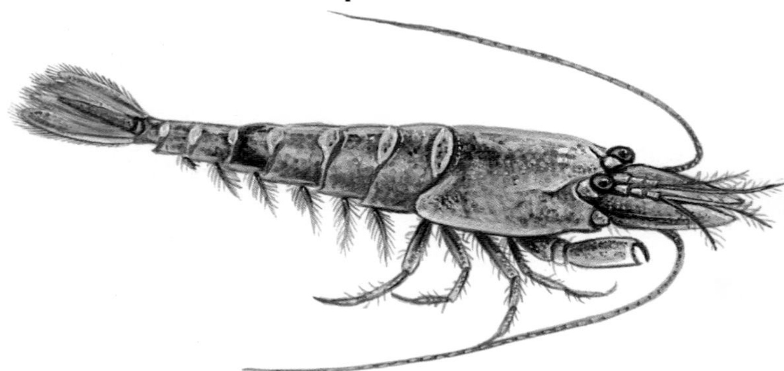

Although the terms prawn and shrimp are often used interchangeably, one way of separating them is by their body plan – shrimps are wide and flat while prawns are tall and narrow. The common shrimp *Crangon crangon* is widespread throughout Europe. It is an active predator, hunting planktonic animals, molluscs, and other shrimps in the hours of darkness on shallow seabeds, and eating up to ten per cent of its own body weight per day. In daylight the shrimp buries itself in sand with only its eyes and antennae sticking out. Shrimps also make an annual migration down the shore into deeper, warmer waters with the onset of winter.

Scientific name	*Crangon crangon*
Classification	Phylum Crustacea; Class Malacostraca;
	Order Decapoda; Crangonidae
Size	Up to 10cm (4in)
Distribution	Eastern North Atlantic; Mediterranean; Baltic
Habitat	Shallow shorelines, just below low-tide mark
Diet	Plankton; small invertebrates
Reproduction	Sexual, 4–5 times a year

Pistol or snapping shrimp

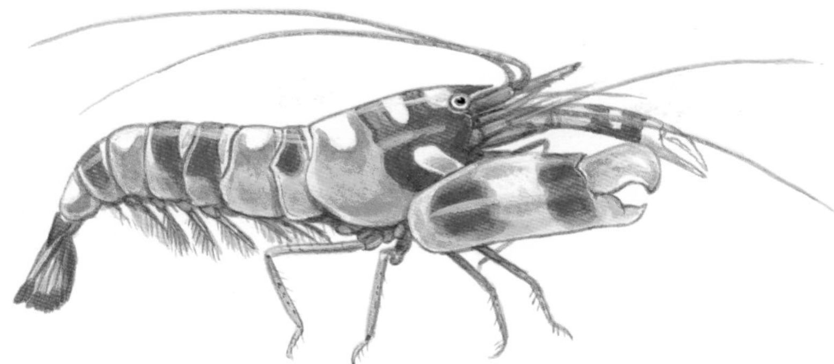

The pistol shrimp is a remarkable little shrimp with an unusual weapon. By snapping its claw closed at high speed, the shrimp can create a powerful sound wave that can stun or even kill nearby prey or predators. It is not the snapping of the claw itself which makes the sound, but the expansion and collapse of nearby microscopic air bubbles disturbed by the high-speed water movements. Pistol shrimps also form unusual symbiotic relationships with goby fish, often allowing the fish to share their burrows and food. In exchange the fish uses its better eyesight to watch for danger and alert the shrimp.

Scientific name	*Alpheus randalli*
Classification	Phylum Crustacea; Class Malacostraca;
	Order Decapoda; Family Alpheidae
Size	About 2.5cm (1in) long
Distribution	Indo-Pacific
Habitat	Shallow sandy seabeds, mostly around reefs
Diet	Small fish; crustaceans
Reproduction	Sexual, through copulation

Common lobster

Lobsters are large, ten-footed crustaceans with huge claws on their first pair of legs. They are normally blue-black in colour (cooked lobster is red because its pigments are destroyed by boiling), and can grow to around 1m (40in) long, from tail to claw. In order to keep growing, the lobster must slough its shell every year, after which it expands slightly before its new shell hardens (shrimps, prawns, and crabs moult in a similar way). Lobsters usually live among rocks and crevices, ideally with sandy seabeds that they can burrow in. They hunt a wide variety of food, using some ingenious hunting strategies, and will also scavenge.

Scientific name	*Homarus gammarus*
Classification	Phylum Crustacea; Class Malacostraca;
	Order Decapoda; Family Astacidae
Size	Up to 75cm (30in) long
Distribution	Eastern North Atlantic; Mediterranean
Habitat	Rocky seabeds
Diet	Crustaceans; fish; molluscs
Reproduction	Sexual; spawns once a year after moulting

Spiny lobster or crayfish

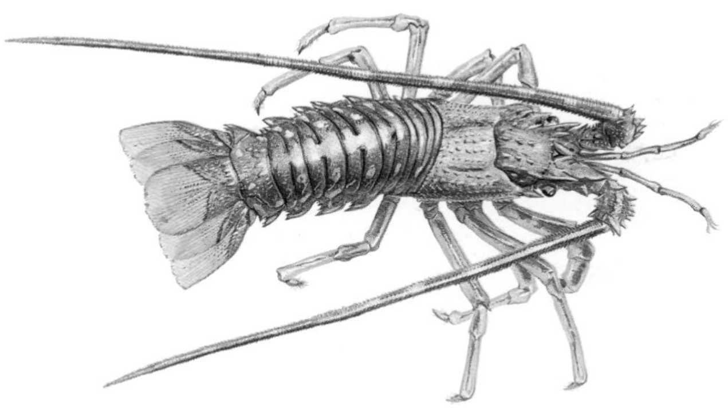

The spiny lobster, crayfish, or crawfish is a close relative of the common lobster, but with several differences – most noticeably the front three pairs of legs all bear claws (though much smaller than the lobster's), and most of the body is covered in sharp defensive spines. Crayfish are generally smaller than lobsters and there are freshwater as well as marine species. They are usually orange on the back and white on their underside. Crayfish hide in the sand during the day, and emerge to hunt a variety of prey at night. If threatened, they can escape at high speed with flicks of their tail.

Scientific name	*Palinurus elephas*
Classification	Phylum Crustacea; Class Malacostraca;
	Order Decapoda; Family Astacidae
Size	Up to 60cm (24in)
Distribution	Eastern North Atlantic and Mediterranean
Habitat	Rock-strewn, sandy seabeds
Diet	Crustaceans; fish; molluscs
Reproduction	Sexual; spawns once a year after moulting

Hermit crab

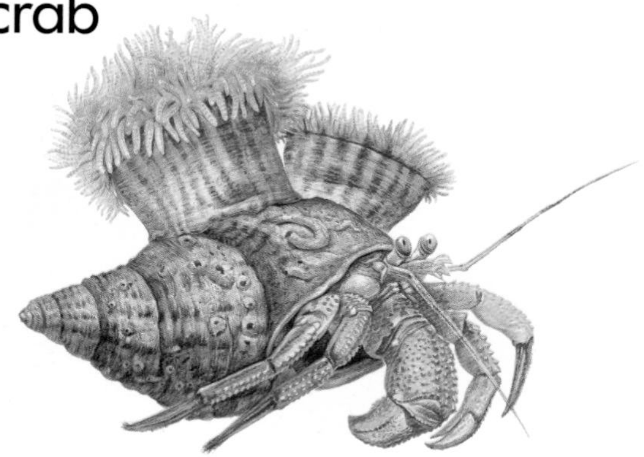

Hermit crabs are unusual malacostracans because they have an unarmoured and vulnerable abdomen. To protect themselves, they hide these body parts in empty gastropod shells, which they hold onto with their reduced hind legs. When threatened, the crab can withdraw into the shell completely, with just one enlarged pincer left outside. When the crab outgrows the shell, it simply finds another one, evicting the mollusc inside it if necessary. Hermit crabs often allow anemones and polyps to grow on their shells – the crab benefits from camouflage and protection, while the squatters feed on the debris of the crab's meals.

Scientific name	*Eupagurus bernhardus*
Classification	Phylum Crustacea; Class Malacostraca;
	Order Decapoda; Family Paguridea
Size	Up to 10cm (4in) total
Distribution	Eastern North Atlantic; Mediterranean
Habitat	Shallow sea floors down to 30m (100ft)
Diet	Small crustaceans; molluscs; carrion
Reproduction	Sexual; males carry females during mating

Striated hermit crab

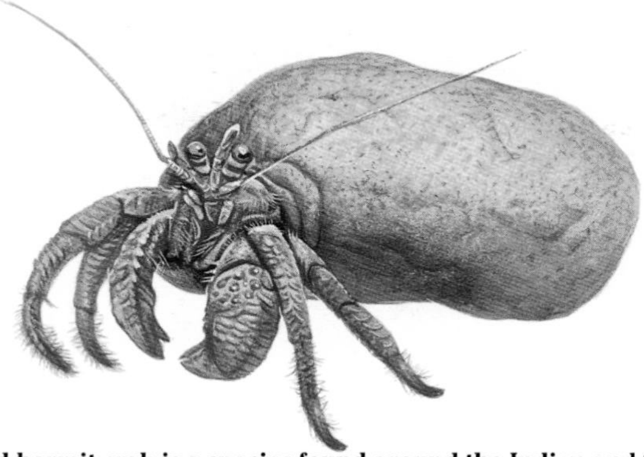

The striated hermit crab is a species found around the Indian and South Pacific oceans, marked with distinctive red and white stripes and a highly developed left claw. It is frequently completely disguised by a red-coloured sponge, *Suberites domuncula*, or covered by several anemones whose stings may help to fend off predators. Hermit crabs are not true crabs – they are members of a sub-order called Anomura, in which the two hindmost legs are reduced, leaving only six main legs for walking and two for pincers. In hermit crabs, the two reduced legs help hold on to the shell.

Scientific name	*Dardanus arosor*
Classification	Phylum Crustacea; Class Malacostraca;
	Order Decapoda; Family Diogenidae
Size	Up to 14cm (5⅜in) long
Distribution	Indo-Pacific
Habitat	Seafloors down to 200m (660ft)
Diet	Small crustaceans; molluscs; carrion
Reproduction	Sexual; males carry females during mating

Porcelain crab

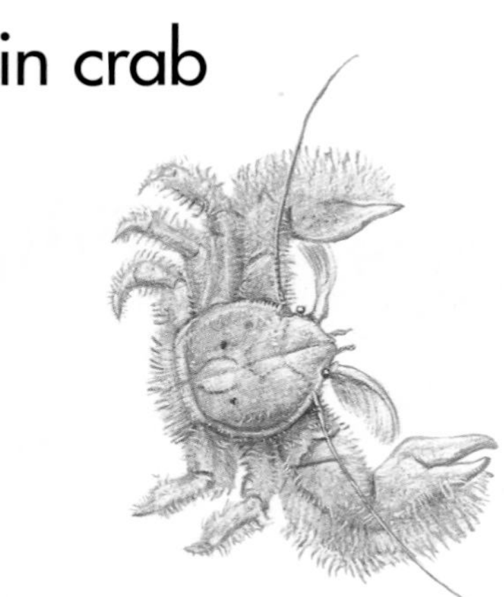

Porcelain crabs, like hermit crabs, are anomurans, with a reduced fifth pair of legs that are often completely hidden. These tiny crabs are typically less than 2.5cm (1in) across, and cling tightly to rocks with spikes that prevent them being washed away. *Porcellana platycheles*, the broad-clawed porcelain crab of Europe, has a 'hairy' shell and two very well-developed front pincers. It collects mud on the hairs, which help to disguise its body, and it can filter organic matter from the sediment on its pincers. It can also use the claws to snip chunks of flesh from any dead animals that it finds on the beach.

Scientific name	*Porcellana platycheles*
Classification	Phylum Crustacea; Class Malacostraca;
	Order Decapoda; Family Diogenidae
Size	Up to 15mm (⅗in)
Distribution	Eastern North Atlantic; Mediterranean
Habitat	Among stones on muddy shores
Diet	Organic debris; carrion
Reproduction	Sexual, through copulation

Squat lobster

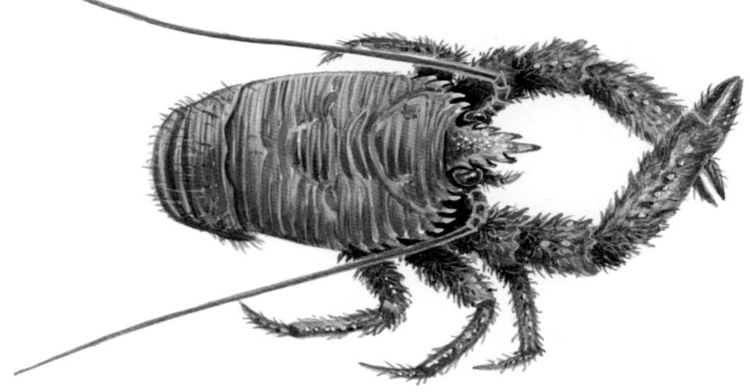

Squat lobsters are another group of crab-like decapods with reduced back legs. They have flattened bodies that allow them to lurk among rocks in the day, emerging at night to feed. They are mainly scavengers, though they are also well equipped to catch their own prey. *Galathea strigosa*, the spiny squat lobster from western Europe, has distinctive colouring with a rusty-orange carapace and blue stripes. The large front claws are covered in defensive spines, while much of the abdomen is folded back under the body, from where it can uncurl rapidly to flip the lobster through the water if it is threatened.

Scientific name	*Galathea strigosa*
Classification	Phylum Crustacea; Class Malacostraca;
	Order Decapoda; Family Galatheidae
Size	Up to around 15cm (6in) long
Distribution	Eastern North Atlantic; Mediterranean
Habitat	Rocky seabeds
Diet	Carrion; small crustaceans
Reproduction	Sexual, breeding once a year

Common or shore crab

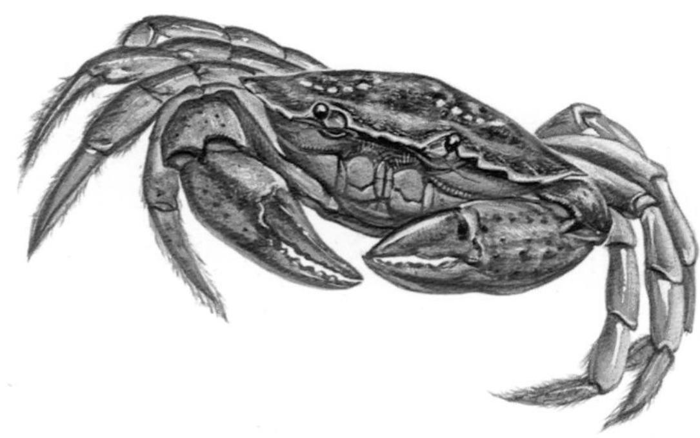

True crabs have ten fully developed legs – eight to walk on and a front pair of 'chelipeds' equipped with pincers. Not all can swim, but those that can, such as the shore crab *Carcinus maenas*, have paddle-shaped hind limbs that help propel them through the water. Shore crabs are scavengers and predators, generally scuttling sideways on the seashore or in shallow water, searching for anything they can find. When the crab moults, it leaves an empty shell, complete with claw cases, on the beach. Shore crabs are extremely successful and adaptable animals, and have become an invasive species in some areas of North America.

Scientific name	*Carcinus maenas*
Classification	Phylum Crustacea; Class Malacostraca;
	Order Decapoda; Family Portunidae
Size	About 10cm (4in) across
Distribution	Eastern North Atlantic; Mediterranean
Habitat	Seashores and shallow waters
Diet	Crustaceans; molluscs; carrion
Reproduction	Sexual, through copulation

Blue swimmer crab

While many crabs can paddle a little, wimming crabs have pecially adapted back legs quipped with broad spoon-haped scoops. The blue wimmer from Pacific and ndian Ocean waters has ttractive colouring (orange nd brown in females, blues nd purples in males), istinctive long straight incers, and a carapace with pikes to either side. *Portunus elagicus* is a highly skilled wimmer that cannot survive or long out of water – it ormally hunts in shallow ffshore seaweed beds, but omes inshore at high tides to atch fish in coastal mangrove wamps and estuaries.

Scientific name	*Portunus pelagicus*
Classification	Phylum Crustacea; Class Malacostraca;
	Order Decapoda; Family Portunidae
Size	Up to about 21cm (8½in) across the carapace
Distribution	Indo-Pacific
Habitat	Offshore seaweed beds; mangrove swamps
Diet	Crustaceans; fish
Reproduction	Sexual, mating once a year

Scorpion spider crab

Spider crabs are so-called because they often have extremely long legs, and their pincered front legs (known as chelipeds) are usually not much longer than the other pairs. They are also distinguished by the triangular shape of their carapace, which narrows towards the front and often extends to form a pointed rostrum. The scorpion spider crab, *Inachus dorsemensis*, has relatively stout pincers compared to most. Spider crabs frequently use their pincers to pick up sponges, seaweed, and other materials, which they attach to hooks on their carapace and claws to decorate and disguise themselves.

Scientific name	*Inachus dorsemensis*
Classification	Phylum Crustacea; Class Malacostraca;
	Order Decapoda; Family Majidae
Size	Carapace up to 30mm (1¼in) long
Distribution	Eastern North Atlantic
Habitat	Plant-strewn seabeds at depths up to 200m (660ft)
Diet	Algae; molluscs; carrion
Reproduction	Sexual, through copulation

Homolid spider crab

A few spider crabs, in the family Homolidae, have roughly square carapaces with forward-facing spikes along the upper front edge. Homolid crabs also have pincer-bearing chelipeds that are shorter than their other legs. Another distinctive feature is that the back pair of legs are thin, short and doubled back on themselves, ending in a hook-shaped 'subchela' claw. Homolids live on the seabed in moderate to deep waters and, like other spider crabs, they frequently attach shells and living polyps to their shells for camouflage. They have even been know to change their decorations when forced to change habitat.

Scientific name	*Homola barbata*
Classification	Phylum Crustacea; Class Malacostraca;
	Order Decapoda; Family Homolidae
Size	Carapace up to 5cm (2in) long
Distribution	Mediterranean and into North Atlantic
Habitat	Shelly, sandy, and muddy seabeds from 40–400m (130–1300ft)
Diet	Algae; molluscs; carrion
Reproduction	Sexual, through copulation

Pea crab

The pea crabs are tiny crustaceans with bodies about the size of a garden pea. They are found living within a wide variety of bivalves, including mussels, oysters, and pen shells (pinnidae), and frequently have bizarre life cycles – the females are much larger than the males and are sometimes mistaken for a different species entirely. Apart from a brief period spent swarming in open water during the mating season, the crabs spend all their lives inside the shell of the host, thriving on nutrients produced by the mollusc. They are usually commensal (doing no harm to the host), but some are damaging parasites.

Scientific name	*Pinnotheres piscum*
Classification	Phylum Crustacea; Class Malacostraca;
	Order Decapoda; Family Pinnotheridae
Size	Carapace up to 1cm (⅜in)
Distribution	Eastern North Pacific; Mediterranean
Habitat	Commensal with bivalves
Diet	Algae and organic particles filtered by the bivalve; chemicals from host
Reproduction	Sexual, through copulation

Fiddler crab

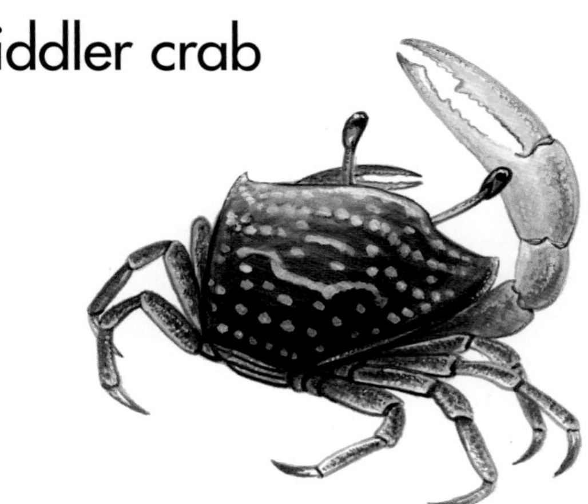

There are at least 75 known species and subspecies of fiddler crab, united by one distinctive feature – the single huge claw on the male that can account for up to half of its body weight. The crabs live largely on land, burrowing in mud and feeding on organic matter buried in sediments. They feed only with their smaller claw, and its rapid movements back and forth to the mouth while the larger claw is held still give fiddler crabs their name. The huge claw, which can be either on the left or the right side, is used in mating rituals for attracting females and challenging rival males, though grappling matches between males rarely end in injury.

Scientific name	*Uca vocans*
Classification	Phylum Crustacea; Class Malacostraca;
	Order Decapoda; Family Ocypodidae
Size	Around 3–4 cm (1⅛–1⅜in) across
Distribution	Indian Ocean
Habitat	Shallow sandy coastlines and mangrove swamps
Diet	Algae and organic debris
Reproduction	Sexual; female broods eggs until they hatch

King or horseshoe crab

The prehistoric-looking horseshoe crab is a living fossil, and a close relative of the trilobites that roamed the sea floors and beaches 300 million years ago. Despite its name, it is closer to an arachnid than a true crab, though it does not bear much resemblance to any other living animal. The head and thorax form a single unit, with six pairs of appendages attached – two feeding palps, two claws, and eight walking legs. The head and abdomen are covered by a horseshoe-shaped shell and a long tail extends from the back. Horseshoe crabs are burrowing predators that feed on molluscs, worms, and other invertebrates.

Scientific name	*Limulus polyphemus*
Classification	Phylum Arthropoda; Class Merostomata;
	Order Xiphosura; Family Limulidae
Size	Up to 60cm (24in) long, including tail
Distribution	Western North Atlantic
Habitat	Shallow sandy offshore seabeds
Diet	Molluscs, worms, and other small invertebrates
Reproduction	Spawns on land annually; eggs laid on sand are then fertilized by males

Sea spider

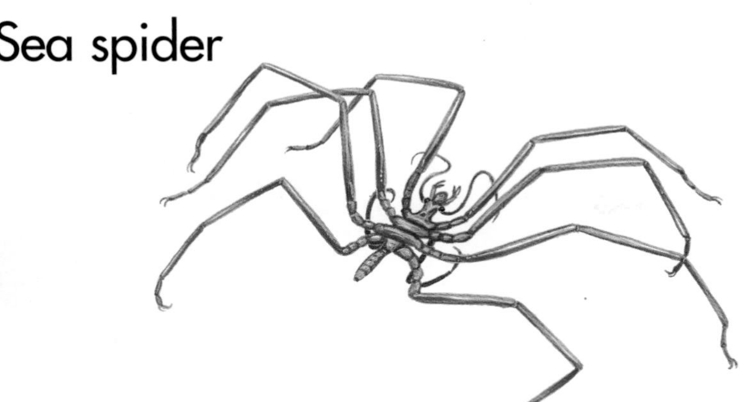

The sea spiders or Pycnogonida are marine arthropods, cousins of terrestrial arachnids. Most have eight walking legs, though some have more. Although a few types can swim, most sea spiders live on the ocean floor, feeding on corals, hydroids, and anemones, by puncturing the outer membrane with a long proboscis and sucking at the internal tissues. Sea spiders have no gut and no gills – they absorb and release gases, nutrients, and waste by simple diffusion through their thin body walls. Most are tiny, but some, such as *Colossondeis colossea*, reach monstrous proportions.

Scientific name	*Colossondeis colossea*
Classification	Phylum Arthropoda; Class Pycnogonida;
	Order Pantopoda; Family Colossendeidae
Size	Up to 75cm (30in) across
Distribution	Cosmopolitan
Habitat	Deep-ocean seabeds
Diet	Corals; hydroids; sea anemones
Reproduction	External fertilization; male gathers fertilized eggs and broods them

Sea lily

Sea lilies are members of the echinoderm phylum – a group of unique animals with no brain but a remarkably sophisticated system for moving and feeding. All show a five-fold symmetry and have a body made largely of calcium carbonate plates. The sea lilies are actually crinoids, the simplest echinoderms. They live permanently attached to the sea floor by a root called a peduncle, and complex branching arms collect floating organic debris with water-filled tentacles called tube feet. Food is then passed down the arms to the upturned mouth, where it is digested. In between the tube feet on each arm are numerous defensive spines of calcium carbonate.

Scientific name	*Rhizocrinus lofotensis*
Classification	Phylum Echinodermata; Class Crinoidea;
	Order Bourgueticrinida; Family Bourgueticrinidae
Size	Around 15cm (6in) long
Distribution	Seabeds down to 2000m (6600ft)
Habitat	Eastern North Atlantic; Baltic
Diet	Algae and organic debris
Reproduction	Sexual with external fertilization

Sea lily

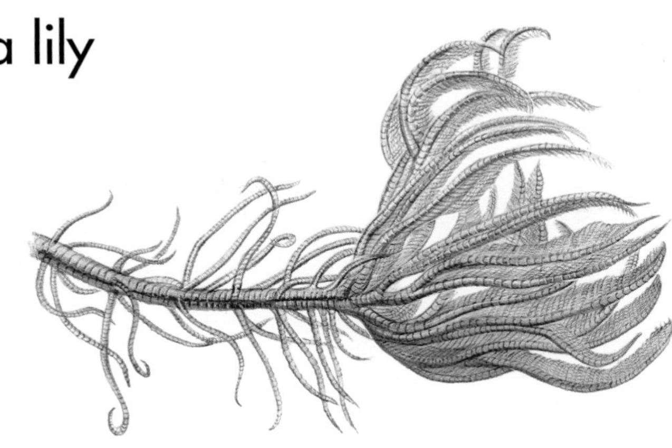

Sea lilies display a unique echinoderm anatomical feature called a water vascular system. It consists of water-carrying vessels spreading out from a ring around the mouth, along the arms, and into the tube feet, controlled by a loose network of nerves that runs throughout the creature's body. A sea lily is rather like an upside-down starfish attached by a stalk to the ocean floor, and like some starfish, it is capable of self-repair, regrowing an arm if it is lost. *Cenocrinus asterius* is a large form, found at moderate depths in the Caribbean and Atlantic, growing on a long peduncle with its arms spreading out in a fan shape.

Scientific name	*Cenocrinus asteria*
Classification	Phylum Echinodermata; Class Crinoidea;
	Order Isocrinida
Size	Up to 25cm (10in) long
Distribution	Caribbean; Central Atlantic
Habitat	Seabed and outcrops, 300–900m (1000–3000ft)
Diet	Algae and organic debris
Reproduction	Sexual with external fertilization

Mediterranean feather star

Feather stars are close relatives of sea lilies, but are free-swimming. They start life as larvae rooted to the ground by a peduncle, but detach from this on reaching maturity and float free in the water, or crawl along the seabed by pumping water in and out of their tube feet. They usually display ten arms and resemble lightweight starfish. A set of small appendages on the opposite side to the mouth (normally the underside) can temporarily attach the feather star to the seabed. The Mediterranean feather star is found in several colours, including red, yellow and white. It often hides among coral reefs, extending only its arms to feed.

Scientific name	*Antedon mediterranea*
Classification	Phylum Echinodermata; Class Crinoidea;
	Order Comatulida; Family Antedonidae
Size	Up to 20cm (8in) across
Distribution	Mediterranean
Habitat	Shallow seabeds and surface waters
Diet	Algae and organic debris
Reproduction	Sexual with external fertilization

Sea cucumber

Although sea cucumbers look very different from other echinoderms, they are in fact members of the group, with the same five-fold symmetry in their bodies, calcareous plates, and flexible tube feet covering their bodies. They are mostly filter feeders, and make their way along the sea floor with movements of their lower tube feet. A group of adapted tentacles around the mouth catch food from the water. Most sea cucumbers have separate sexes, but *Cucumaria planci* is hermaphroditic, and capable of asexual reproduction by cell division. All sea cucumbers have the ability to regenerate missing limbs.

Scientific name	*Cucumaria planci*
Classification	Phylum Echinodermata; Class Holothuroidea;
	Order Dendrochirotida; Family Cucumariidae
Size	Up to around 15cm (6in) long
Distribution	Mediterranean
Habitat	Shallow seabeds among plantlife
Diet	Algae and organic particles
Reproduction	Sexual and asexual

Swimming sea cucumber

Not all sea cucumbers are restricted to crawling along the sea floor. A few species have become free-swimming, by evolving extended tentacles around the mouth joined together by a thin web-like membrane. This allows them to swim around rather like jellyfish, and their bodies are similarly soft, light and gelatinous. Swimming sea cucumbers feed on plankton and organic debris suspended in the water. They are a stark contrast to the seabed-dwelling species, which mostly feed on organic matter in the sediment, and frequently end up with bodies full of mud, from which their digestive system extracts any available nutrients.

Scientific name	*Pelagothuria ludwigi*
Classification	Phylum Echinodermata; Class Holothuroidea;
	Order Elasipodida; Family Pelagothuridae
Size	Around 15cm (6in) across
Distribution	Cosmopolitan in deep seas
Habitat	Free-swimming a few metres above seabed
Diet	Plankton and organic particles
Reproduction	Sexual, with external fertilization

3urrowing sea cucumber

Some sea cucumbers have abandoned their mobile festyles in favour of a safer :atic or sessile one. One xample is *Rhopalodina ıgeniformis*, which buries self in the seabed with just a roboscis protruding through ıe sand or mud. The animal's ntire body plan has changed, ɔ both its mouth and its anus e at the end of the proboscis, nd it feeds by filtering ıicroorganisms from the vater. Other sea cucumber efences include an ability in ome species to produce fine ıreads of toxic mucus, or in thers a reflex that violently xpels the viscera (internal soft arts), allowing the animal to scape and regrow them later.

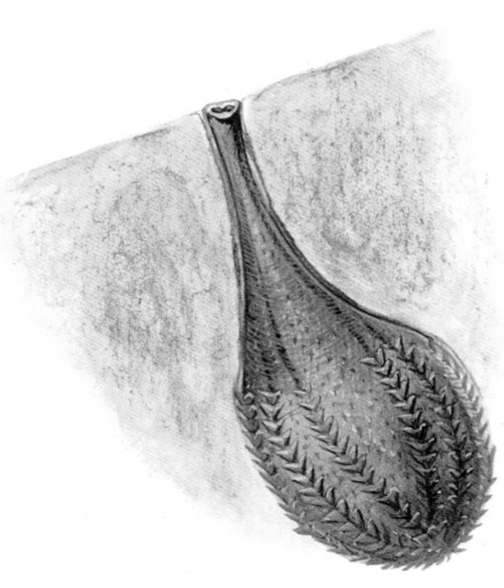

Scientific name	*Rhopalodina lageniformis*
Classification	Phylum Echinodermata; Class Holothuroidea;
	Order Dactylochirotida; Family Rhopalodinidae
Size	Around 10cm (4in) across
Distribution	South-east Atlantic
Habitat	Buried in the sand of deep seabeds
Diet	Plankton; organic debris
Reproduction	Sexual, with external fertilization

Melon urchin

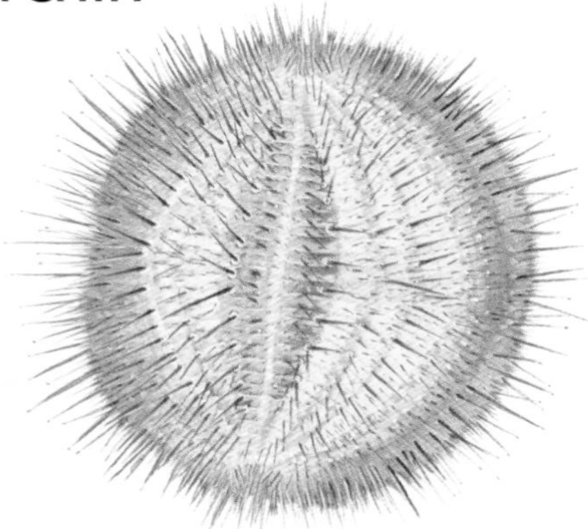

Sea urchins are armless echinoderms in which the body plates form a sphere or near-sphere called a 'test'. They graze over seabeds with their mouth downward, and dispose of waste through an anus in their upper surface. Sea urchins are covered in long calcareous spines, with suckered tube feet in between them and tentacles around the mouth for crawling slowly over the sea floor. *Echinus melo*, the melon urchin, is yellow-white in colour and has fewer spines than some species, though they are of two different sizes and colours – short pale green ones and longer yellow ones.

Scientific name	*Echinus melo*
Classification	Phylum Echinodermata; Class Echinoidea;
	Order Echinoida; Family Echnidae
Size	Up to around 14cm (5½in)
Distribution	Eastern North Atlantic, Mediterranean
Habitat	Rocky seabeds and coral reefs, 20–100m (65–330ft)
Diet	Algae; seaweed; polyps; hydroids
Reproduction	Sexual, with external fertilization

urple sea urchin

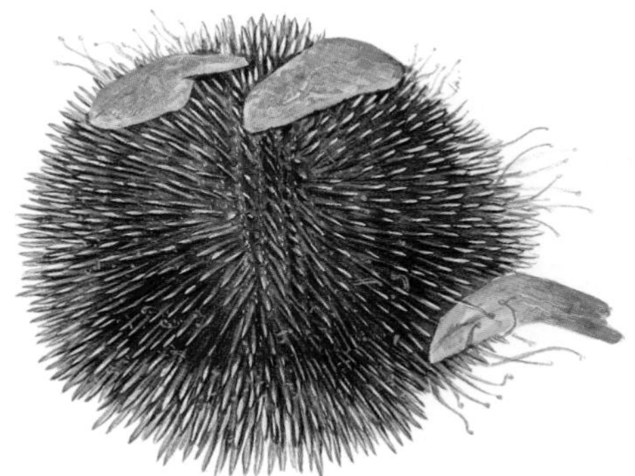

Not all sea urchins are perfectly spherical – most are slightly flattened, such as the purple sea urchin *Sphaerechinus granularis,* whose sex organs are a elicacy in parts of the Mediterranean. All urchins have a unique feeding apparatus nown as 'Aristotle's lantern', first noted by the Greek philosopher more than two illennia ago. The organ does indeed look like a five-sided glass lantern, with alcareous struts supporting it on the inside of the body, and only the sharp teeth icking out through the creature's mouth. It is worked by a total of 60 internal uscles and is very efficient at mashing up the urchin's food.

Scientific name	*Sphaerechinus granularis*
Classification	Phylum Echinodermata; Class Echinoidea;
	Order Temnopleuroida; Family Toxopneustidae
Size	Up to around 15cm (6in)
Distribution	Northern Mediterranean; Eastern North Atlantic
Habitat	Shallow rocky and weed-strewn sea floors
Diet	Algae and organic debris
Reproduction	Sexual, with external fertilization

Pencil urchin

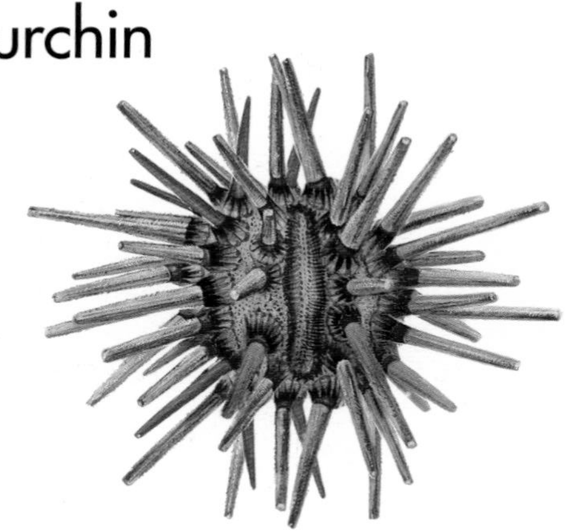

Some sea urchins do not use their spines defensively – they have thicker, sturdier, and relatively sparse spines that look like pencil leads, with the shell clearly visible between them. *Eucidaris tribuloides*, the pencil urchin of the Caribbean, is a small example. It uses its spines to wedge itself into cavities in rocks and coral reefs during the day, only emerging at night to feed. Other sea urchins employ a variety of defensive tactics – many dig burrows or bore holes into rock for shelter, while some have poison sacs on the end of their spines. Some even seem to use deliberate camouflage, collecting a variety of other organisms on their spines.

Scientific name	*Eucidaris tribuloides*
Classification	Phylum Echinodermata; Class Echinoidea;
	Order Cidaroida; Family Cidaridae
Size	Up to 7.5cm (3in) across
Distribution	Caribbean; Western Atlantic
Habitat	Reefs and turtle grass beds
Diet	Algae; hydroids; molluscs; carrion
Reproduction	Sexual, with external fertilisation

Sand dollar

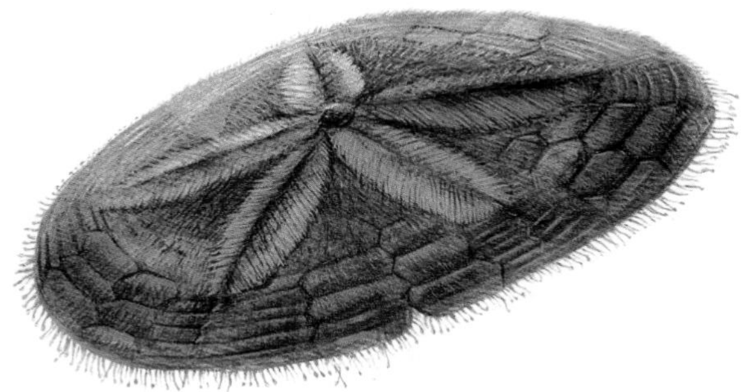

The flattened sand dollars or Scutellidae are close relatives of sea urchins that have evolved specifically for burrowing in sandy and muddy seabeds. Their spines are shortened into a bristly coat of 'fur' and collect food which hair-like cilia transfer on the underside of the body to the mouth. When the creature dies, it loses its outer skin of spines and only the internal discoid skeleton washes up on the beach, looking rather like it is moulded from compressed sand. The undersides of these skeletons clearly show five symmetrical apertures where water enters the animal to be used in the water vascular system.

Scientific name	*Echinarachnius parma*
Classification	Phylum Echinodermata; Class Echinoidea;
	Order Clypeasteroida; Family Scutellidae
Size	Around 8cm (3⅛in) across
Distribution	Atlantic and Pacific coasts of North America
Habitat	Sandy seabeds to 1500m (5000ft) deep
Diet	Algae; organic debris
Reproduction	Sexual, with external fertilization

Sea-potato

Sea potatoes are heart urchins – unevenly shaped burrowing urchins that are covered in short, spiny fur that is generally swept towards the back of the animal. As their name suggests, they have a distinctive heart shape, with a dip at the front. They are burrowers, digging some 10–15cm (4–6in) beneath sandy seabeds, where their position can be revealed by circular depressions on the surface. The sea potato feeds on organic detritus, passing food back to the mouth using its front-facing sets of tube feet. Burrowing urchins perform an important function in seabed communities by churning over and mixing the upper layers of the sand.

Scientific name	*Echinocardium cordata*
Classification	Phylum Echinodermata; Class Echinoidea;
	Order Spatangoida; Family Loveniidae
Size	Around 7cm (2¾in) across
Distribution	Cosmopolitan in warm and temperate seas
Habitat	Sandy and muddy seabeds
Diet	Organic detritus
Reproduction	Sexual, with external fertilization

Brittle-star

Brittle-stars are echinoderms related to starfish, but with a less robust structure, their five arms emerging from a central disc-shaped body. They are highly obile, and are either scavengers or suspension feeders – they are too fragile to ınt larger prey on their own. They are capable of regenerating lost body parts, ıd in some cases an entire new brittle-star can also grow from a severed limb. ıey reproduce sexually – some species are hermaphrodites but most have two enders. In a few cases, such as *Ophiocomina nigra*, a smaller male attaches to the male during breeding.

Scientific name	*Ophiocomina nigra*
Classification	Phylum Echinodermata; Class Ophiuroidea;
	Order Laemophiurina; Family Ophiacanthidae
Size	Body disc up to 25mm (1in) across; arms about 12.5cm (5in) long
Distribution	Eastern North Atlantic
Habitat	Sheltered seabeds to 400m (1300ft)
Diet	Plankton; organic detritus; carrion
Reproduction	Sexual, with external fertilization

Brittle-star

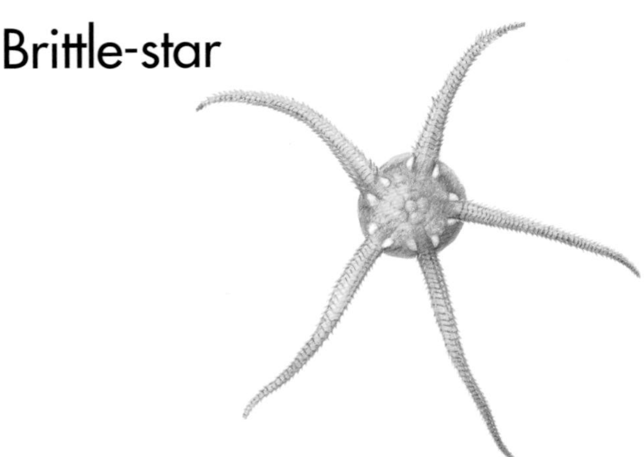

Brittle-stars such as *Ophiura albida* are members of the class Ophiuroidea, along with their close relatives the basket stars. These have multiple branching arms which they hold aloft to filter the waters. *O. albida* is widespread around western Europe, and is distinctive because of the heart-shaped plates where its arms join the central disc. The arms are lined with spines, but they lie almost flat against the arm itself – brittle-stars often catch their food on a sticky mucus strung between the spines rather than relying on spiking food directly. As with many of its relatives, this small brittle-star grows at a remarkably slow rate, taking up to six years to reach maturity.

Scientific name	*Ophiura albida*
Classification	Phylum Echinodermata; Class Ophiuroidea;
	Order Chilophiurina; Family Ophiuridae
Size	Body disc up to 1.5cm (⅜in) across; arms about 6cm (2⅜in) long
Distribution	Eastern North Atlantic; Mediterranean
Habitat	Sandy seabeds down to 1,000m (3,300ft)
Diet	Plankton; organic detritus; carrion
Reproduction	Sexual, with external fertilization

Common brittle-star

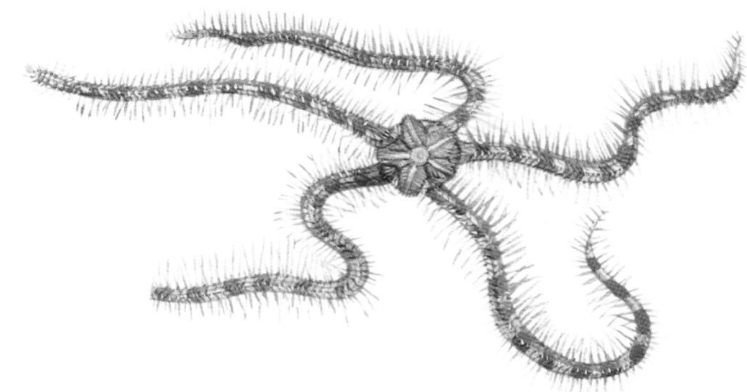

The common brittle-star *Ophiothrix fragilis* is relatively large (its central disc reaches around 20mm [⅘in] across, and its arms grow to 10cm [4in] long) and is ery widespread around the entire eastern Atlantic. It comes in a variety of colours, s covered in untidy spines, and, as the name suggests, is very fragile – though it can egenerate lost limbs and spawn new individuals from the severed limbs hemselves. As well as being found scattered on coastlines, it accumulates in huge ffshore beds where tidal flows can bring it a plentiful supply of food. Within these eds, up to 2000 individuals can occupy a square metre (11 sq ft) of sea floor.

Scientific name	*Ophiothrix fragilis*
Classification	Phylum Echinodermata; Class Ophiuroidea;
	Order Ophiurida; Family Ophiotrichidae
Size	Body disc up to 2cm (⅘in) across; arms about 10cm (4in) long
Distribution	Eastern Atlantic Ocean
Habitat	Coastlines and offshore sea floor
Diet	Plankton; organic detritus; carrion
Reproduction	Sexual, with external fertilization

Striped brittle-star

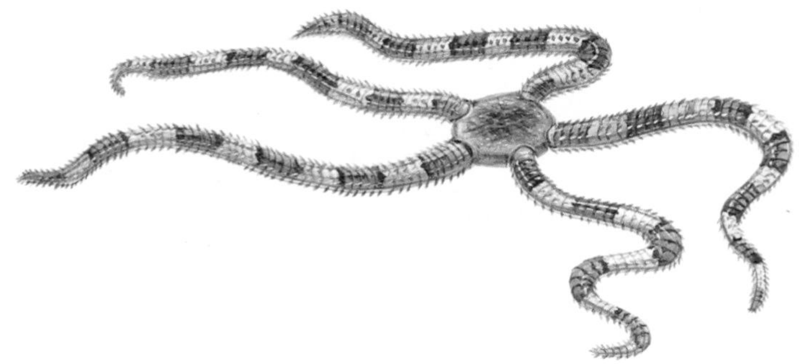

The striped brittle-star *Ophioderma longicauda* is a large and active western European species, distinguished by the broad stripes along its arms. This brittlestar is relatively fast-moving and will hide from bright sources of light. Scientists think most echinoderms sense light through reactive pigments in their skin, but a recently discovered species turns out to have a much more sophisticated visual system – its entire body is covered in crystalline lenses that are thought to function as an all-directional compound eye. Scientists are now looking again at whether other echinoderms have similar surprises in store.

Scientific name	*Ophioderma longicauda*
Classification	Phylum Echinodermata; Class Ophiuroidea;
	Order Ophiurida; Family Ophidermatidae
Size	Body disc up to 40mm (1⅜in) across; arms about 12cm (4⅘in) long
Distribution	Eastern North Atlantic; Mediterranean
Habitat	Shallow sandy and rocky seabeds with plant life
Diet	Plankton; organic detritus; carrion
Reproduction	Sexual, with external fertilization

Crown-of-thorns starfish

The crown-of-thorns starfish is an unusual and very efficient predator on corals. It has up to twenty arms, all protected with extremely sharp thorn-like spines, coated with a venomous nerve toxin. It feeds on corals in a remarkable way – it crawls on top of them, then uses its tube feet to pull its large yellow stomach out of its mouth and spread it over the coral. The digestive juices dissolve the living tissue from the coral, leaving just the skeleton behind. Since the 1960s this starfish has had a devastating effect on coral reefs – it is thought to have thrived due to overfishing of one of its main predators, the triton gastropods.

Scientific name	*Acanthaster planci*
Classification	Phylum Echinodermata; Class Asteroidea;
	Order Valvatida; Family Acanthasteridae
Size	Around 40cm (16in) across
Distribution	Indo-Pacific
Habitat	Coral reefs
Diet	Coral polyps
Reproduction	Sexual, with external fertilization

Common sunstar

Sunstars, also called rose stars, are some of the most attractive echinoderms, with a brightly coloured centre and striped arms in a variety of colours. Starfish bodies are more robust than those of brittlestars, with strong muscles in their arms, and spikes and powerful suckers on their undersides. They typically have 10–12 arms, but can have fewer or still more. Although the body retains its pentagonal symmetry, the varying number of arms is a result of their willingness to grow (and grow back). Sunstars swallow their prey – such as shellfish, sea anemones and other echinoderms – whole, ejecting the inedible parts later.

Scientific name	*Crossaster papposus*
Classification	Phylum Echinodermata; Class Asteroidea;
	Order Velatida; Family Solasteridae
Size	Up to around 25cm (10in) across
Distribution	North Atlantic and Pacific
Habitat	Hard sea floors down to 50m (165ft)
Diet	Shellfish; sea anemones; sea cucumbers
Reproduction	Sexual, with external fertilization

Combtooth starfish

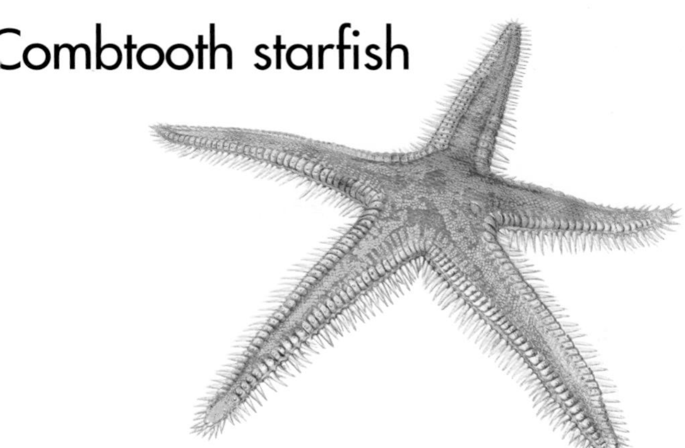

The classic starfish have five arms and are vividly coloured, such as the combtooth starfish *Astropecten aranciacus*. This large starfish from the Mediterranean grows up to 30cm (12in) across, and has a bright orange upper surface and a yellow underside. The arms are lined with two rows of long spines that stick out to either side and give the creature its common name. Between them runs a long furrow from the centre which contains two lines of unsuckered tube feet for locomotion. Each arm contains a set of sexual organs, and the tips also have a chemical-sensing olfactory organ and a light-sensitive red spot.

Scientific name	*Astropecten aranciacus*
Classification	Phylum Echinodermata; Class Asteroidea;
	Order Paxillosida; Family Astropectinidae
Size	Up to 30cm (12in) across
Distribution	Mediterranean and surrounding waters
Habitat	Sandy and rocky seabeds down to around 25m (85ft)
Diet	Molluscs; corals; anemones
Reproduction	Sexual, with external fertilization

Blue starfish

The brightly coloured blue starfish *Linckia laevigata* is found on coral reefs throughout the western Pacific and Indian oceans, frequently hiding in crevices in the rock or coral. It usually has five arms, though occasionally it may have between three and seven, and can grow up to 30cm (12in) across. Blue starfish are omnivores, feeding largely on algae and organic detritus by extruding their stomach and rolling it over the reef surface. Blue starfish are particularly good at regenerating themselves, with new animals growing from the very tip of a severed arm (sometimes called a 'comet').

Scientific name	*Linckia laevigata*
Classification	Phylum Echinodermata; Class Asteroidea;
	Order Valvatida; Family Ophidiasteridae
Size	Up to 30cm (12in) across
Distribution	Indo-Pacific
Habitat	Coral reefs
Diet	Algae; plankton; organic detritus
Reproduction	Sexual, with external fertilization

Spotted starfish

The genus *Fromia* consists of medium-sized, slow-moving and generally placid starfish, most of which dwell on reefs across the Indian and Pacific oceans. Most are red or orange in colour, usually with blue or white symmetrical patterns of spots on their upper surfaces. In some species these spots form scales that end up covering most of the arms. *Fromia ghardaqana*, from the Red Sea, generally has sparse white (but sometimes blue) spots. It is an omnivore, generally feeding on algae and detritus that collects on the living reef, but also on any other creature too slow to escape.

Scientific name	*Fromia ghardaqana*
Classification	Phylum Echinodermata; Class Asteroidea;
	Order Valvatida; Family Ophidiasteridae
Size	Up to 7.5cm (3in) across
Distribution	Red Sea and surrounding waters
Habitat	Coral reefs
Diet	Algae; organic detritus; carrion
Reproduction	Sexual, with external fertilization

Common European sea squirt

They do not look it, but sea squirts represent a key evolutionary stage between invertebrates and vertebrates such as fishes and mammals. They are the most primitive chordates – the wider group that takes in vertebrates. Adult sea squirts consist simply of a translucent bag, attached to a rock, with two syphons, or spouts. They are filter-feeders: internal hairs waft water into the side syphon and out of the top, and small plankton – floating animals and plants – are filtered from it. The clue to their evolutionary position comes from their larvae, which look like transparent tadpoles; they have a stiff rudimentary backbone called a notochord.

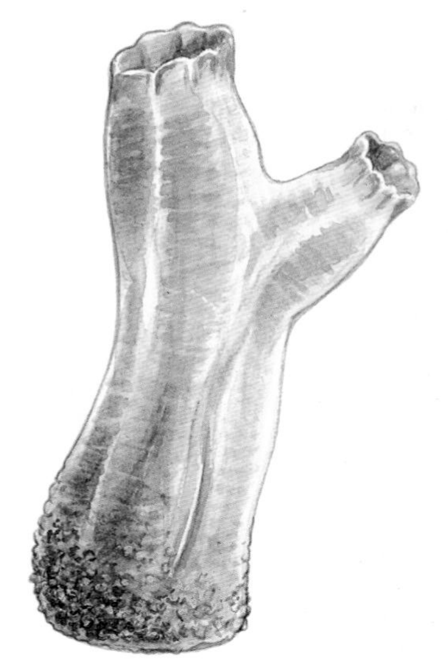

Scientific name	*Ciona intestinalis*
Classification	Class Ascidiacea (sessile tunicates or sea squirts)
	Order Enterogona (solitary sea squirts)
Size	Adult up to about 15cm (6in) long
Distribution	North-western European coastal waters; Mediterranean
Habitat	Shallow water up to low-water mark, attached to rock or seaweed
Diet	Plankton
Reproduction	Hermaphrodite. Eggs fertilized within syphon; larvae free-swimming

Hagfish

Direct descendants of the armoured ostracoderms of 500 million years ago, the jawless fishes are the most primitive living fish species. They have no scales, no skull, no paired fins, no backbone – in fact, no true bones – although (like sea-squirt larvae; *see opposite*) they do have a stiffening notochord made of cartilage. They have a simple mouth opening in place of jaws. Hagfish are slimy, eel-like blind fish that find their food prey by smell. They are scavengers, attacking dead and dying fish on the seabed and rasping at the flesh with two horny 'teeth' attached to a tongue-like piston. They often clean out the prey's insides, leaving the skin intact.

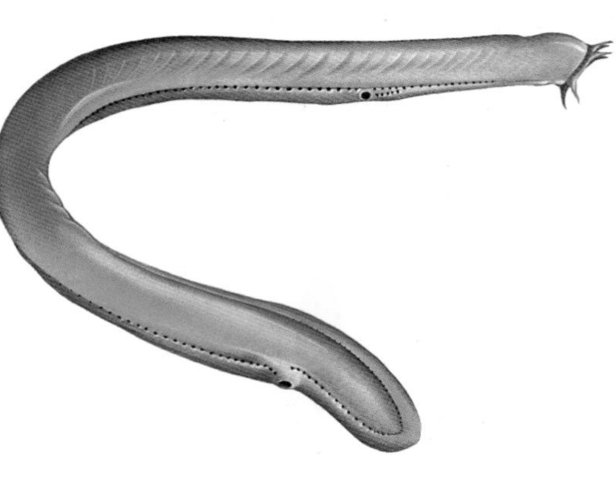

Scientific name	*Myxine glutinosa*
Classification	Superclass (formerly class) Agnatha; class Myxini
	Order Myxiniformes (formerly Cyclostomata); family Myxinidae
Size	Up to about 60cm (24in) long
Distribution	Eastern and western North Atlantic; western Mediterranean; Arctic
Habitat	Cool coastal waters; burrows in bottom mud, to 600m (2000ft) deep
Diet	Invertebrates; internal tissues and organs of dead or sickly fish
Reproduction	Spawns in summer; few (20–30) very large eggs up to 25mm (1in) long

Sea lamprey

With their sucker-like mouth, lampreys are classed with the hagfish (*see p.173*) as jawless fishes, but scientists now believe that lampreys evolved separately, later than hagfish. Adult lampreys are parasites. They attach themselves to a fish, rasp at its skin with their short, sharp teeth, then suck its blood (aided by a chemical that prevents the victim's blood clotting). Sea lampreys live mainly in coastal waters but swim up a river to spawn and then die. Eggs hatch into small worm-like larvae, which take several years to develop into adults and return to the sea. Sea lampreys kill many commercially caught fish – especially in the North American Great Lakes.

Scientific name	*Petromyzon marinus*
Classification	Superclass (formerly class) Agnatha; class Cephalaspidomorphi
	Order Petromyzoniformes (ex-Cyclostomata); family Petromyzonidae
Size	Up to about 90cm (3ft) long
Distribution	Eastern, western North Atlantic; western Mediterranean; Great Lakes
Habitat	Coastal waters; some fresh water lakes; breeds in rivers
Diet	External parasite: sucks host fish's blood and body fluids
Reproduction	Spawns in sandy or gravelly river bottom; larvae mature after 3–6 years

Port Jackson shark

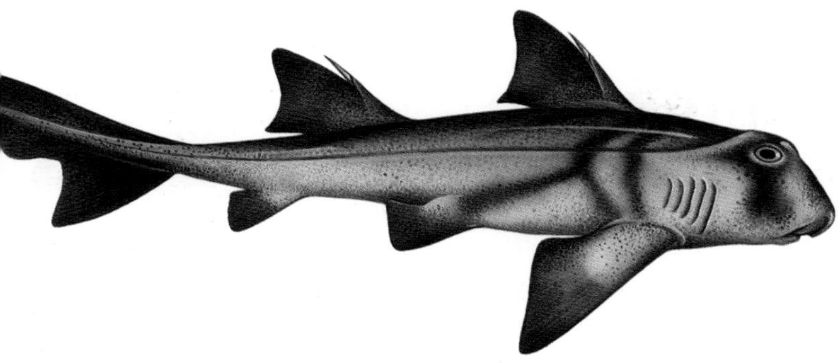

Sharks, rays and other members of the Chondrichthyes are called cartilaginous fishes because their skeleton is made of gristly cartilage instead of bone; but they do have a proper jaw, unlike the hagfish and lampreys (*see pp.173–174*). The Port Jackson shark is one of the most primitive types, closely related to shark species that lived in the Devonian period, 400 million years ago. It has a bulbous head and a venomous spine on each dorsal fin. Its upper jaw is fixed to the cranium, so it does not have the big bite of many other sharks. It is a rather slow swimmer, but migrates each year to the same shallow, rocky waters to deposit its cased eggs in crevices.

Scientific name	*Heterodontus portusjacksoni*
Classification	Order Heterodontiformes (horn or bullhead sharks)
	Family Heterodontidae
Size	Up to 1.5m (5ft) long
Distribution	Southern Pacific and Indian oceans; Southern Ocean
Habitat	Temperate offshore waters to 200m (650ft) deep; breeds in shallows
Diet	Molluscs; crustaceans; sea urchins
Reproduction	Spawns winter; 10–16 eggs in helix-shaped cases; hatch in 10–12 months

Spotted wobbegong

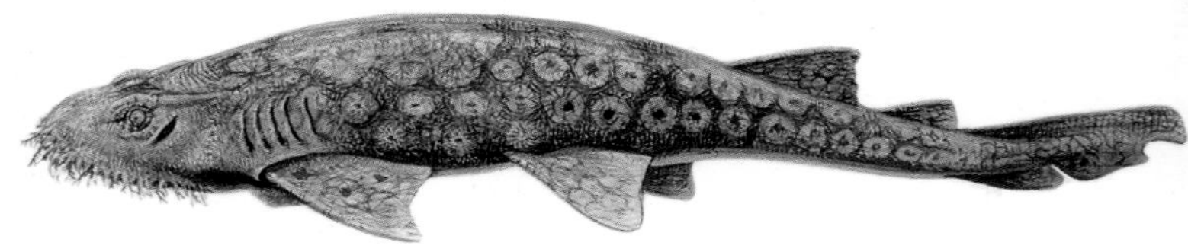

Wobbegong is the Australian aboriginal name for this relatively small, bottom-living shark. Its irregularly spotted back pattern gives it good camouflage as it rests or creeps across the sea-floor; the closely related ornate wobbegong (*Orectolobus ornatus*) is very similar but with a different pattern. Wobbegongs are usually inactive by day and forage at night, using their beard-like fringe of nasal barbels, or feelers, to help them to locate food. They are not aggressive, but often rest in tide pools and reef shallows, and may well attack anyone who accidentally disturbs them. They have long, dagger-like teeth and can inflict serious wounds.

Scientific name	*Orectolobus maculatus*
Classification	Order Orectolobiformes (carpet sharks and allies)
	Family Orectolobidae
Size	Up to 3m (10ft) long, usually less
Distribution	Coasts of south-western, southern and south-eastern Australia
Habitat	Cool waters, up to 110m (360ft) deep, with sandy or rocky bottom
Diet	Bottom-living fish, crustaceans, octopuses and other invertebrates
Reproduction	Ovoviviparous; up to about 20 young; gestation period uncertain

Whale shark

The whale shark is the biggest known fish, but it poses little threat to people. It is a slow-swimming filter-feeder that sucks in seawater and filters from it masses of small crustaceans, squid and other floating organisms. Sometimes it bobs up and down vertically, holding its mouth open at the surface to allow food-bearing water to rush in. The food is separated out by stacks of spongy tissue in the gaps between the fish's gill bars; the filtered water passes out through the gill slits. The whale shark's mouth is so big that it often takes in fish – mainly small sardines, anchovies and mackerel, but sometimes species as big as tuna – as well as smaller creatures.

Scientific name	*Rhincodon typus*
Classification	Order Orectolobiformes (carpet sharks and allies)
	Family Rhincodontidae
Size	Up to about 15–18m (50–60ft) long; up to 20 tonnes
Distribution	Tropical parts of Atlantic, Indian and Pacific oceans
Habitat	Warm surface waters
Diet	Plankton; fish
Reproduction	Ovoviviparous; details little known, but one female had 301 embryos

Basking shark

Second only in size (among sharks and all fish) to the whale shark (*see p.177*), the basking shark is also a normally peaceful plankton-feeder. It has a huge mouth which it holds wide-open while cruising at all depths, from the surface to 550m (1800ft), to catch shrimps and other small crustaceans. It has more than 150 rows of tiny hooked teeth, but filters its food with bristle-like attachments to its gills. Its gill slits are extremely long, almost meeting behind the head. Basking sharks have long been hunted in both the Atlantic and Pacific, mainly for their huge liver, which may yield over 2000 litres (440 Imp gal; 530 US gal) of oil, rich in vitamin A, per fish.

Scientific name	*Cetorhinus maximus*
Classification	Order Lamniformes (mackerel sharks and allies)
	Family Cetorhinidae
Size	Up to about 9–11m (30–36ft) long; up to 4 tonnes
Distribution	Worldwide except tropics
Habitat	Warm temperate to cold waters, from inshore to open ocean
Diet	Plankton – mainly small crustaceans
Reproduction	Ovoviviparous; number of young uncertain; gestation probably 3½ years

Sand-tiger shark

The sand-tiger – also known as the sand shark, in Australia as the grey nurse, and in South Africa as the spotted ragged-tooth – is one of the best-known aquarium and marine-park sharks. It looks streamlined and aggressive as it cruises with mouth open, exposing its long, sharp teeth. Yet it is rather slow-moving and docile, and most experts agree that it probably attacks only when provoked. It is certainly less dangerous than the similarly named tiger shark (*Galeocerdo cuvier*). In one respect, sand-tigers are aggressive: the largest or strongest embryo in each part of a female's uterus (womb) eats all the other embryos, ensuring that only two are born.

Scientific name	*Carcharias* (or *Odontaspis* or *Eugomphodus*) *taurus*
Classification	Order Lamniformes (mackerel sharks and allies)
	Family Carchariidae; sometimes included in Odontaspididae
Size	Up to about 3.2m (10½ft) long
Distribution	Widely distributed in temperate and tropical seas
Habitat	Shallow waters, to 200m (650ft): reefs, sandy bays, estuaries
Diet	Many kinds of fish; squid; crabs and lobsters
Reproduction	Ovoviviparous; two young (*see above*) born after 9–12 month gestation

Thresher shark

Thresher sharks are instantly recognizable by their long, whip-like tail, which accounts for half of the fish's total length. When feeding, they thrash the water with their tail to herd their prey, which consists mainly of fish such as herring, mackerel, sardines, bluefish and other small species that naturally swim in schools or groups. Threshers have even been observed using their tail to stun a fish. Where prey is abundant, they often hunt in pairs or small groups. The tail also helps thresher sharks to swim powerfully, and they sometimes leap completely clear of the water. They are caught by both sports fishermen and commercial fishing fleets.

Scientific name	*Alopias vulpinus*
Classification	Order Lamniformes (mackerel sharks and allies)
	Family Alopiidae
Size	Up to 5.5m (18ft) or even 6m (20ft) long; up to about 350kg (770lb)
Distribution	Almost worldwide in cool and warm seas
Habitat	Coastal zone to far offshore in tropical and temperate waters
Diet	Mainly schooling fish; also squid, octopuses and deep-sea crustaceans
Reproduction	Ovoviviparous; usually two to four young; gestation period unknown

Great white shark, or white pointer

No shark is more feared than the great white, 'star' of the film *Jaws*, although the tiger shark (*Galeocerdo cuvier*) comes a close second as a threat to swimmers. In some ways, the great white's reputation is unjustified; shark experts believe that it has no more taste for human flesh than any other shark – in fact, it rarely consumes its human victims – but its size, speed and aggression make it the most dangerous species. It accounts for one-third of all deaths from shark attacks, despite the fact that it prefers relatively cold water where few people swim. The truth is that it will attack almost anything smaller than itself – seals, whales and people included.

Scientific name	*Carcharodon carcharias*
Classification	Order Lamniformes (mackerel sharks and allies)
	Family Lamnidae
Size	Up to about 7.5m (25ft) long and about 2.5 tonnes, sometimes more
Distribution	Almost worldwide between 60°S and 60°N
Habitat	Mainly cool temperate inshore and offshore waters; also open ocean
Diet	'Top' predator, eating vast range of marine organisms, including sharks
Reproduction	Ovoviviparous; usually up to ten young born after 12-month gestation

Lesser spotted dogfish

The common dogfish of British waters, this species is caught commercially and sold as rock fish or 'rock salmon'. It is not a true dogfish but one of the catshark family – whose members are distinguished by the number and position of their fins. Unlike true dogfishes (*see p.186*), they have an anal fin under the body, just in front of the tail, and both dorsal (back) fins are set well back, behind the pelvic fins. The lesser spotted dogfish is a well-camouflaged bottom-dweller. Its egg cases have fine tendrils that anchor them to seaweed until the young fish, about 10cm (4in) long, hatch. The cases, sometimes washed up on shore, are known as mermaids' purses.

Scientific name	*Scyliorhinus canicula*
Classification	Order Carcharhiniformes (ground or whaler sharks)
	Family Scyliorhinidae
Size	Up to about 1m (3¼ft) long
Distribution	Eastern North Atlantic; Mediterranean
Habitat	Shallow waters (to 400m [1300ft] in Mediterranean) over sand or mud
Diet	Bottom-living invertebrates; small fish
Reproduction	Eggs encased in horny, tendrilled cases; hatch after 5–11 months

Smooth hammerhead shark

The extraordinary T-shaped 'hammer' forming the head of hammerhead sharks makes them unmistakable, but has long puzzled shark biologists. The sharks' eyes and nostrils are located at the ends of the hammer, and many experts believe that they increase the sensitivity and accuracy of the fishes' senses – in particular allowing them to smell in 'stereo', as it were. This idea is backed up by the fact that hammerheads are often the first on the scene when a fishery ship dumps offal. Its second purpose is probably to increase the sharks' manoeuvrability, acting like a hydroplane, or underwater wing. Hammerhead sharks sometimes attack people.

Scientific name	*Sphyrna zygaena*
Classification	Order Carcharhiniformes (ground or whaler sharks)
	Family Sphyrnidae
Size	Up to about 4.25m (14ft) long
Distribution	Atlantic, Indian and Pacific oceans; Mediterranean
Habitat	Coastal to open seas, to 400m (1300ft), in tropical and temperate waters
Diet	Mostly fish (especially rays); offal and other dead matter
Reproduction	Ovoviviparous; up to 37 young, born with 'hammer' folded

Blue shark

With its streamlined body and long, wing-like pectoral fins, the blue shark is a long-range cruiser and voracious feeder that sometimes attacks swimmers. But it mostly travels the open oceans, far from land, commonly migrating 3000km (1900 miles) or more with the seasons. The longest journey on record is nearly 6000km (about 3700 miles), and its maximum speed 69km/h (43mph). It usually travels near the surface, its dorsal and tail fins often projecting. It has big eyes that help it to spot prey – which is scarce in mid-ocean – and finger-like gill-rakers to filter any small fish and other creatures from water passing from its mouth out through its gills.

Scientific name	*Prionace glauca*
Classification	Order Carchariniformes (ground or whaler sharks)
	Family Carcharhinidae
Size	Up to about 4m (13ft) long; up to 206kg (455lb)
Distribution	Worldwide, in temperate and tropical zones
Habitat	Mostly open ocean, near surface, but sometimes inshore
Diet	Fish (especially schooling species); squid and other invertebrates
Reproduction	Viviparous; often 50 or more young, born after 9–12 month gestation

rilled shark

With its slim body and fins, the frilled shark looks more like a giant eel than a typical shark. It is a deep-water species, rarely seen except in the nets of deep-a trawlers, and may be responsible for some stories of 'sea-serpents'. Like a few her species of the related order Hexanchiformes (the cow sharks; within which me biologists also place the frilled shark), it has six gill-slits – resembling a frilled llar – on each side; most sharks have five. The mouth opening is at the very front its head, rather than being underslung as in most sharks; inside it has about 300 eth, each three-pointed like a trident. It probably strikes snake-like at its prey.

Scientific name	*Chlamydoselachus anguineus*
Classification	Order Chlamydoselachiformes (frilled sharks) or Hexanchiformes
	Family Chlamydoselachidae
Size	Male up to 2m (6½ft) long; female up to 1.5m (5ft)
Distribution	Worldwide, in temperate and tropical zones
Habitat	Offshore waters, to 1200m (4000ft) deep
Diet	Mainly deep-sea squid and fish
Reproduction	Ovoviviparous; 4–12 young born after up to 3½-year gestation

Spiny dogfish

This true dogfish is distinguished from the lesser spotted dogfish (*see p.182*) by its lack of an anal fin, and by the sharp spines at the front of each dorsal fin, which also lie farther forward on its body. Also known as the spurdog or piked dogfish, it has been fished commercially for centuries (and sold as rock fish, 'rock salmon' or flake), but is probably still the most abundant shark. However, fishermen have to beware the spines; they are not venomous, but are coated with slime that contains bacteria, and these can cause illness if the skin is punctured. It is very long-lived (to at least 70 years), and females cannot breed until they are 20 or more years old.

Scientific name	*Squalus acanthias*
Classification	Order Squaliformes (dogfish sharks)
	Family Squalidae
Size	Male up to about 1m (3¼ft) long; female up to 1.2m (4ft)
Distribution	Worldwide in cool temperate seas; also deep tropical waters
Habitat	Mainly bottom-living, in coastal to oceanic waters, to 900m (3000ft)
Diet	Schooling and bottom-living fish; marine invertebrates
Reproduction	Ovoviviparous; up to 20 young born after 18–24 month gestation

Angular rough shark

This strange-looking small shark is sometimes caught by fishermen, but is rarely seen otherwise, because it is a relatively deep-sea species living on the sea-floor mainly near the edge of the continental shelf. It has a stout, high-backed body that is almost triangular in cross-section, and a short blunt snout; in several European languages it is known as the pigfish or sea-pig. It has two large but rather floppy dorsal fins, each with a large spine embedded within the fin. Large, prickly scales give its skin a rough surface, and at one time this was sometimes used as sandpaper. A similar fish living off South Africa may belong to the same or a different species.

Scientific name	*Oxynotus centrina*
Classification	Order Squaliformes (dogfish sharks)
	Family Oxynotidae or Dalatiidae
Size	Up to about 1.5m (5ft) long, usually much less; male smaller than female
Distribution	Eastern Atlantic; Mediterranean
Habitat	Warm temperate and tropical offshore waters, at 60–660m (200–2200ft)
Diet	Mainly invertebrates such as molluscs and worms
Reproduction	Ovoviviparous; usually seven or eight young; gestation period uncertain

European angel shark

Angel sharks look rather like a cross between a shark and a ray (*see pp.190–196*), with their flattened body and wide pectoral and pelvic fins. But the position of the mouth (near the tip of the snout) and gill slits (on the back) shows that they are true sharks; in rays, both are on the ventral (lower) surface. Angel sharks spend long periods – often days or even weeks – lying half-buried in the sand or mud of the seabed waiting for prey to come within range of their snapping jaws. Although sometimes called the monkfish, this Mediterranean and eastern Atlantic species is quite different from the angler fish (*see p.230*) sold by fishmongers as monkfish.

Scientific name	*Squatina squatina*
Classification	Order Squatiniformes (angel sharks)
	Family Squatinidae
Size	Usually up to 1.8m (6ft) long; female sometimes 2m (6½ft) or more
Distribution	Eastern North Atlantic; Mediterranean
Habitat	Bottom-living in temperate coastal waters, to 100m (330ft) or more
Diet	Bottom-living fish; crustaceans; octopuses; shellfish
Reproduction	Ovoviviparous; up to 25 young, born after about 10-month gestation

Smalltooth or greater sawfish

Sawfishes are instantly recognizable by their long, toothed rostrum, or snout – the 'saw' – which they use to stun prey and stir up the seabed when feeding. In other ways they look more like sharks than rays, but the position of the gills and mouth *see opposite*) shows that they belong among the rays. The smalltooth sawfish is one f the biggest species, with 24 to 32 pairs of teeth on its saw. It used to be common in nany areas, including the western Atlantic and Gulf coast, but like several other awfishes is now seriously endangered. It was often caught in fishing nets, and its word was (and still is) collected as a souvenir and for its supposed magical powers.

Scientific name	*Pristis pectinata*
Classification	Order Pristiformes (sawfishes)
	Family Pristidae
Size	Up to 7.5m (25ft) long including saw, but 5.5m (18ft) more common
Distribution	Worldwide (but rare) in tropical and temperate waters
Habitat	Mainly shallow coastal waters and estuaries; sometimes enters rivers
Diet	Schooling fish; bottom-living invertebrates
Reproduction	Ovoviviparous; 15–20 young, born with soft saw in protective sheath

Common guitarfish

The guitarfishes are another group that are intermediate in shape between rays and sharks. The head and front part of the body are flattened and arrow-shaped with a pointed snout and wing-like pectoral fins, while the hind part looks shark-like. However, the mouth and gill slits are on the underside of the body, showing that they are rays. The common guitarfish of European and west African waters is a rather slow-moving, bottom-living fish that often half-buries itself in the sand or mud of the seabed, up to 100m (330ft) down. It is caught commercially in some parts of the Mediterranean. There are more than 40 other species worldwide.

Scientific name	*Rhinobatos rhinobatos*
Classification	Order Rhinobatiformes or Rhynchobatiformes (shovelnose guitarfishes);
	sometimes included in Rajiformes. Family Rhinobatidae
Size	Up to 1m (3¼ft) long
Distribution	Eastern Atlantic; Mediterranean
Habitat	Shallow tropical and warm temperate waters, near coasts
Diet	Bottom-living fish and invertebrates
Reproduction	Ovoviviparous; one or two litters per year of 4–10 young

Eyed electric ray, or common torpedo

Electric rays have a small kidney-shaped muscular rgan on each side of their body hat, when contracted, can enerate an electrical discharge. ome species generate only 20 r 30 volts, but the common orpedo, or eyed electric ray, an inflict a shock of up to 200 olts. (A related species, the uch larger *Torpedo obiliana*, generates as much as 20 volts.) The electricity is used o defend the ray against attack, nd also to stun or kill its prey, nd is quite enough to give a erson a shock if touched. All lectric rays have a rounded hape, with a blunt snout and hick body. The common orpedo has five bright blue, ark-edged spots on its back.

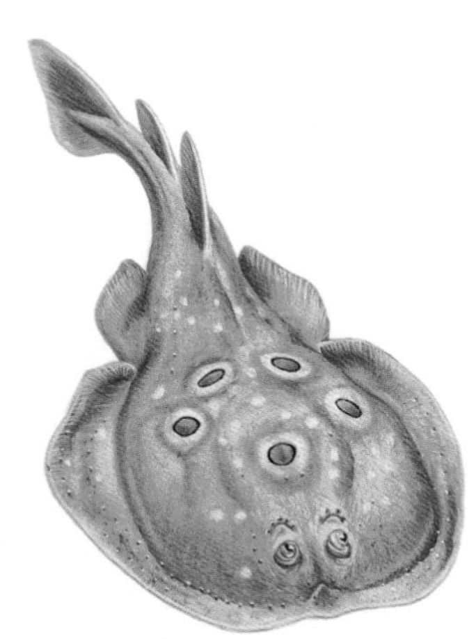

Scientific name	*Torpedo torpedo*
Classification	Order Torpediniformes (electric rays and allies)
	Family Torpedinidae
Size	About 60cm (24in) long; female smaller
Distribution	Eastern Atlantic; Mediterranean
Habitat	Tropical and warm temperate waters, usually near coasts
Diet	Mainly small fish; also bottom-living invertebrates
Reproduction	Ovoviviparous; up to 21 young born after about 5-month gestation

Brown ray

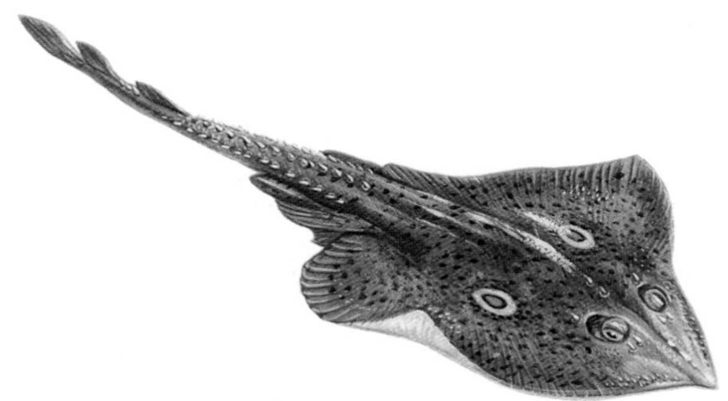

In true rays and skates (order Rajiformes) and stingrays (order Myliobatiformes; *see pp.194–196*), the body and the wing-like pectoral and pelvic fins together form a single distinct unit called the pectoral disc; it is usually diamond-shaped. There is no real biological distinction between rays and skates, but skates generally have a much more pointed snout than rays; both have a slender tail. The brown ray, one of many species found in European and African waters, has a distinctive bright blue and yellow 'eye' spot on each side of the brown, speckled back. Males have three rows of spines along the centre of the tail, females five rows. The underside is white

Scientific name	*Raja miraletus*
Classification	Order Rajiformes (skates and true rays)
	Family Rajidae
Size	Up to about 63cm (25in) long; female slightly smaller
Distribution	Eastern Atlantic; Mediterraean; south-western Indian Ocean
Habitat	Warm temperate and tropical waters, to depth of 300m (1000ft)
Diet	Bottom-living fish and invertebrates; remains of dead creatures
Reproduction	Up to 70 eggs, laid in 4.5cm (1¾in) capsules on sandy or muddy flats

Common Atlantic skate

Known also as the grey or blue skate, this has long been an important catch for commerical fishermen off European shores as far north as Iceland and the rctic coast of Norway. Most of those traditionally caught were relatively small and oung fish living on the floor of the continental shelf at depths of up to 200m (650ft), ut catches there have dropped sharply and the common skate is now seriously ndangered in these areas. Fishermen have switched to deeper waters – where ome much larger specimens live – in an effort to maintain catches, but experts elieve that the species will be in serious danger unless catches are curtailed.

Scientific name	*Dipturus* (or *Raja*) *batis*
Classification	Order Rajiformes (skates and true rays)
	Family Rajidae
Size	Female up to 2.4m (8ft) long; male up to 2m (6½ft); up to 98kg (216lb)
Distribution	Eastern and northern North Atlantic; western Mediterranean
Habitat	Temperate and cold waters, from shallows to depth of 600m (2000ft)
Diet	Mainly bottom-living fish and crustaceans; also other fish and octopuses
Reproduction	About 40 eggs per year, laid in capsules up to 24.5cm (9½in) long

Common stingray

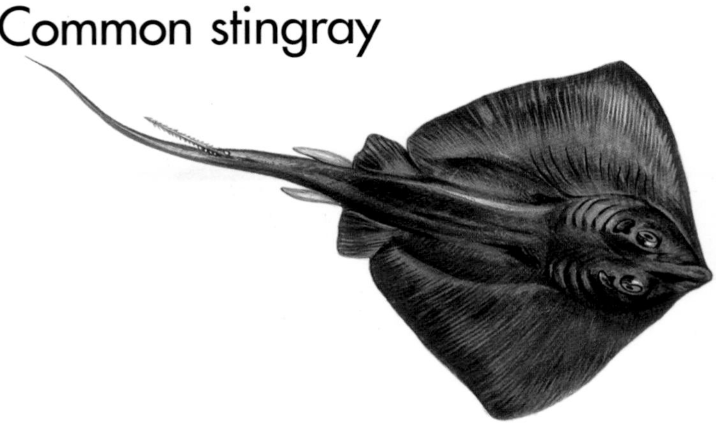

Slightly more rounded in outline than skates and true rays (*see pp.192–193*), the common eastern Atlantic and Mediterranean stingray lives mostly in shallow water. One or sometimes two saw-toothed poisonous barbs, up to 35cm (14in) long, project from the top of its tail. If disturbed – perhaps by a diver or fisherman, or even by a bather stepping on the half-buried fish – it will lash with its tail and may stab or cut its victim seriously. Poison entering the wound from a gland at the base of the barb causes intense pain, but deaths are rare. However, a few people die worldwide each year from stingray stings, usually to the upper part of their body.

Scientific name	*Dasyatis* (or *Trygon*) *pastinaca*
Classification	Order Myliobatiformes (great rays); sometimes included in Rajiformes
	Family Dasyatidae
Size	Up to about 60cm (24in) wide; to about 1.5m (5ft) long
Distribution	Eastern Atlantic; Mediterranean
Habitat	Temperate coastal waters and estuaries, to 200m (650ft) deep
Diet	Bottom-living fish; crustaceans; molluscs
Reproduction	Ovoviviparous; four to seven young, born after 4-month gestation

Common eagle ray

Eagle rays are aptly named, because their pectoral disc (*see p.192*) is much wider than it is long, so the fish appears to have wings. They are also (along with the manta rays; *see p.196*) much more active swimmers than most other rays, 'flying' through the water by flapping their wings, and even leaping into the air. They use their flat, plate-like teeth to crush crustacean and mollusc shells. The common eagle ray has a venomous tail spine but is not regarded as dangerous. The huge spotted eagle ray (*Aetobatus narinari*), up to 3m (10ft) wide, is common worldwide in the tropics and subtropics, including waters off the southern and south-eastern USA.

Scientific name	*Myliobatis aquila*
Classification	Order Myliobatiformes (great rays); sometimes included in Rajiformes
	Family Myliobatidae
Size	Up to about 1.8m (6ft) wide
Distribution	Eastern Atlantic from British Isles to South Africa; Mediterranean
Habitat	Temperate and tropical coastal waters; offshore to 300m (1000ft) deep
Diet	Mainly bottom-living crustaceans and molluscs; also fish
Reproduction	Ovoviviparous; three to seven young born after 6–8-month gestation

Giant manta ray

This is truly the giant among rays, the biggest living species and one of the so-called devil rays. Apart from its size, it is distinguished by strange paddle-like fins or lobes projecting from the front of its body, with the eyes on either side. These lobes look threatening, but are merely scoops that the ray unfurls when feeding, to direct food into its large, rectangular mouth. Giant mantas feed mainly on plankton – floating organisms – and some schooling fish. In spite of their size, they sometimes leap out of the water; this may be part of their courtship ritual, which is known to involve one or more males chasing a female for up to 30 minutes before mating.

Scientific name	*Manta birostris*
Classification	Order Myliobatiformes (great rays); sometimes included in Rajiformes
	Family Myliobatidae; sometimes placed in separate family Mobulidae
Size	Up to 8m (26ft) wide and possibly up to 3 tonnes
Distribution	Worldwide in tropical and subtropical seas
Habitat	Surface waters, mainly near shores and reefs, but also in open ocean
Diet	Mainly plankton; some small and medium-sized fish
Reproduction	Ovoviviparous; one or two young; gestation period uncertain

Rat or rabbit fish

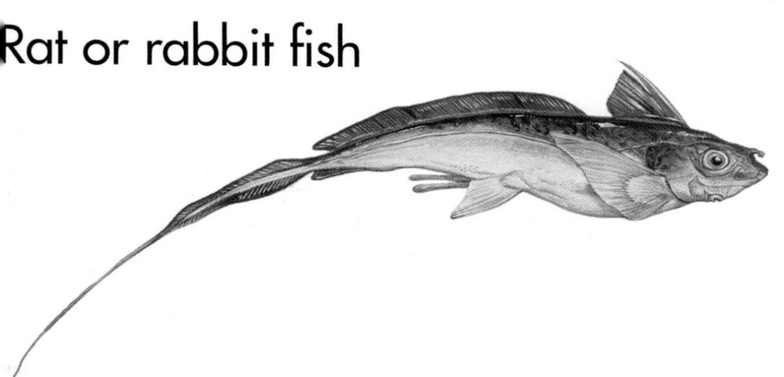

Most fishes with a skeleton of cartilage rather than bone belong to the rays and sharks (suborder Elsamobranchii; *see pp. 175–196*). A small second group, the himaeras of the suborder Holocephali, are strange-looking deep-sea fishes. The rat ish or rabbit fish (not to be confused with the warm-water rabbit fishes of the family iganidae, sometimes kept in aquariums) is an example. It has a long whip-like tail, ig staring eyes, large pectoral fins, and a large dorsal fin with a long spine behind he head. Its small mouth has lips and rabbit-like tooth plates. Around Iceland and orway it migrates to shallow seas to breed, and is sometimes caught by fishermen.

Scientific name	*Chimaera monstrosa*
Classification	Subclass Holocephali. Order Chimaeriformes (chimaeras)
	Family Chimaeridae
Size	Up to about 1.5m (5ft) long
Distribution	Eastern and northern Atlantic; Mediterranean; possibly other oceans
Habitat	Deep temperate and cold waters, mainly at 300–500m (1000–1600ft)
Diet	Mainly bottom-living invertebrates
Reproduction	Spawns in spring; eggs in slender cases, 18cm (7in) long

Coelacanth

Coelacanths are sometimes called 'living fossils' because, until the first specimen was caught off South Africa and identified in 1938, they were thought to have been extinct for at least 65 million years. They are similar to the prehistoric fishes with fleshy, lobed fins that evolved into the amphibians, the first land animals. Their internal features show other ways in which fishes have evolved; the heart, for example, is much more primitive than that of other fishes. The coelacanth is a rare, endangered species; fortunately, only a few are caught each year – accidentally – by Comoran fishermen. Its eggs, which develop internally, are huge: 9cm (3½in) across.

Scientific name	*Latimeria chalumnae*
Classification	Subclass Sarcopterygii (fleshy-finned fishes)
	Order Coelacanthiformes; family Latimeriidae
Size	Up to about 1.8m (6ft) long; male smaller
Distribution	Indian Ocean, especially near Comoros Islands
Habitat	Cool water among rocky reefs and caves, at 150–750m (500–2500ft)
Diet	Fish; squid
Reproduction	Ovoviviparous; up to 25 young born after 13-month gestation

Atlantic sturgeon

Sturgeons are best known – and have long been caught – as the source of caviar, their immature eggs, which are salted to make a luxury food. These may be cut from the female's body, killing her, or may be stripped and the female returned to the water – much preferable for conservation reasons. Sturgeon flesh is also eaten, and it is now an endangered species. It is a primitive fish, and has rows of bony plates along its body. It breeds in fresh water; the young stay in the river of their birth for up to three years before returning to the sea. A similar (perhaps identical) species, *Acipenser oxyrhynchus*, lives along the North American Atlantic coast.

Scientific name	*Acipenser sturio*
Classification	Subclass Actinopterygii (ray-finned fishes; includes all fish species on following pages); order Acipenseriformes; family Acipenseridae
Size	Up to 3.5m (11½ft) long – female smaller; up to 400kg (880lb)
Distribution	Eastern Atlantic; Baltic; Mediterranean; *see also above*
Habitat	Shallow coastal waters (bottom-living); enters rivers to breed
Diet	Worms; crustaceans; molluscs; some fish
Reproduction	Spawns in spring and early summer on gravelly bottom of fast rivers

Atlantic tarpon

A huge silvery fish looking rather like a giant herring, the tarpon may weigh 125kg (275lb, or 19½ stones) or more. It fights fiercely and leaps when caught by game fishermen. It has a deep, compressed body (flattened from side to side) and large scales. The tarpon sometimes comes into brackish or fresh water. It is regarded by biologists as one of the most primitive of the Teleostei, the very large group that contains almost all bony fish species alive today. They all have a well-developed skull and spine, and a symmetrical tail fin (unlike the sturgeons, whose tail fin is bigger at the top). Most have a gas-filled swim bladder which helps the fish to float.

Scientific name	*Megalops* (or *Tarpon*) *atlanticus*
Classification	Order Elopiformes (tarpons and allies)
	Family Megalopidae
Size	Up to 2.4m (8ft) long
Distribution	Eastern and western Atlantic, to Argentina, Nova Scotia and Ireland
Habitat	Warm tropical, subtropical and Gulf Stream inshore waters
Diet	Mainly schooling fish; crabs
Reproduction	Spawns in spring and summer; vast numbers of eggs

Bonefish

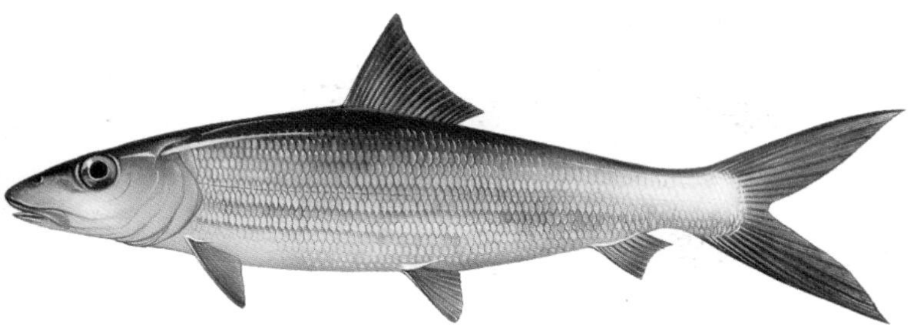

Even though they are so bony as to be almost inedible, bonefish are eagerly sought by game fishermen, using imitation shrimps and fish as bait, for the fierce fight they put up if hooked. Bonefish feed in the shallows, their body almost vertical as they forage for small, bottom-living creatures. They are slender and streamlined, with a deeply forked tail fin. It was long thought that a single species extended throughout the tropics, but biochemical and DNA studies have shown that the almost identical-looking fish in fact belong to at least five separate species. They all produce almost transparent larvae which eventually change into the adult form.

Scientific name	*Albula vulpes*
Classification	Order Albuliformes (bonefishes and allies)
	Family Albulidae
Size	Up to about 90cm (3ft) long
Distribution	Worldwide in tropical waters (*but see above*)
Habitat	Shallow inshore waters, especially over sand
Diet	Crabs; prawns; shellfish; small bottom-feeding fish
Reproduction	Spawns in shallow waters; eggs hatch to eel-like larvae

European eel

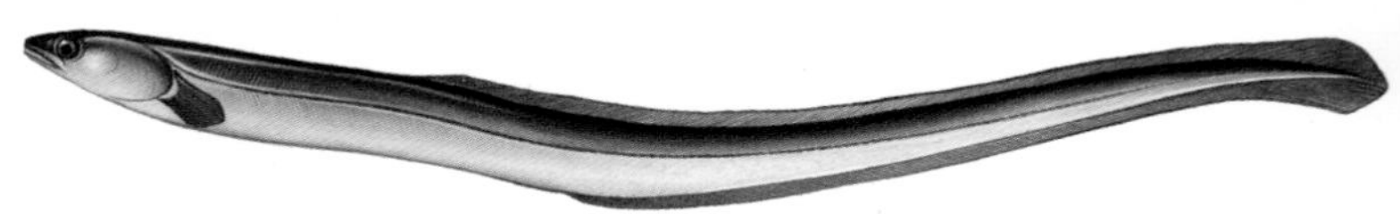

The life history of the European eel is extraordinary and still a mystery in some of its details. Eels spend most of their lives in rivers, where they have yellowish underparts. When mature and ready to breed, they turn silvery (as illustrated), develop enlarged eyes, and their gut shrivels; they will never eat again. They swim to the sea in autumn, and apparently in deep water to the Sargasso Sea, in the southwestern North Atlantic. There they spawn in spring at about 100–450m (300–1500ft), then die. The transparent larvae drift in the Gulf Stream and re-enter fresh water as small elvers. The American eel (*Anguilla rostrata*) has a similar life history.

Scientific name	*Anguilla anguilla*
Classification	Order Anguilliformes (true eels)
	Family Anguillidae
Size	Up to 1.4m (4½ft) long; female generally longer than male
Distribution	Breeds in Atlantic; spends most of life in fresh water
Habitat	Deep water during breeding migration; larvae drift near surface
Diet	Insects, crustaceans and fish in fresh water; adults do not eat at sea
Reproduction	Spawns in Sargasso Sea (western Atlantic); larvae drift in Gulf Stream

Mediterranean moray eel

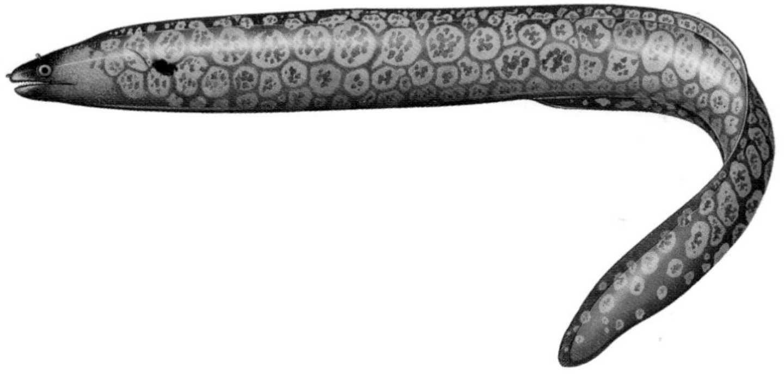

Moray eels live in rocky crevices and reefs throughout the tropical, subtropical and warm temperate seas of the world. They have a reputation for ferocity, and they are certainly voracious predators, lunging from their lair (where they lurk with only the head showing) to snatch their prey. They have a large mouth and sharp teeth, and if disturbed will give a diver a nasty bite. However, experts believe that the similarity of human fingers to an octopus's tentacles may often be to blame for attacks. Like most moray eels, the Mediterranean species has a boldly patterned body, mottled and banded. All morays lack scales and both pectoral and pelvic fins.

Scientific name	*Muraena helena*
Classification	Order Anguilliformes (true eels)
	Family Muraenidae
Size	Up to about 1.3m (4¼ft) long
Distribution	Mediterranean; adjacent areas of eastern Atlantic
Habitat	Rocky shores of warm temperate seas
Diet	Mainly fish, squid and cuttlefish
Reproduction	Spawns in summer; large (5mm; ⅕in) floating eggs

Conger eel

Huge fish with large jaws and extremely sharp teeth, conger eels are powerful predators that hunt mainly at night for fish such as pollack, hake, wrasse and sole, as well as squid, octopuses and crustaceans. By day, they hide among rocks or other 'cover', and divers exploring wrecks often find them inhabited by many large congers. They are distinguished from moray eels (*see p.203*) by their colouring and the fact that they have pectoral fins. They breed in deep water like the European eel (*see p.202*), and their larvae take one to two years to drift back to their coastal adult habitat. A similar species, *Conger oceanicus*, lives off eastern North America.

Scientific name	*Conger conger*
Classification	Order Anguilliformes (true eels)
	Family Congridae
Size	Up to 3m (10ft) long or more; weight up to 110kg (over 240lb)
Distribution	Eastern North Altantic; Mediterranean; breeds mid-Atlantic
Habitat	Rocky shores to 200m (650ft); old wrecks; breeds in deep water
Diet	Fish; crabs and other crustaceans; squid and octopuses. Feeds at night
Reproduction	Spawns at 3000-4000m (10 000–13 000ft) in summer

Brown garden eel

The name garden eel was coined in the early 20th entury by American zoologist Villiam Beebe, who first lescribed the creatures living in lense colonies, half-buried, waying in the current like a garden' or 'meadow' of sea-grass tems. The fish spend their whole ife anchored in the sandy sea-ottom like this, eating passing ood particles and always ready o retreat into their burrow if hreatened by a predator. Males nd females even mate part-uried, intertwining their bodies. 'he brown garden eel is the best-nown Atlantic species. The potted garden eel *Heteroconger hassi*) lives in varm water from the Red Sea to 'ahiti and California.

Scientific name	*Heteroconger* (or *Taenioconger*) *longissimus*, or *H.* (or *T.*) *halis*
Classification	Order Anguilliformes (true eels)
	Family Congridae; subfamily Heterocongrinae
Size	Up to about 60cm (24in) long
Distribution	Eastern and western Atlantic (Canaries to West Africa; Florida to Brazil)
Habitat	Sandy bottom of inshore warm waters, to 50m (165ft)
Diet	Small planktonic creatures and detritus
Reproduction	Mate while anchored in sand; juveniles burrow into sand

Atlantic or slender snipe eel

A very long, slender and fragile fish, with dorsal and anal fins that run almost the entire length of its body and a tail that ends in a whip-like filament, the snipe eel is named after its long, beak-like jaws. These resemble the beak of the snipe (a wading bird). The fish feeds by swimming along with its mouth open, using its sharp, backward-facing teeth to trap shrimps and other small creatures that swim into its gape. Only females and younger males have these long jaws; they degenerate in older males, which develop long, tubular front nostrils – possibly to help to locate females. Both males and females are believed to die after breeding.

Scientific name	*Nemichthys scolopaceus*
Classification	Order Anguilliformes (true eels), or separately in Saccopharyngiformes
	Family Nemichthyidae
Size	Up to about 1.3m (4¼ft) long
Distribution	Worldwide in tropical and temperate seas
Habitat	Mostly at 400–2000m (1300–6500ft); sometimes shallower in north
Diet	Mainly small crustaceans; some small fish
Reproduction	Eggs hatch into planktonic larvae

?elican or gulper eel

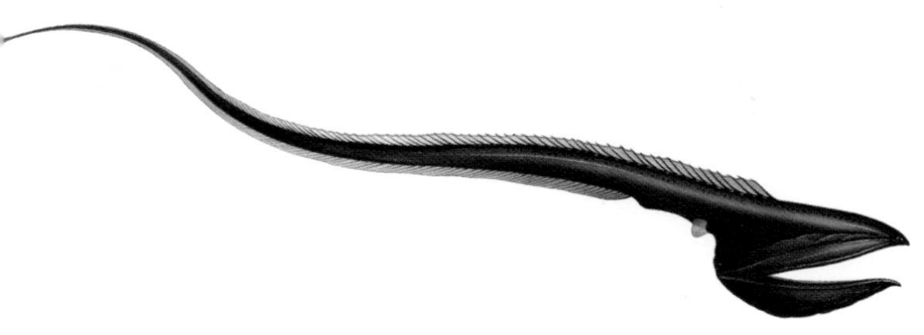

This is one of the most extraordinary-looking of all fish, with its slender body, long whip-like tail, and disproportionately large head and mouth (making up nore than half of its true body length), with tiny teeth. Its gape is formed by a black lastic membrane, making the name 'pelican eel' an apt one. (Another name for it is umbrella-mouth gulper eel.) It has a flashing luminous organ at the tip of its tail – ›ut no one knows whether the fish holds this in front of its mouth to lure prey, or vhether it simply swims along with its mouth open, gulping whatever comes its way. The fish's stomach can expand to contain the rare catch of a large amount of prey.

Scientific name	*Eurypharynx pelecanoides*
Classification	Order Anguilliformes (true eels), or separately in Saccopharyngiformes
	Family Eurypharyngidae
Size	Up to about 75–100cm (30–39in) long
Distribution	Worldwide in temperate and tropical seas
Habitat	Deep water, mostly at 2000–7500m (6500–24 500ft)
Diet	Mainly small crustaceans; also fish, squid and other invertebrates
Reproduction	Eggs hatch into planktonic larvae which develop in shallower water

Atlantic herring

One of the most important commercial fishery species, herrings have been over-fished in recent years, and stocks are seriously depleted in many areas. Several distinct races live in different parts of their overall range, migrating to various spawning grounds – the floor of shallow bays and offshore banks – at different seasons. They swim in large schools, mostly near the surface at night, but deeper in daylight. Herrings breed rapidly, and can double their numbers in just over a year if not fished. The larvae swim to the surface in large schools, and reach maturity in three to nine years. The North Pacific herring, *Clupea pallasii*, is a similar species.

Scientific name	*Clupea harengus*
Classification	Order Clupeiformes (sardines, herrings and allies)
	Family Clupeidae
Size	Up to about 45cm (18in) long
Distribution	North Atlantic (Arctic to Carolinas and Bay of Biscay)
Habitat	Cool coastal waters and open sea; mainly near surface, to 200m (650ft)
Diet	Mainly small crustaceans; some small fish; sometimes filter-feeds
Reproduction	Races spawn at various seasons, on shallow sea-floor

Twaite shad

Shads are rather similar to herrings, but have a deeper body; it is silvery with a greenish or bluish cast. The twaite shad has a series of dark blotches – usually six to eight – along its sides, while the closely related but rarer allis shad (*Alosa alosa*) has only one or a few blotches. Twaite shads spend most of the year in shallow waters, feeding on shrimps, small fish and other floating organisms. They swim into the lower reaches of rivers in late spring to breed, before returning to the sea in late summer. The young return to the sea after about a year, when they are about 13cm (5in) long. Some shad populations live permanently in landlocked freshwater lakes.

Scientific name	*Allosa fallax*
Classification	Order Clupeiformes (sardines, herrings and allies)
	Family Clupeidae
Size	Up to about 60cm (24in) long
Distribution	Eastern North Atlantic; Baltic, Mediterranean and Black seas
Habitat	Inshore and coastal waters; estuaries; enters rivers to breed
Diet	Mainly crustaceans and small fish
Reproduction	Spawns spring and early summer on gravel beds in lower parts of rivers

European anchovy

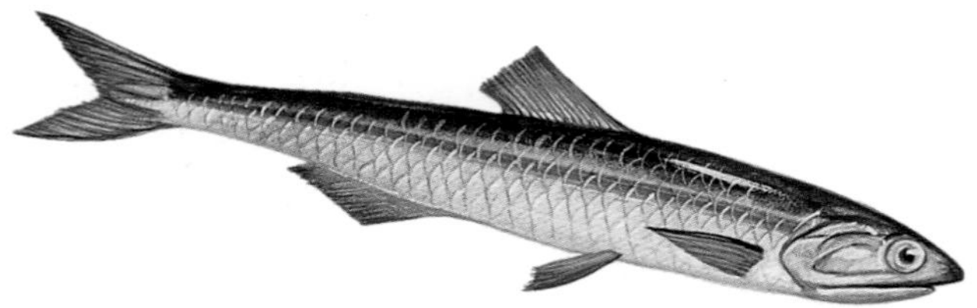

More than 100 species of anchovies live in the world's oceans, and many are an important commercial catch. They are small fish that swim in large schools, and are also eaten by larger species, such as tunas. Anchovies are recognizable by their long snout and long, underslung mouth, which extends well behind the eyes. When feeding – mainly at night – they swim with their mouth agape to filter small floating creatures. One of the most important Pacific species is the anchoveta (*Engraulis ringens*), which feeds on plankton brought by the cold Peruvian current; when the *El Niño* phenomenon stops this current, the anchovies disappear.

Scientific name	*Engraulis encrasicholus*
Classification	Order Clupeiformes (sardines, herrings and allies)
	Family Engraulidae
Size	Up to about 20cm (8in) long
Distribution	Eastern Atlantic; Mediterranean and Black seas; western Indian Ocean
Habitat	Coastal and inshore temperate and tropical waters, usually near surface
Diet	Filter-feeds on small planktonic organisms
Reproduction	Spawns spring to autumn, often in estuaries and lagoons; eggs float

Dorab wolf-herring

This large tropical and subtropical fish is very appropriately named, for it is a voracious predator of small schooling fish – such as its relatives the herrings and anchovies. Known also, particularly in south-western Asia and India, simply as the dorab, it has large, fang-like teeth and is very similar to its close relative the whitefin wolf-herring (*Chirocentrus nudus*). The only easy distinguishing features are the dorab's shorter pectoral fins and the black markings on the upper part of its dorsal fin. Both are very bony fish, but are important commercially in southern and south-east Asia, where more than 50 000 tonnes of the two are caught each year.

Scientific name	*Chirocentrus dorab*
Classification	Order Clupeiformes (sardines, herrings and allies)
	Family Chirocentridae
Size	Up to about 1m (3¼ft) long, possibly more
Distribution	Indian and western Pacific oceans (Red Sea to Australia and Japan)
Habitat	Warm coastal and shallow seas; also brackish waters
Diet	Mainly small schooling fish; probably also crustaceans
Reproduction	Details uncertain, but probably spawns in shallow water

Milkfish

Big silvery fish of warm waters, milkfish have no teeth and are filter-feeders. They swim in schools near coasts and around island reefs, and lay their eggs in the sea – where the larvae remain for about two weeks. The larvae then move inshore, into river estuaries, brackish lagoons or mangrove swamps, where they grow into immature adults before returning to the sea. In many parts of south-east Asia and around the South China Sea, the larvae are collected and raised in village ponds until big enough to eat. Human manure may be used to encourage the growth of algae on which the fish feed. Milkfish thrive in water as warm as 32°C (90°F).

Scientific name	*Chanos chanos*
Classification	Order Gonorynchiformes (milkfish and allies)
	Family Chanidae
Size	Up to about 1.8m (6ft) long; weight up to 14kg (31lb)
Distribution	Indian and Pacific oceans (Red Sea and South Africa to California)
Habitat	Mainly shallow coastal waters (to 12m; 40ft) in tropics and subtropics
Diet	Filter-feeder on planktonic plants and animals
Reproduction	Spawns near surface at spring tides; larvae develop in brackish waters

Common jollytail, or inanga

Inanga is the Maori (native New Zealand) name for the fish called by European settlers the minnow (or, when young, whitebait); jollytail is the Australian name. The fish spends most of its adult life in the lower reaches of rivers, but migrates downstream to estuaries to breed. It spawns among vegetation at high spring tide (an extremely high tide), and the eggs hatch only after they have been covered again by the next spring tide. The larvae are washed into the sea and develop there for some months before returning to fresh water. Some fish have been caught far from land, and the species must have spread across the world by long sea journeys.

Scientific name	*Galaxias maculatus* or *G. attenuatus*
Classification	Order Osmeriformes (smelts and allies) or Galaxiiformes; sometimes included in Salmoniformes (salmon and allies); family Galaxiidae
Size	Up to about 18cm (7in) long
Distribution	Australia, New Zealand and South America, and adjacent islands
Habitat	Temperate fresh and salt water
Diet	Aquatic and surface-floating invertebrates
Reproduction	Spawns in estuaries at high tide; eggs hatch at next spring tide

European smelt

A curious feature of all smelts – the reason for which is unknown – is their cucumber-like smell. They are rather like slender trout, and (like trout) have a fleshy second dorsal fin near the tail. The European species, like most of its close relatives, spends most of its life at sea, rarely far from the shore, but it migrates to fresh water to breed. It swims upstream in early spring and sheds its eggs over the pebbles or gravel of the river bed, to which the eggs attach by a thin stalk. The adults return to the sea after some weeks or months, and the young fish later follow them. In some Scandinavian lakes there are permanent freshwater populations.

Scientific name	*Osmerus eperlanus*
Classification	Order Osmeriformes (smelts and allies); sometimes included in
	Salmoniformes (salmon and allies); family Osmeridae
Size	Up to about 46cm (18in) long
Distribution	North-east Atlantic; White Sea; Baltic
Habitat	Cool to cold coastal waters, to 50m (165ft); estuaries; rivers
Diet	Mainly shrimps and other small crustaceans; some small fish
Reproduction	Spawns in spring in gravel-bottomed rivers

Atlantic salmon

Often called the 'king of fish', the Atlantic salmon is one of the finest game and food fish. It spends its early years in a river, changing its appearance as it develops; the various stages have special names: alevin (larva), parr and smolt. The last, up to 25cm (10in) long, is the form that returns to the sea, where it lives and grows, usually for several years. Adults then find their way – probably by smell – back to the river where they were born, often leaping high waterfalls to reach their spawning grounds. These are the fish that anglers and fishermen catch. Many die after spawning, but emaciated 'kelts' may return to the sea and later breed again.

Scientific name	*Salmo salar*
Classification	Order Salmoniformes (salmon and allies)
	Family Salmonidae
Size	Up to about 1.5m (5ft) long; weight up to 47kg (104lb)
Distribution	Eastern and Western North Atlantic; some lakes; farmed in sea lochs
Habitat	Open sea, mostly in cold surface waters, to 10m (33ft); rivers and lakes
Diet	Squid; crustaceans; fish. Young feed on small invertebrates and fish
Reproduction	Spawns in river of birth; young return to sea after one to six years

Rainbow trout, or steelhead

Rainbow trout are named for the fine colouring of adult fish that spawn in fast-flowing streams; those living permanently in large inland lakes are a more uniform silver colour. The species originated in the American north-west, where populations that regularly migrate to the sea are known as steelheads; these are the biggest rainbow trout, and return to fresh water to breed after several years at sea. However, it seems to be naturally a freshwater species, and has been introduced to rivers and lakes worldwide – even to tropical lakes above about 1200m (4000ft). It is also widely farmed, and captive-bred fish are used to stock fishing lakes and ponds.

Scientific name	*Oncorhynchus mykiss* or *Salmo gairdneri*
Classification	Order Salmoniformes (salmon and allies)
	Family Salmonidae
Size	Up to about 1.2m (4ft) long; weight up to 26kg (57lb)
Distribution	Eastern Pacific (Alaska to Mexico); widely introduced around world
Habitat	Open temperate and warm waters, to 10m (33ft); rivers and lakes
Diet	Various invertebrates; small fish
Reproduction	In wild, spawns in spring in hollow in gravel of fast-flowing stream

Sockeye salmon; kokanee

These are two forms of the same Pacific salmon species, both of which breed in freshwater lakes and streams. The name sockeye applies to fish that return to the sea at the age of one to three years, and spend their adult life there before returning to their breeding grounds – a run of up to 2400km (1500 miles). Kokanee remain in fresh water; they never grow as big as sockeyes, which are among the most important commercially fished Pacific salmon (although endangered in some river systems). At spawning time, the fish turn from a silvery colour to red; the male is particularly brilliant, and develops a humped back, as illustrated. They then die.

Scientific name	*Oncorhynchus* (or *Salmo*) *nerka*
Classification	Order Salmoniformes (salmon and allies)
	Family Salmonidae
Size	Up to about 84cm (33in) long; weight up to 7.7kg (17lb)
Distribution	North Pacific rim, from Japan and Kamchatka to Alaska and California
Habitat	Open sea and coastal waters, to 240m (800ft); rivers and lakes
Diet	Mainly small invertebrates; sea-going adults also eat fish
Reproduction	Spawn in lakes or streams, then die; young sockeyes migrate to sea

Pacific hatchetfish

Despite its common name, this species is found in the Atlantic and Indian oceans as well as the Pacific. And despite their fearsome appearance, hatchetfishes are small, harmless fish that feed on small invertebrates. They, in turn, are important food for deep-swimming tuna in many areas. Hatchetfishes are middle to deep-water species with a short silvery body that is compressed from side to side. They have light-generating organs on their lower surface; the colour and pattern of light produced varies from species to species. The hatchetfish's mouth and the large, bulging eyes point upwards, suggesting that it usually attacks its prey from below.

Scientific name	*Argyroplectus affinis*
Classification	Order Stomiiformes (dragonfishes and relatives)
	Family Sternoptychidae
Size	Up to about 8.5cm (3⅓in) long
Distribution	Worldwide in tropical and warm temperate waters
Habitat	Mid-levels of deep ocean, but sometimes to 3870m (12 700ft)
Diet	Small crustaceans and other invertebrates
Reproduction	Eggs and larvae planktonic; swim to deep water as they mature

Sloane's viperfish

A fierce predator in spite of its relatively small size, the viperfish is armed with long, fang-like teeth set in jaws that are specially built to open extremely wide for attacking prey. Yet the lower teeth are so long that they extend above the fish's head when its jaws are closed. The frontmost ray of the viperfish's dorsal fin is lengthened into a filament like a fishing line; it is tipped with a light-generating organ to lure prey in the deep gloom in which it lives. The fish's ventral (lower) surface also has numerous light organs, which glow red, scattered all over it. Viperfish live at least 1000m (3300ft) deep, but are believed to move up to around 500m (1650ft) or even shallower levels at night, in order to feed.

Scientific name	*Chauliodus sloani*
Classification	Order Stomiiformes (dragonfishes and relatives)
	Family Stomiidae; sometimes classified separately in Chauliodontidae
Size	Up to about 35cm (14in) long
Distribution	Tropical and temperate parts of all oceans, but patchily distributed
Habitat	Deep oceanic waters, to 1000m (3300ft) or more
Diet	Fish; crustaceans
Reproduction	Spawns at any time of year; eggs and larvae planktonic

Scaly dragonfish, or boa fish

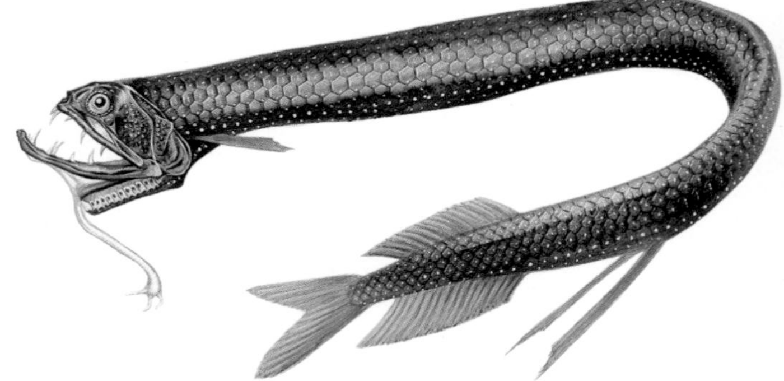

This dragonfish fully deserves its common names, with its fearsome fangs and its head and mouth wider than its body (and able to swallow prey larger than itself). It also has a strange-looking barbel (ending in a light-emitting organ and three short filaments) hanging from its mouth. There are several known subspecies, with minor differences, living in various parts of the deep oceans, but all have rows of hexagonal (six-sided) scales along the sides of their body and a series of about 90 photophores (light-emitters) along the belly. Little is known of their habits, but they are believed to move from the deeps nearer the surface at night in order to feed.

Scientific name	*Stomias boa*
Classification	Order Stomiiformes (dragonfishes and relatives)
	Family Stomiidae or Stomiatidae
Size	Up to about 40cm (16in) long
Distribution	Atlantic, Indian and Pacific oceans, including Arctic and Antarctic waters
Habitat	Deep waters to 1000–4000m (3300–13 000ft); shallower at night
Diet	Fish; crustaceans
Reproduction	Eggs and larvae planktonic

Black dragonfish

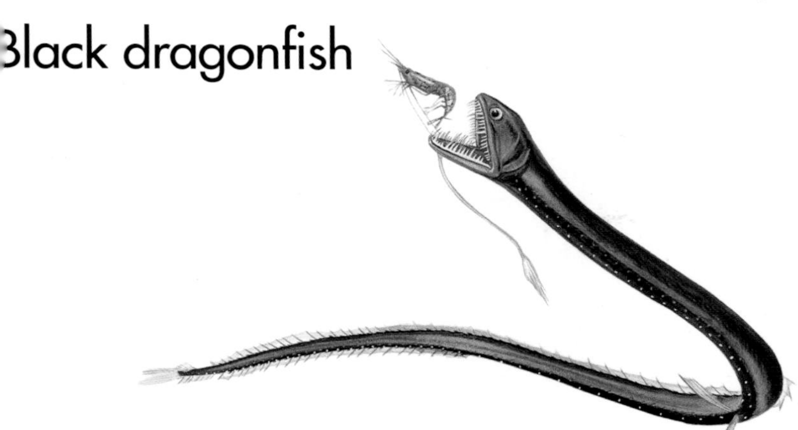

Known also as the ribbon sawtail fish, this deep-water species is rather like the scaly dragonfish (*opposite*), but has no scales on its body. However, its most extraordinary feature is its life history. Female larvae and adults are much bigger than their male counterparts. Female larvae grow to a length of about 7cm (2¾in), and have eyes at the end of stalks up to 2cm (¾in) long. As the larvae grow into the adult shape, the stalks are gradually absorbed until the eyes are in the normal position in the creature's head. Male larvae, on the other hand, remain small and, when adult, have no teeth and do not eat. They live only long enough to mate.

Scientific name	*Idiacanthus fasciola*
Classification	Order Stomiiformes (dragonfishes and relatives)
	Family Stomiidae; sometimes classified separately in Idiacanthidae
Size	Female up to about 50cm (19½in) long: male about 8cm (3in) long
Distribution	Probably worldwide in deep waters, except polar regions
Habitat	Deep waters, to 500–2000m (1650–6500ft); female shallower at night
Diet	Fish; crustaceans
Reproduction	Eggs planktonic; larvae differ according to sex (*see above*)

Showy bristlemouth

Some marine biologists believe that there are more individual creatures among bristlemouths of the genus *Cyclostoma* than of any other genus of vertebrates (animals with backbones) on Earth. This is because the oceanic plankton – the mass of floating organisms that drift around the world's oceans – contains billions upon billions of these tiny fish. Many species of bristlemouths (also sometimes known as lightfish) are even smaller than the so-called 'showy' species, and even the biggest is no more than 7.5cm (3in) long. Yet, like other members of their group, they have a relatively large mouth, and hunt small planktonic crustaceans and other creatures.

Scientific name	*Cyclothone signata*
Classification	Order Stomiiformes (dragonfishes and relatives)
	Family Gonostomatidae
Size	Up to about 3cm (just over 1in) long
Distribution	Pacific and Indian oceans
Habitat	Open ocean; mostly found near surface and at 400–500m (1300–1650ft)
Diet	Small planktonic creatures
Reproduction	Eggs and larvae planktonic

Spotted lantern fish

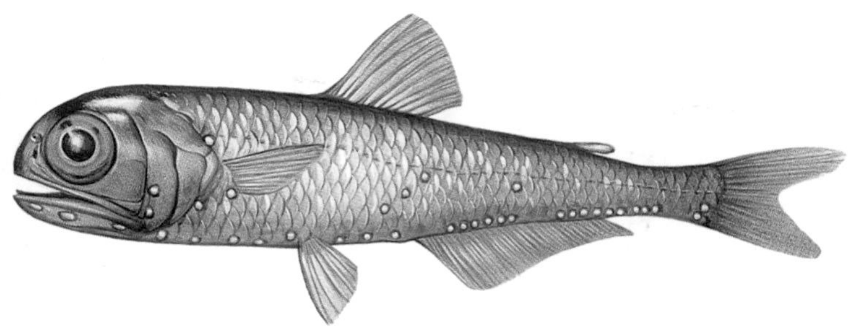

The species name *punctatum* means 'spotted', and this fish has light-producing photophores scattered over its head and body. There are many related species f lantern fish, all with a blunt, rounded head, long jaws and large eyes. Each has its wn unique pattern of glowing spots, which is sometimes the only method of lentification. In fact, the fish themselves may identify other members of their own pecies in the same way, for breeding. Lantern fishes are among the most abundant f all fish – more so even than sardines and anchovies. They are eaten by many arger species, and could become an important commercial catch in many areas.

Scientific name	*Myctophum punctatum*
Classification	Order Myctophiformes (lantern fishes and allies)
	Family Myctophidae
Size	Up to about 11cm (4½in) long
Distribution	North Atlantic (tropics to Arctic); Mediterranean
Habitat	Deep ocean, mostly at 700–800m (2300–2600ft); nearer surface at night
Diet	Small crustaceans; fish larvae
Reproduction	Female produces about 800–900 eggs in spring to summer; planktonic

Sea catfish

There are more than 2000 catfish species, easily recognized by the barbels around their mouth. Most live in fresh water, but this – the hardhead sea catfish – is one of more than 100 marine species. It swims in large shoals in shallow, often muddy water, and can make loud sounds by vibrating its swim-bladder. The most extraordinary feature of sea catfish of the family Ariidae is their breeding habits. Females produce relatively small numbers of large eggs, up to 2cm (¾in) across. The male holds as many as 55 eggs in his mouth until they hatch, and cannot eat during this time. After hatching, the young fish also hide from danger in his mouth.

Scientific name	*Arius felis*
Classification	Order Siluriformes (catfishes and allies); suborder Siluroidei
	Family Ariidae
Size	Up to about 70cm (27½in) long
Distribution	Western Atlantic (Massachusetts to Mexico)
Habitat	Coastal waters; estuaries
Diet	Bottom feeder, mostly at night, on crabs, shrimps and some small fish
Reproduction	Mouth-brooder (*see above*)

₹ed or diamond lizardfish

The lizardfishes have a large head, with a wide, toothy mouth, that looks very lizard-like especially when seen from the side. They are voracious carnivores, ɑd habitually lie on the sea-bottom, propped on their lower fins, with their head aised in a lizard-like manner. Some species half-bury themselves in the sand, but ıe red lizardfish prefers a rocky bottom. The cryptic coloration of most species' ack hides them well; whenever suitable prey passes, they suddenly lurch forward ɔ catch it. A related species of the subfamily Harpadontinae, *Harpadon nehereus*, ; widely caught in south and south-east Asia, dried and sold as the 'Bombay duck'.

Scientific name	*Synodus synodus*
Classification	Order Aulopiformes (lizardfishes, lancetfishes and allies)
	Family Synodontidae; subfamily Synodontinae
Size	Up to about 33cm (13in) long
Distribution	Tropical and subtropical parts of Atlantic; Caribbean
Habitat	Mainly shallow inshore waters; sometimes to 90m (300ft)
Diet	Mainly fish
Reproduction	Spawns near bottom in open waters

Atlantic cod

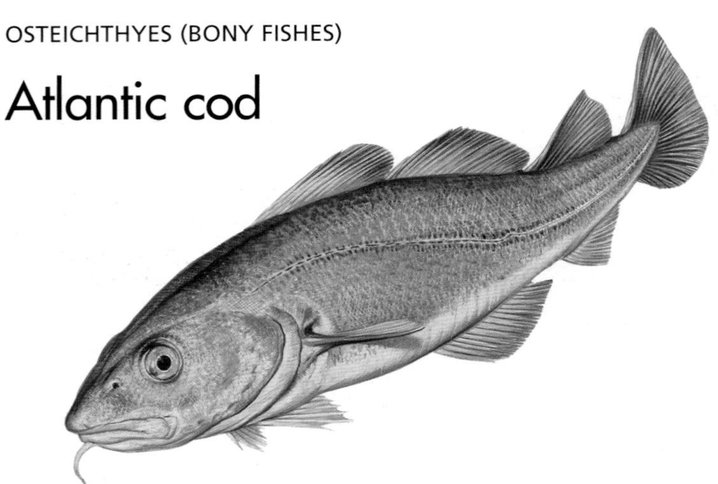

Many of the most important commerically caught fish, including hake, ling, whiting and haddock (*opposite*), belong to the cod family and its relatives, but few are as important as the common Atlantic cod. However, overfishing in recent decades has reduced stocks drastically, and some populations – particularly around Greenland and Newfoundland – are particularly endangered. Cod are prolific breeders, however, and with conservation measures their numbers could increase again quite rapidly. The similar but rather larger-headed Pacific cod (*Gadus macrocephalus*) is widely caught in the eastern and western far North Pacific.

Scientific name	*Gadus morrhua*
Classification	Order Gaddiformes (codfishes and allies)
	Family Gadidae
Size	Up to 2m (6½ft) long and 96kg (212lb); usually much less, to 1.3m (4¼ft)
Distribution	Atlantic north of Cape Hatteras and Bay of Biscay, to 78°N; Baltic
Habitat	Cool or cold inshore and offshore waters, to 600m (2000ft)
Diet	Fish; invertebrates
Reproduction	Spawns at various seasons, at or near sea-bottom

Haddock

Another important North Atlantic fishing catch, haddock do not grow as big as cod, and are easily distinguished by their sharply pointed first dorsal fin. (Both od and haddock have three dorsal fins, but in cod the first one is rounded.) laddock also have a much smaller chin barbel than cod. They have never been aught in quite such large quantities as cod, but they are less prolific breeders and re also threatened by overfishing. Young haddock live at first near the surface mong the tentacles of a large jellyfish before heading for deep waters. Both cod nd haddock may make long migrations between feeding and spawning grounds.

Scientific name	*Melanogrammus* (formerly *Gadus*) *aelgefinus*
Classification	Order Gaddiformes (codfishes and allies)
	Family Gadidae
Size	Rarely more than 1m (3¼ft) long; weight up to 17kg (37½lb)
Distribution	Atlantic north of Delaware Bay and Bay of Biscay, to 78°N; Barents Sea
Habitat	Cold inshore and offshore waters, mostly at 80–200m (260–650ft)
Diet	Mainly bottom-living crustaceans, molluscs, starfish, worms and fish
Reproduction	Spawns late winter to early summer at depth of 50–150m (165–500ft)

Alaska or walleye pollack

Since the 1980s, a greater tonnage of Alaska or walleye pollack has been caught than of any other fish species – almost 7 million tonnes a year at its peak in 1986, although less than 5 million tonnes by 1995. At one time, it was used only to make animal feed, but has become an important food for humans – mostly in the form of fish fingers and other frozen blocks, or as salted fish. Its roe is also eaten, and the flesh is processed to make surimi, or fish mince, for making 'crab sticks'. It is widely distributed, with at least 12 major populations. The fish swim near the sea-bottom in vast schools during the day, but often move to higher levels at night in order to feed

Scientific name	*Theragra chalcogramma* (formerly *Gadus chalcogrammus)*
Classification	Order Gaddiformes (codfishes and allies)
	Family Gadidae
Size	Up to 80–90cm (31½–36in) long
Distribution	North Pacific, from Alaska to Sea of Japan and California
Habitat	Open sea, from near surface to almost 1000m (3300ft) deep
Diet	Fish; krill and other crustaceans
Reproduction	Spawns winter to summer in dense schools at 50–250m (165–800ft)

Rat-tail, or grenadier

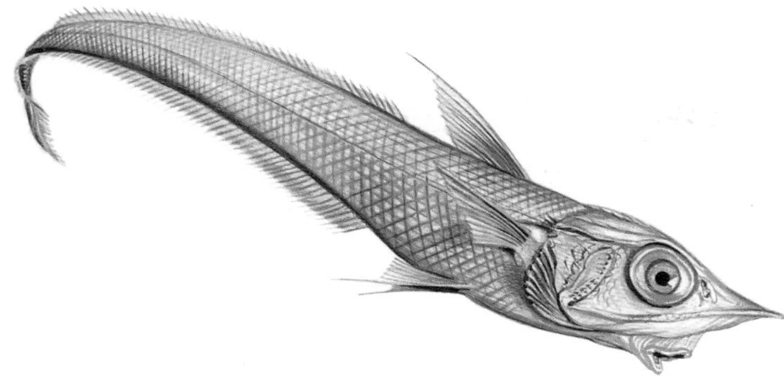

The various rat-tail or grenadier species are probably the most numerous and varied of all deep-water fish. They are curious-looking, with a large head and a long tapering tail; many, such as the species illustrated, have a pronounced snout. This and some others have a large light-producing organ on their belly, between the base of the pelvic fins. Rat-tails are rather slow swimmers with a characteristic head-down posture, eating more or less any small creatures or other food material – alive or dead – they encounter. Their large eyes suggest that they hunt luminescent deep-sea creatures, but they may also possibly feed nearer to the surface at night.

Scientific name	*Caelorinchus caelorhincus*; often spelt *Coelorinchus* or *Coelorhynchus*
Classification	Order Gaddiformes (codfishes and allies)
	Family Macrouridae
Size	Up to about 40cm (16in) long
Distribution	Warmer parts of Atlantic; Mediterranean
Habitat	Mainly deep water, to at least 1250m (4100ft); some species deeper
Diet	Bottom-living invertebrates and fish; also scavenges on dead creatures
Reproduction	Details uncertain, but eggs and larvae probably planktonic

Angler fish or goosefish

The angler fish makes excellent eating, but it looks so hideous that it is almost always displayed with the head and skin removed, and is sold as monkfish. The name angler fish is very apt, however, since it has a 'fishing rod' – a long, flexible spine properly called the *illicium* – growing from its head; this ends in a fleshy bait or lure called the *esca*. The fish lies on the bottom, well disguised by its colouring and fringe of skin flaps, and sometimes half-buried, until the lure attracts suitable prey. The slightest touch on the esca provokes a snapping reflex by its huge jaws. A similar but smaller species, *Lophius americanus*, lives off eastern North America.

Scientific name	*Lophius piscatorius*
Classification	Order Lophiiformes (angler fishes, frogfishes and allies)
	Family Lophiidae
Size	Up to about 2m (6½ft) long; weight up to 58kg (128lb)
Distribution	Eastern Atlantic (Barents Sea to West Africa); Mediterranean; Black Sea
Habitat	Inshore and offshore waters at 20–1000m (65–3300ft)
Diet	Fish; larger invertebrates
Reproduction	Spawns spring and summer; eggs planktonic, in gelatinous ribbon

Longnose batfish

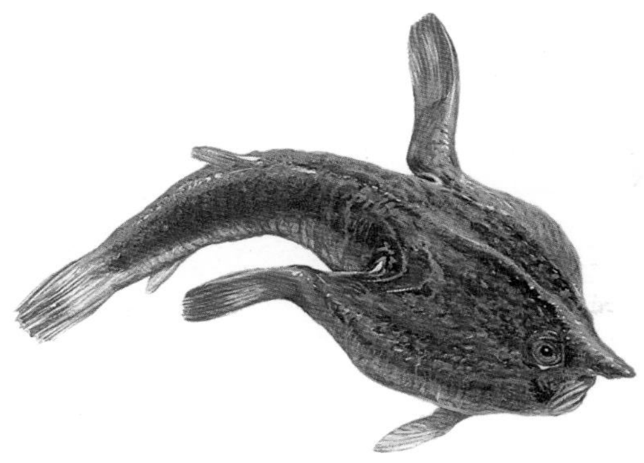

Batfishes are bottom-living fish that lure their prey in a similar way to the related angler fishes (*opposite*). However, in batfishes, the lure and its 'fishing rod' are retractable into a tube just above the mouth when the fish is resting. When feeding, the lure is extended and vibrated to attract small prey – which the batfish snaps up. Batfishes are poor swimmers; they push themselves along the seabed with their fleshy pectoral fins. The longnose batfish was thought to be a single species, but fish found from the Bahamas north are now classified separately, as *Ogcocephalus corniger*, from those living from the West Indies to Uruguay, *O. vespertilio*.

Scientific name	*Ogcocephalus vespertilio* and *O. corniger*
Classification	Order Lophiiformes (angler fishes, frogfishes and allies)
	Family Ogcocephalidae
Size	Up to about 30cm (12in) long; *O. corniger* smaller
Distribution	Tropical and subtropical western Atlantic (*see above*)
Habitat	seabed, to depths of 30–240m (100–800ft)
Diet	Small crustaceans, worms and other invertebrates; small fish
Reproduction	Little is known of their biology

Garfish

The garfish, like all members of its family, has a long, slim body with the dorsal and anal fins set well back, and extremely elongated jaws armed with many needle-like teeth. It is a surface-swimming predator which chases its prey and often leaps well out of the water. Young garfish pass through a 'halfbeak' stage when the upper jaw is much shorter than the lower; these feed on plankton. (The upper jaw is permanently short in the halfbeaks of the related family Hemiramphidae.) Three distinct subspecies of garfish live in the northern Atlantic and Baltic, in the Mediterranean and warmer parts of the Atlantic, and in the Black Sea respectively.

Scientific name	*Belone belone*
Classification	Order Beloniformes (needlefishes, flying fishes and allies)
	Family Belonidae
Size	Up to about 94cm (37in) long
Distribution	Eastern North Atlantic; Baltic; Mediterranean; Black Sea
Habitat	Surface waters, mostly in open sea, but inshore and estuaries in summer
Diet	Small fish; some crustaceans
Reproduction	Spawns spring and summer; eggs have threads that attach to seaweed

Atlantic or Mediterranean flying fish

Flying fishes glide rather than actively fly through the air, and do so mainly to escape predators. They swim forwards at high speed in the water, boost themselves with a rapid vibration of the tail as they break the surface, then glide on their greatly enlarged fins. The Atlantic species is a so-called four-wing flying fish, using both its pectoral and smaller pelvic fins as wings. The tropical flying fish, *Exocoetus volitans*, which is widespread around the world, is a two-wing species, with only its pectoral fins enlarged. It is fished commercially in many areas, but the Atlantic species is also good to eat and could be exploited.

Scientific name	*Cheilopgon* (or *Cyselurus*) *heterurus*
Classification	Order Beloniformes (needlefishes, flying fishes and allies)
	Family Exocoetidae
Size	Up to about 40cm (16in) long
Distribution	Eastern and western Atlantic; western Mediterranean
Habitat	Temperate and subtropical inshore waters, near surface
Diet	Small crustaceans and other planktonic creatures
Reproduction	Spawns spring and summer; planktonic eggs with filaments

Mediterranean sand smelt

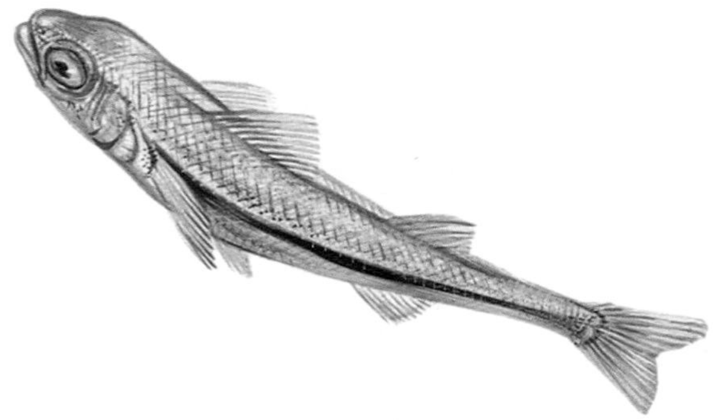

Several very similar species of sand smelts live along various parts of the African and European shoreline. *Atherina presbyter* (known simply as the sand smelt) is the most northerly, living along Atlantic coasts from Denmark to West Africa, while *A. hepsetus* and *A. boyeri* (the big-scaled sand smelt) are mostly Mediterranean species. All are silvery fish with a slender body and two widely spaced dorsal fins; some can be told apart only by small details such as the number of scales along the body and their relative eye size. They swim in large schools, and several species are widely caught for eating, sometimes as small 'whitebait'; they breed rapidly.

Scientific name	*Atherina hepsetus*
Classification	Order Atheriniformes (silversides and allies)
	Family Atherinidae
Size	Up to about 20cm (8in) long
Distribution	Mediterranean and adjacent parts of Atlantic; Black Sea
Habitat	Warm coastal waters; also brackish lagoons and estuaries
Diet	Bottom-living and floating crustaceans
Reproduction	Spawns near seabed; eggs anchored by filaments

California grunion

The 'grunion run' is a favourite spectacle for southern Californians. Every two weeks from March to August, for a few days after the new and full moons, female California grunion ride the surf at the spring (extra-high) tide, and swim and wriggle as far up the beach as they can. They half-bury themselves in the sand and lay their eggs, which are immediately fertilized by males. The eggs incubate in the damp sand until the next spring tide, about 10–12 days later; they then hatch within minutes of being immersed. Females may spawn several times at successive spring tides. Catching of spawning grunion is strictly controlled, using the hands only.

Scientific name	*Leuresthes tenuis*
Classification	Order Atheriniformes (silversides and allies)
	Family Atherinidae
Size	Up to about 19cm (7½in) long
Distribution	Eastern Pacific from Monterey Bay to southern Baja California
Habitat	Coastal waters; near surface, to 18m (60ft)
Diet	Small planktonic creatures
Reproduction	Spawns on beach at high spring tide; eggs hatch next high spring tide

Ribbon fish

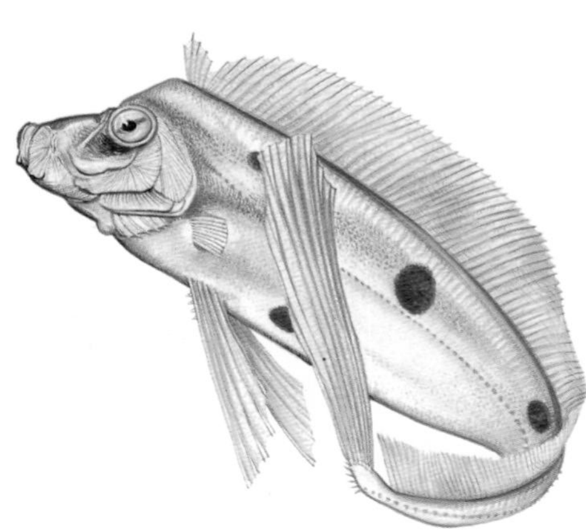

The ribbonfish and the closely related dealfishes (which belong to the same genus, *Trachipterus*) have an extraordinarily elongated but narrow body that tapers to the tail, with the dorsal fin extending along most of its length. They are rare ocean fish that mostly live at considerable depths, but they sometimes come to the surface and (together with the even larger oarfish, *Regalecus glesne*) are said to have originated many myths of sea-serpents. One curious feature of all fish of the order Lampridiformes is their extendible jaws; the upper jaw is not connected to the cheek bones, so it can protrude, expanding the mouth cavity by as much as 40 times.

Scientific name	*Trachipterus* (or *Trachypterus*) *trachypterus*
Classification	Order Lampridiformes or Lampriformes (oarfishes and allies)
	Family Trachipteridae
Size	Up to 3m (10ft) long
Distribution	Parts of Atlantic and Pacific oceans; Mediterranean
Habitat	Open ocean, mostly at mid-levels, to depth of 500m (1650ft)
Diet	Squid; midwater fish
Reproduction	Planktonic eggs incubate near surface; larvae feed on plankton

Opah or moonfish

Despite its very different shape – almost round when seen from the side, but highly compressed from side to side – the opah's extendible jaws show that it is a member of the same group as the ribbonfish and its allies (*see opposite*). It is a huge, brilliantly coloured fish that has been found in virtually every ocean, but only in very small numbers; it seems to spend most of its life alone. It is a strong swimmer, propelled by its large, muscular pectoral fins. It is occasionally caught by fishermen whose target is other fish – mainly tuna – and makes good eating. The smaller southern opah (*Lampris immaculatus*) of the Southern Ocean has no spots.

Scientific name	*Lampris guttatus* or *L. regius*
Classification	Order Lampridiformes or Lampriformes (oarfishes and allies)
	Family Lamprididae
Size	Up to 2m (6½ft) long; weight up to 270kg (600lb)
Distribution	Probably worldwide apart from Arctic and Antarctic
Habitat	Open ocean, mainly at depths of 100–400m (330–1300ft)
Diet	Squid, octopuses, crabs and other invertebrates; midwater fish
Reproduction	Planktonic eggs incubate near surface; larvae feed on plankton

Fifteen-spined or sea stickleback

Sticklebacks are found in fresh and salt water throughout much of the Northern Hemisphere, and have for generations fascinated young nature-explorers and aquarium-keepers. All are small fish with spines on their back (the origin of their common name), but this species (which may in fact have 14 to 17 spines) is much more slender and elongated than others. Unlike most sticklebacks, it lives only in seawater – in pools or among seaweeds and eel grasses along the shore. As with all species, the male makes a nest among the weeds and entices several females, one after the other, to spawn there. He fertilizes and guards the eggs until they hatch.

Scientific name	*Spinachia spinachia*
Classification	Order Gasterosteiformes (pipefishes and allies); Suborder Gasterosteoidei; Family Gasterosteidae
Size	Up to about 22cm (8½in) long
Distribution	North-eastern North Atlantic (northern Norway to Bay of Biscay); Baltic
Habitat	Shallow coastal waters; rock pools
Diet	Small bottom-living invertebrates
Reproduction	Male makes nest by gluing together seaweeds, and guards eggs

Tubesnout

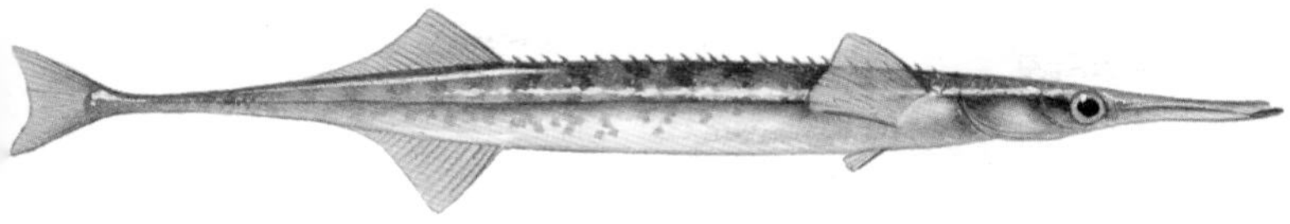

The tubesnout's body and snout are even more elongated than the 15-spined stickleback's (*opposite*) and it has even more spines – up to 27 – on its back, but it is very much the Pacific counterpart of the sea stickleback. (Another similar species, *Aulichthys japonicus*, lives along seashores of northern Japan and Korea.) A major difference is that, while sticklebacks tend to be solitary or live in pairs, the tubesnout is found in large shoals of hundreds or even thousands of fish – mostly among kelp beds and patches of eel grass, or in rocky areas where the seabed is sandy. But schools also sometimes swim much farther offshore, near the surface.

Scientific name	*Aulorhynchus flavidus*
Classification	Order Gasterosteiformes (pipefishes and allies); Suborder
	Gasterosteoidei; Family Aulorhynchidae
Size	Up to about 18cm (7in) long
Distribution	Eastern North Pacific (Alaska to Baja California)
Habitat	Usually shallow coastal waters; sometimes in schools well offshore
Diet	Small crustaceans; fish larvae
Reproduction	Male makes nest by gluing together seaweeds, and guards eggs

Lesser pipefish

Sometimes called Nilsson's pipefish after the naturalist who identified and named it in the 1850s, this is one of numerous similar pipefish species, all of which have a long tubular snout and an elongated tubular body encased in bony, jointed rings. The fish vary in size and coloration, but some species may be distinguishable only by the number of rings; in the lesser pipefish there are 13 to 17 body rings and a further 37 to 42 along the tail. In all pipefishes, the male has a pouch of skin on his abdomen in which the female deposits about 100 eggs; he fertilizes and keeps them in the pouch until they hatch and the young are about 14mm (just over ½in) long.

Scientific name	*Syngnathus rostellatus*
Classification	Order Gasterosteiformes (pipefishes and allies); suborder Syngnathoidei
	(but sometimes classified as Syngnathiformes); Family Syngnathidae
Size	Up to about 17cm (6½in) long
Distribution	Eastern North Atlantic (Norway to Bay of Biscay); Kattegat
Habitat	Shallow coastal waters and estuaries
Diet	Small invertebrates; fish larvae
Reproduction	Male carries eggs and larvae in pouch on rear of abdomen

Long-snouted seahorse

Seahorses are unmistakeable, and are among the most fascinating of all bizarre-shaped fishes. They were first described scientifically by Aristotle over 2,300 years ago, and are widely displayed in aquariums. They are, in fact, quite closely related to pipefishes, but have their body bent into an S-shape; the tail is prehensile – it can be wound around a seaweed stem or a branch of coral to anchor the fish. When swimming, the dorsal and pectoral fins oscillate, but the body hardly moves. As with pipefishes, the male seahorse has a brood pouch in which the eggs incubate and the larvae develop until they are 'pumped' out through a small opening.

Scientific name	*Hippocampus guttulatus* or *H. ramulosus*
Classification	Order Gasterosteiformes (pipefishes and allies); suborder Syngnathoidei
	(but sometimes classified as Syngnathiformes); Family Syngnathidae
Size	About 16–18cm (6¼–7in) long
Distribution	Eastern Atlantic (British Isles to Canaries); Mediterranean; Black Sea
Habitat	Shallow inshore waters among seaweeds and eel grass; lagoons
Diet	Small bottom-living invertebrates
Reproduction	Male carries eggs and larvae in abdominal pouch for 3–5 weeks

John dory

The John dory is a rather ugly-looking fish with long dorsal spines, but it makes excellent eating and is caught by fishermen in many parts of the world. However, it is a largely solitary species and is not suitable for large-scale fishing. It is not a strong swimmer, but its body is highly compressed from side to side, making it inconspicuous from the front so that it can approach prey unnoticed. It has greatly extendible jaws which it then shoots forward to seize the prey. According to legend, the round black mark on each side of the John dory's body is the thumb-print of St Peter, and its name in several European languages translates as St Peter's fish.

Scientific name	*Zeus faber*
Classification	Order Zeiformes (dories and allies);
	Family Zeidae
Size	Up to about 90cm (3ft) long and 8kg (17½lb); usually 30–40cm (12–16in)
Distribution	Almost worldwide in temperate waters
Habitat	Offshore waters, to 400m (1300ft); closer inshore in summer
Diet	Mainly schooling fish such as herrings, anchovies, etc.; some crustaceans
Reproduction	Spawns in shallow water inshore; large (2mm [$\frac{1}{12}$in]) floating eggs

Flying gurnard

In spite of its common name and its extremely large, wing-like or fan-like pelvic fins, the flying gurnard cannot fly. (For this reason, some experts prefer the name helmet gurnard – its head is bony.) The fish seems to use its 'wings' to make itself look bigger to potential predators – to ward them off long enough to make an escape. The front part of each pelvic fin forms a separate lobe, and the fish uses this to 'walk' over the sandy, muddy or rocky sea floor, searching for crustaceans, clams and other food items. A rather similar but smaller related species, the oriental flying gurnard (*Dactyloptena orientalis*), lives in the Indian and western Pacific oceans.

Scientific name	*Dactylopterus* (formerly *Trigla*) *volitans*
Classification	Order Scorpaeniformes (scorpionfishes and allies); sometimes classified separately in Dactylopteriformes; Family Dactylopteridae
Size	Up to about 50cm (20in) long
Distribution	Tropical and warm temperate east and west Atlantic; Mediterranean
Habitat	Bottom-living in shallow waters; reefs
Diet	Bottom-living crustaceans (especially crabs); molluscs; small fish
Reproduction	Spawns on seabed

Lionfish

The lionfishes and their close relatives the turkeyfishes (*Dendrochirus* species, also often called lionfishes) are extraordinary-looking, brightly coloured fish that are well described by the alternative name butterfly cod. Their colouring and form are a warning to other reef-dwellers, for the lionfish is venomous: it has poison glands at the base of the extremely sharp dorsal spines. It hides in an inconspicuous place in daytime, and hunts its prey by night. Anyone disturbing the fish with hands or feet is liable to get an extremely painful, but rarely fatal sting. (Heat on the wound relieves the pain.) Yet, despite the risk, it is caught and makes good eating.

Scientific name	*Pterois volitans*
Classification	Order Scorpaeniformes (scorpionfishes and allies);
	Family Scorpaenidae
Size	Up to about 38cm (15in) long
Distribution	Indian; Pacific oceans (Malaysia and Australia to Japan and Polynesia)
Habitat	Tropical and subtropical lagoons and reefs, to 50m (165ft)
Diet	Small fish and crustaceans
Reproduction	Spawns on sea-bottom

Stonefish

If the lionfish (*opposite*) advertises its nature colourfully, the stonefish disguises itself – and is far more dangerous. It and its equally venomous estuarine relative, *Synanceia horrida* or *S. trachynis*, lie half-hidden in sand or mud, motionless for long periods and sometimes encrusted with algae. When prey approaches, suddenly opening jaws suck in the victim. If disturbed, the stonefish raises its dorsal spines, which are needle-sharp and have grooves that inject venom into a wound like a hypodermic needle. It is the most toxic venom in the fish world, causing severe pain and sometimes death. Fortunately, an antidote has been developed in Australia.

Scientific name	*Synanceia verrucosa*
Classification	Order Scorpaeniformes (scorpionfishes and allies);
	Family Scorpaenidae or Synanceiidae
Size	Up to about 40cm (16in) long
Distribution	Indian; Pacific oceans (East Africa to Australia, Ryukyu Is and Polynesia)
Habitat	Bottom-living in warm; shallow lagoons; pools and reefs; to 30m (100ft)
Diet	Bottom-living fish and crustaceans
Reproduction	Details uncertain, but presumably spawns on sea-bottom

Redfish, or ocean perch

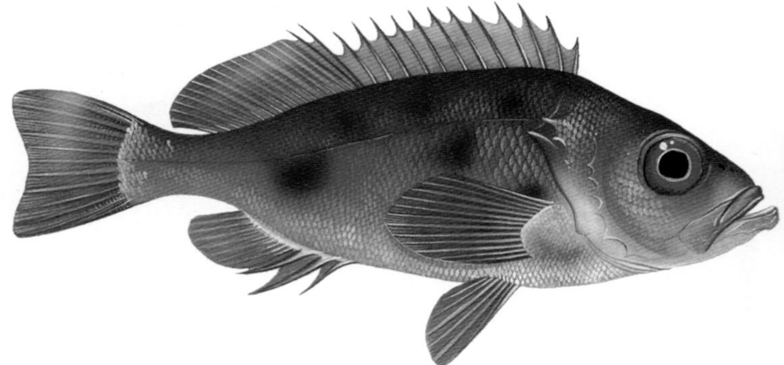

One of the most commercially important species of the scorpionfish group, the redfish, ocean perch or rosefish is sometimes sold as 'Norway haddock'. It is a gregarious fish that swims in schools, and is caught by deep-water trawlers in the northern seas. It is a heavy-bodied, slow-growing species, and most of those caught are much smaller than the maximum size given below. It has spines on the dorsal and anal fins and on the cheeks, and the large head has a protruding lower jaw. The redfish's eggs are fertilized internally; males and females mate in late summer or autumn but fertilization is delayed and the young born six to nine months later.

Scientific name	*Sebastes marinus*
Classification	Order Scorpaeniformes (scorpionfishes and allies)
	Family Scorpaenidae or Sebastidae
Size	Up to about 1m (3¼ft) long; maximum weight 15kg (33lb)
Distribution	Northern Atlantic and Barents Sea, south to North Sea and New Jersey
Habitat	Offshore, at 100–1000m (330–3300ft); nearer surface at night to feed
Diet	Schooling fish such as herring; crustaceans and other invertebrates
Reproduction	Ovoviviparous; young, about 6mm (¼in) long, born spring and summer

Tub gurnard

The true gurnards or sea robins of the family Triglidae look quite similar to the flying gurnard (*see p.243*), but they are classified in a separate order as well as a separate family. The tub gurnard is typical of the family, with a large polygonal head armoured with bony plates, a pointed snout and a steep brow. The front three rays of the pectoral fins are separated to form finger-like feelers, which the fish uses to 'walk' on the sea-bottom and to sense the presence of prey. Like many gurnards, it can make a grunting noise by using muscular contractions to pump air through its swim bladder. This may be the origin of its name, from the Latin *grunnire* (to grunt).

Scientific name	*Chelidonichthys* (or *Trigla*) *lucerna*
Classification	Order Scorpaeniformes (scorpionfishes and allies);
	Family Triglidae
Size	Up to about 75cm (30in) long; maximum weight 6kg (13lb)
Distribution	Eastern Atlantic (Norway to Mauritania); Mediterranean; Black Sea
Habitat	Bottom-living, to 150–300m (500–1000ft), on mud, sand or gravel
Diet	Bottom-living crustaceans; molluscs and fish
Reproduction	Eggs and larvae planktonic

Lumpsucker or lumpfish

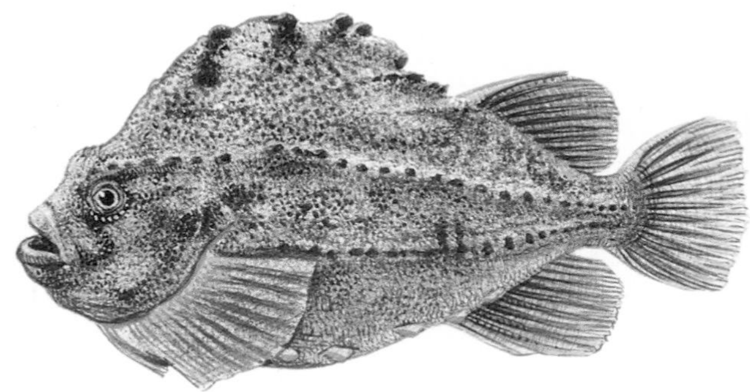

The name lumpsucker comes from the warty bumps that cover the fish's scaleless body, and from the round sucker disc – actually modified pelvic fins – on its underside. The male fish uses this sucker to attach itself to a rock while guarding the eggs that the female lays in shallows in the summer. The male develops reddish underparts (as illustrated) at this time; the female remains bluish-green. While on guard, the male does not feed; he constantly fans fresh water over the eggs with his fins. Lumpsuckers, or lumpfish, are caught for their flesh but particularly for their roe, which is dyed black or orange to make an economical caviar substitute.

Scientific name	*Cyclopterus lumpus*
Classification	Order Scorpaeniformes (scorpionfishes and allies)
	Family Cyclopteridae
Size	Female up to about 60cm (24in) long; male up to about 50cm (20in)
Distribution	North Atlantic (Hudson Bay and Barents Sea to Maryland and Spain)
Habitat	Mainly on rocky seabed, to 50–400m (165–1300ft); breeds inshore
Diet	Jellyfish, worms, small crustaceans and other invertebrates; some fish
Reproduction	Large numbers of sticky eggs, laid in mass on rocks; guarded by male

Dusky grouper or dusky perch

Perch and their allies (order Perciformes) make up the biggest and most varied group of all vertebrates (animals with backbones), although DNA studies result in their classification constantly being reorganized. The biggest species in the group is the 4.6m (15ft) black marlin (*Makaira indica*), but the dusky grouper is one of the biggest inshore fishes in many parts of its range, which includes the Mediterranean. It is a deep-bodied, massive fish that is highly territorial and generally lives alone among rocks. Very little is known about its breeding habits except that all young fish are female and some later become male – but the age of the change is uncertain.

Scientific name	*Epinephelus marginatus* or (incorrectly) *E. guaza*
Classification	Order Perciformes (perches and allies); Suborder Percoidei
	Family Serranidae
Size	Up to about 1.5m (5ft) long; maximum weight 60kg (132lb)
Distribution	Tropical and subtropical parts of Atlantic and southwest Indian oceans
Habitat	Reefs and rocky coasts, at depth of 8–300m (25–1000ft)
Diet	Crabs and other crustaceans; squid and octopuses; fish
Reproduction	Changes sex (*see above*); other details uncertain

Cardinal fish

The brightly coloured cardinal fish looks at first glance rather like a goldfish (*Carassius auratus*), but the eyes and mouth are much bigger and it has two dorsal fins, not one. It is one of some 200 similar species found in warm waters worldwide; freshwater species live in Australia, New Guinea and some Pacific islands. Most, if not all (including this species), are mouth-brooders; the male takes the fertilized eggs into his mouth and keeps them there until the larvae hatch. The normal flow of water through the parent's mouth and gills keeps the eggs supplied with oxygen. Some cardinal fish form schools, but others are found singly.

Scientific name	*Apogon imberbis*
Classification	Order Perciformes (perches and allies); Suborder Percoidei
	Family Apogonidae
Size	Up to about 15cm (6in) long
Distribution	Eastern Atlantic (Portugal to Gulf of Guinea); Mediterranean
Habitat	Rocks, underwater caves and muddy seabeds, at 10–200m (30–650ft)
Diet	Small invertebrates and fish
Reproduction	Breeds in summer; mouth-brooder (*see above*)

Gilthead seabream

Many species of seabreams or porgies (which are completely unrelated to freshwater bream species) are fished commercially, and the gilthead is also an important farmed fish. Its common name comes from the golden mark between its eyes, which fades after death. Like most other members of its family, it has strong teeth for eating shellfish, and is regarded as a nuisance on commercial mussel and oyster beds. All giltheads are born males but become females when about three years old. A similar, related species, *Chrysophrys* (or *Pagrus*) *auratus*, lives in Australian and New Zealand waters, where it is called the snapper or red bream.

Scientific name	*Sparus auratus*
Classification	Order Perciformes (perches and allies); Suborder Percoidei
	Family Sparidae
Size	Up to about 1.4m (4½ft) long and 18kg (40lb); usually less than half this
Distribution	Eastern Atlantic (British Isles to Cape Verde); Mediterranean
Habitat	Bottom-living in coastal waters, to 150m (500ft); also brackish lagoons
Diet	Mostly shellfish and crustaceans; also squid and fish
Reproduction	Changes sex (*see above*); spawns in winter in Mediterranean

Striped red mullet

This species is distinguished from the otherwise very similar plain or common red mullet (*Mullus barbatus*) by the yellow stripes along its body and the very long barbels below its chin. (In the common species, these are no longer than the pectoral fins.) Red mullets use their barbels to locate their prey (they have taste buds at the tips), then often dig it from the sand or mud of the seabed. Both species have been widely caught for food, especially in warm regions, since ancient times; they are rather bony but make excellent eating. The goatfishes of North America, especially the red goatfish (*M. auratus*), are more or less closely related species.

Scientific name	*Mullus surmuletus*
Classification	Order Perciformes (perches and allies); Suborder Percoidei;
	Family Mullidae
Size	Up to about 40cm (16in) long; weight up to 1kg (2¼lb)
Distribution	Eastern Atlantic (Norway to Senegal); Mediterranean and Black Seas
Habitat	Bottom-living in coastal waters, to 60m (200ft)
Diet	Bottom-living small crustaceans, worms, molluscs and fish
Reproduction	Spawns in summer; eggs and larvae float

Long-nosed or copper-banded butterfly fish

Butterfly fishes are small, beautifully patterned and colourful disc-shaped reef fishes that are favourite specimens for salt water aquariums. Many, including the copper-banded species, have a false 'eye' spot on the upper rear part of the body, while the true eye is camouflaged by the body markings; this pattern presumably confuses would-be predators. The closely related margined butterfly fish (*Chelmon marginalis*) is similar but with a slightly different colour pattern. The long nose of these and some other species is adapted to picking small invertebrates from coral crevices; other butterfly fishes have short jaws for biting off coral polyps (*see p.25*).

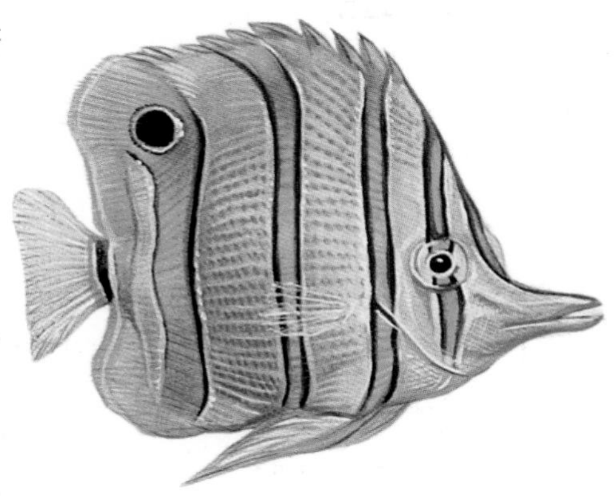

Scientific name	*Chelmon* (or *Chaetodon*) *rostratus*
Classification	Order Perciformes (perches and allies); Suborder Percoidei;
	Family Chaetodontidae
Size	Up to about 20cm (8in) long
Distribution	North-eastern Indian Ocean and western Pacific (Ryukyu Is to Australia)
Habitat	Warm, shallow waters along rocky shores and reefs; lagoons
Diet	Small bottom-living invertebrates
Reproduction	Prolonged larval stage; larvae have characteristic bony head plates

Common remora, or sharksucker

Sharksuckers are not strictly parasites, but they attach themselves to a host with a large sucker on the back of their head. The host is usually a shark (especially, in the case of the common remora, the blue shark; *see p.184*), but may be another large fish, turtle or whale, or even a ship. Young fish swim freely, and the sucker disc develops as they grow. It is in fact a modified dorsal fin with a series of slat-like ridges which the remora moves to create suction. It may damage the host's skin, but does not draw nourishment from the host; instead remoras eat small parasitic crustaceans found on the host's skin and sometimes swim free to catch other prey.

Scientific name	*Remora remora*
Classification	Order Perciformes (perches and allies); Suborder Carangoidei
	Family Echeneidae
Size	Up to about 85cm (33in) long
Distribution	Worldwide in tropical and warm temperate waters
Habitat	Mainly offshore, but anywhere carried by host
Diet	Mainly parasitic copepods (small crustaceans) on host
Reproduction	Eggs float, but other details uncertain

Crevalle jack

Jacks vary widely in body form, but most have two, small, separate spines just in front of the anal fin, and many have a distinct narrowing of the body just in front of the tail. The Mediterranean and Atlantic crevalle jack (*Caranx hippos*) is found over a wide range, from Portugal to Angola and from Nova Scotia to Uruguay. The Pacific crevalle jack (*C. caninus*), found from California to the Galápagos Islands and Peru, is probably the same species, but Indian Ocean specimens probably belong to a separate species, the giant trevally (*C. ignobilis*). Crevalle jacks form fast-swimming schools, and are caught commercially. They often grunt when captured.

Scientific name	*Caranx hippos* and *C. caninus*
Classification	Order Perciformes (perches and allies); Suborder Carangoidei;
	Family Carangidae
Size	Up to about 1.2m (4ft) long; maximum weight 32kg (70lb)
Distribution	Warm temperate and tropical Atlantic and east Pacific; Mediterranean
Habitat	Mainly offshore waters, surface to 350m (1150ft); sometimes in rivers
Diet	Mainly fish; also crustaceans and other invertebrates
Reproduction	Spawns in coastal waters and brackish estuaries

Common dolphinfish

With their beautiful metallic colouring (which fades on death) and distinctive long dorsal fin, the two species of dolphinfish are unmistakeable. Both look similar, but the pompano dolphinfish (*Coryphaena equiselis*) is smaller and its anal fin has a convex (outward-curving) edge. They swim in small schools, hunting surface-swimming fish such as flying fish (*see p.233*), which rarely escape even by leaping from the water. Both commercial and sports fishermen catch dolphinfish, and they are farmed in some regions; they are excellent to eat. They are sometimes called simply dolphins, risking confusion with the small whales (*see pp.299–300*).

Scientific name	*Coryphaena hippurus*
Classification	Order Perciformes (perches and allies); Suborder Carangoidei;
	Family Coryphaenidae
Size	Up to about 2.1m (7ft) long; maximum weight 40kg (88lb)
Distribution	Worldwide in tropical and subtropical waters
Habitat	Open waters and near coast, to 85m (275ft)
Diet	Wide range of fish; also squid and crustaceans
Reproduction	Spawns in open sea and inshore

Striped or flathead mullet

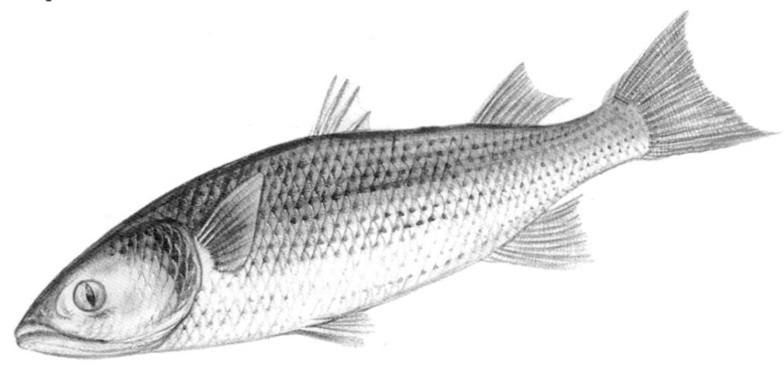

Only distantly related to the red mullets of the family Mullidae (*see p.252*), fishes of this family are generally known as grey mullets or simply mullets. There are a number of similar species, all quite elongated, cylindrical, silvery fish, which can be difficult to distinguish despite belonging to several different genera. The striped or flathead mullet is an important commercial catch, and is widely farmed in freshwater ponds in south-east Asia. Like other members of the group, it swims in large schools and is adapted to feeding on the detritus of the sea-bottom, sucking up mud and sand and digesting food from it with its muscular gizzard and long gut.

Scientific name	*Mugil cephalus*
Classification	Order Perciformes (perches and allies); Suborder Mugiloidei;
	Family Mugilidae
Size	Up to about 1.2m (4ft) long; maximum weight 8kg (17½lb)
Distribution	Worldwide in tropical and warm temperate waters
Habitat	Mainly bottom-living in coastal and offshore waters; estuaries and rivers
Diet	Small algae and planktonic animals in bottom detritus; algae in rivers
Reproduction	Spawns at sea, on bottom

Clown fish

More correctly called the orange clownfish or clown anemone fish, this is one of 27 *Amphiprion* species that live among the tentacles of sea anemones on reefs. The fish are protected from the anemone's sting by a thick layer of mucus and by their undulating swimming motion, which does not trigger the anemone's stinging response. The anemone is preened by the fish and cleaned of debris, but the fish gets the main advantage by being protected from its predators. Almost all fish of the family Pomacentridae (known as damselfishes) are brightly coloured, but this and the very similar *A. ocellaris* (often kept in aquariums) are among the best known.

Scientific name	*Amphiprion percula*
Classification	Order Perciformes (perches and allies); Suborder Labroidei;
	Family Pomacentridae
Size	Up to about 11cm (4¼in) long
Distribution	South-western Pacific (north Queensland to New Guinea and Vanuatu)
Habitat	Reefs and lagoons, to 15m (50ft)
Diet	Very small crustaceans and other reef organisms
Reproduction	Eggs laid in prepared nest on coral or rock; guarded by both parents

Rainbow wrasse

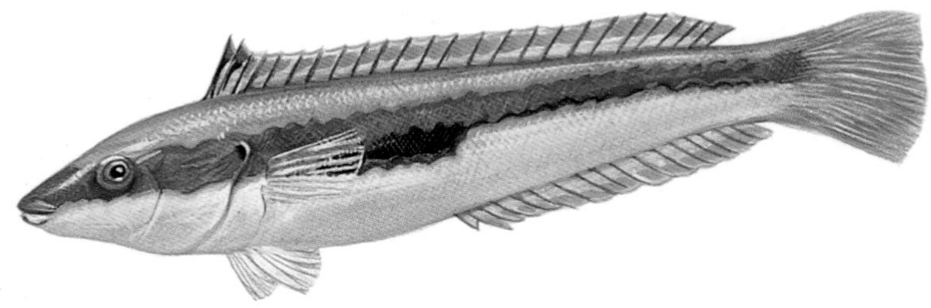

Many wrasses are colourful but in this species, like some others, mature males are much more so than females and young fish, which are coppery-brown with a broad white stripe. However, to confuse matters, some old females change their sex. Like other members of the family Labridae, it has a modified throat structure that acts like a second set of jaws to help to crush and grind its hard-shelled prey. It is sometimes called the Mediterranean rainbow wrasse to distinguish it from the rainbow or painted wrasse of the West Indies, *Halichoeres pictus*. Those found south of Cape Verde, West Africa, may belong to a separate species, *Coris atlantica*.

Scientific name	*Coris julis*
Classification	Order Perciformes (perches and allies); Suborder Labroidei;
	Family Labridae
Size	Up to about 30cm (12in) long
Distribution	Eastern Atlantic (Norway to Gabon; *but see above*); Mediterranean
Habitat	Shallow water along rocky shores and weed beds; mature males deeper
Diet	Small crustaceans, sea urchins and other invertebrates
Reproduction	Eggs planktonic; some old females become males

Queen parrotfish

Parrotfishes get their name from their beak-like mouth. This is formed by their fused front teeth, and is well adapted to grazing algae from coral and rocks, at the same time biting off coral chunks. They grind it all into paste with plate-like teeth in their throat, releasing nutrients in the algae (like a cow chewing the cud), and converting the coral into sand. Until they realized that male and female parrotfish look very different, scientists used to think there were many more than the 84 species now recognized. Female queen parrotfish are brown and white. It is one of several species that excretes a mucus cocoon at night; it probably repels predators.

Scientific name	*Scarus vetula*
Classification	Order Perciformes (perches and allies); Suborder Labroidei;
	Family Scaridae
Size	Up to about 60cm (24in) long
Distribution	Western Atlantic (Bermuda to northern South America); Caribbean
Habitat	Warm waters on and near coral reefs
Diet	Algae scraped from rocks and dead coral
Reproduction	Eggs scattered; mature females may change into males

Atlantic wolf fish

Wolf fishes used to be grouped with blennies – small fishes mostly found in rock pools and along rocky shores – but are now classified in a separate suborder with the eelpouts and their allies, many of which are deep-water species. They are big fish with a big head and sharp fang-like teeth, which they use to break open clams and other hard-shelled invertebrates; they then crush these with their broad molar teeth. They are an important commercial catch. The larger, similar-shaped but browner spotted wolf fish or spotted cat (*Anarhichas minor*) lives in the same waters, while the Bering wolf fish (*A. orientalis*) is found in the northern Pacific.

Scientific name	*Anarhichas lupus*
Classification	Order Perciformes (perches and allies); Suborder Zoarcoidei;
	Family Anarhichadidae
Size	Up to about 1.5m (5ft) long; maximum weight 24kg (53lb)
Distribution	Atlantic (Spitsbergen and Greenland to British Isles and New Jersey)
Habitat	Bottom-living (mostly on rocks) in offshore waters, to 500m (1650ft)
Diet	Crabs, lobsters, shellfish, sea urchins and other invertebrates
Reproduction	Spawns in winter, laying clusters of sticky eggs on seabed

Greater weever

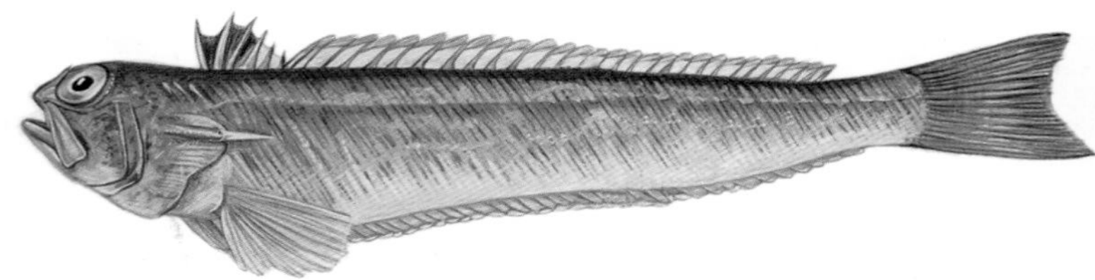

Weevers are wedge-shaped fish that have poison glands along the spines of their front dorsal fin and also on the spine on their gill-covers. They often bury themselves in the sand with only their eyes and back showing, and spread the venomous spines in defence if they are disturbed. A person who accidentally treads on the fish is liable to get an extremely painful wound that causes swelling, although rarely death. The greater weever is one of the largest species, but the lesser weever (*Echiichthys vipera*), which is less than half the length, is more common. Most weevers live off Europe and Africa, but one possible species is known from Chile.

Scientific name	*Trachinus draco*
Classification	Order Perciformes (perches and allies); Suborder Trachinoidei;
	Family Trachinidae
Size	Up to about 53cm (21in) long
Distribution	Eastern North Atlantic (Norway to Canary Is); Mediterranean; Black Sea
Habitat	Bottom-living, on sand, mud or gravel; shallows to about 150m (500ft)
Diet	Small fish and bottom-living crustaceans, mainly at night
Reproduction	Eggs planktonic, laid in summer

Sand eel

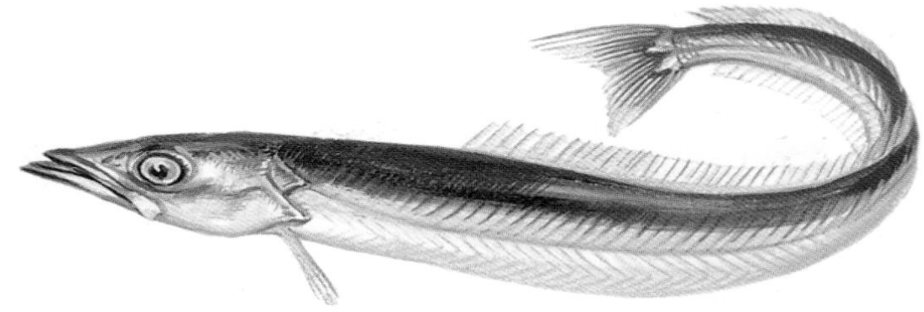

Various species of sand eels (which are unrelated to true eels; *see p.202*) live in temperate and tropical waters in most parts of the world. They vary in size, but are all similar to the lesser (or small) sand eel illustrated. They are sometimes called sand lances, because of their habit of diving into sand or fine gravel; they alternate between lying buried in this way and swimming freely in schools. Sand eels are an important part of the marine food chain because they eat plankton and are in turn food for larger creatures – fish, mammals and birds. In areas such as the North Sea their numbers have been greatly reduced by industrial fishing to make animal feed.

Scientific name	*Ammodytes tobianus* and other species
Classification	Order Perciformes (perches and allies); Suborder Trachinoidei;
	Family Ammodytidae
Size	Up to about 20cm (8in) long; other species up to 40cm (16in)
Distribution	Eastern North Alantic (Spitsbergen to Spain); Mediterranean
Habitat	Sandy-bottomed inshore waters; hibernates in winter buried in sand
Diet	Very small planktonic plants and animals
Reproduction	Spawns on sea-bottom, but larvae planktonic

Atlantic mudskipper

Mudskippers are among the most bizarre of all fish. They live on and in shallow mudflats of the mangrove swamps that fringe many tropical shores, and spend as much or more time out of the water as in it. When the tide falls, they emerge from a burrow and walk or skip across the mud and mangrove roots using their muscular pectoral fins. Their skin is richly supplied with blood vessels and can absorb oxygen directly from the air, making them truly amphibious. Mudskippers' eyes protude from the top of their head, enabling them to spot insects and other prey easily and to watch for predators such as birds. As the tide rises, they retreat into their burrow.

Scientific name	*Periophthalamus barbarus* or *P. koelreuteri*
Classification	Order Perciformes (perches and allies); Suborder Goboidei;
	Family Gobidae
Size	Up to about 25cm (10in) long
Distribution	Coasts of tropical West Africa (Senegal to Angola) and offshore islands
Habitat	Shallows and mudflats of estuarine mangrove swamps (*see above*)
Diet	Crabs, insects and other invertebrates of mud surface; plant material
Reproduction	Spawns in burrow in mud

Blue tang

The blue tang is one of the most distinctively coloured members of its family – the surgeonfishes – found in the tropical and subtropical western Atlantic. Juveniles are a beautiful clear yellow colour, becoming blue with a yellow tail as they grow, and finally maturing all-blue. Surgeonfishes are so called because they have a sharp scalpel-like spine projecting from each side of their body, just in front of the tail. The blue tang is a deep-bodied fish with a prominent 'scalpel'; this can inflict a painful wound on a diver who ventures too close, for the fish is not afraid of humans. It is rarely seen north of Florida, but is also found as far east as Ascension Island.

Scientific name	*Acanthurus coeruleus*
Classification	Order Perciformes (perches and allies); Suborder Acanthuroidei;
	Family Acanthuridae
Size	Up to about 39cm (15½in) long
Distribution	Atlantic (New York [rarely] and Bermuda to Gulf of Mexico and Brazil)
Habitat	Warm waters of coral reefs; inshore weed beds and rocky areas
Diet	Algae
Reproduction	Scatters eggs on and near reef

Great barracuda

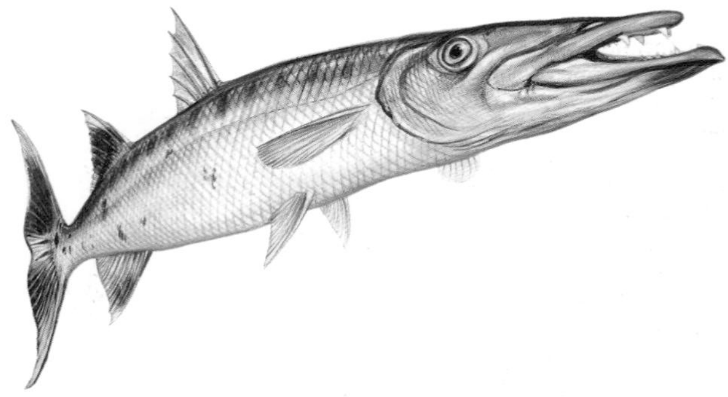

The biggest of the 20 or more barracuda species, the great barracuda is a slender, swift and powerful swimming machine. It swims mostly at or near the surface, usually on its own or in small groups. (Some other barracuda species form dense schools.) Their pointed jaws and prominent sharp teeth give barracudas a fierce appearance, and they show great curiosity, approaching boats, divers and other objects. They do sometimes attack humans – usually with a single fierce strike – but this is rare unless they are provoked. They can cause a severe wound, but barracuda attacks are rarely fatal. They are a popular prey of game fishermen.

Scientific name	*Sphyraena barracuda*
Classification	Order Perciformes (perches and allies); Suborder Scombroidei;
	Family Sphyraenidae
Size	Up to about 2m (6½ft) long; maximum weight about 50kg (110lb)
Distribution	Worldwide in tropical and subtropical waters, except eastern Pacific
Habitat	Muddy estuaries to open sea; young in lagoons, estuaries, mangroves
Diet	Mainly fish; also squid, cuttlefish and crustaceans
Reproduction	Spawns in inshore waters

Swordfish

With a huge, flattened 'sword' making up as much as one-third of its total length and a tall, sickle-shaped dorsal fin, the swordfish is one of the biggest and most spectacular of all the so-called billfishes. (This group includes the marlins and sailfishes of the family Istiophoridae. The black marlin, *Makaira indica*, is about the same size as the swordfish, but is heavier, with a smaller bill.) Swordfish use their sword to slash at and kill their prey; they have no teeth. They are widely sought by game and commercial fishermen, some of whom use harpoons, but their numbers are threatened by overfishing. Large swordfish may be toxic because of high levels of mercury in their flesh.

Scientific name	*Xipias gladius*
Classification	Order Perciformes (perches and allies); Suborder Scombroidei;
	Family Xiphiidae
Size	Up to about 4.5m (15ft) long; maximum weight 650kg (over 1400lb)
Distribution	Virtually worldwide, including cold waters in summer; migratory
Habitat	Mainly open sea, from surface to 800m (2600ft); also coastal waters
Diet	Wide range of fish; squid and octopuses; crustaceans
Reproduction	Spawns near surface in tropical and warm temperate spawning grounds

Northern or Atlantic bluefin tuna

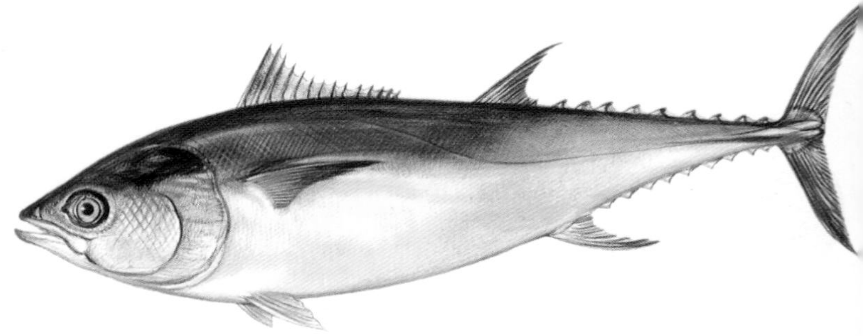

Sailfish (*Istiophorus* species) are the fastest fish measured in short bursts, at over 110km/h (68mph), but the northern bluefin tuna is unmatched for endurance; one tagged specimen covered 7700km (4785 miles) in 119 days. The reason is that fish of the Scombridae family have a high proportion of red muscle, which is well adapted to prolonged effort. This muscle is also what makes tuna so 'meaty' and valuable for eating cooked or raw (as sashimi). However, despite producing millions of eggs, bluefin numbers increase only slowly, and all bluefin species around the world – as well as many other tuna species – are severely threatened by overfishing.

Scientific name	*Thunnus thynnus*
Classification	Order Perciformes (perches and allies); Suborder Scombroidei;
	Family Scombridae
Size	Up to about 4.6m (15ft) long; maximum weight 684kg (1507lb)
Distribution	Throughout most of Atlantic; Mediterranean; southern Black Sea
Habitat	Mainly open ocean; also inshore
Diet	Small schooling fish; squid; crabs
Reproduction	Spawns at various seasons, in open water; very large numbers of eggs

Black-finned icefish

Members of the suborder Notothenioidei are found only in Antarctic waters, and some have a special blood protein that acts like an antifreeze, enabling them to survive at the temperature of freezing seawater, –1.9°C (28.6°F). Icefish are strange, semi-transparent fish that completely lack the oxygen-carrying red pigment haemoglobin in their blood – which, like their gills and flesh, is white. Apart from one species of larval eel (which develops haemoglobin as it matures), no other fish is known to lack the pigment; the reason is unknown. Icefish have to rely on oxygen simply dissolving in their blood plasma, and as a result can move only sluggishly.

Scientific name	*Chaenocephalus aceratus*
Classification	Order Perciformes (perches and allies); suborder Notothenioidei;
	Family Channichthyidae
Size	Up to about 72cm (28in) long
Distribution	Atlantic part of Southern Ocean, south of Falklands and South Georgia
Habitat	Mainly bottom-living, to about 750m (2500ft)
Diet	Small fish; krill and other crustaceans
Reproduction	Details uncertain

Atlantic halibut

Unlike other fishes of similar shape, true flatfishes live on their side, one of their eyes having migrated, or moved, close to the other during larval development; the fins on either side are in fact the dorsal and anal fins. Flatfishes are classified as right- or left-eyed, depending on which side of the fish has both eyes and is usually uppermost. The Atlantic halibut – one of the biggest and best to eat – belongs to the right-eyed flounder family. It has a relatively elongated body. Females live longer and grow larger than males. They shed up to 2 million eggs, but halibut grow slowly and start to breed only at 10 to 14 years old, so are very vulnerable to overfishing.

Scientific name	*Hippoglossus hippoglossus*
Classification	Order Pleuronectiformes (flatfishes); Suborder Pleuronectoidei;
	Family Pleuronectidae
Size	Up to about 2.4–3m (8–10ft) long; maximum weight 320kg (700lb)
Distribution	Atlantic (Virginia and Bay of Biscay to Greenland and Barents Sea)
Habitat	Mainly bottom-living, to 2000m (6500ft); sometimes in midwater
Diet	Mainly fish; also squid, large crustaceans and other invertebrates
Reproduction	Spawns in winter and early spring; eggs float in midwater

Turbot

Despite its relatively small size, the turbot is probably the most prized of all the flatfishes for its fine flavour and texture; some people claim that it is the finest-tasting of all sea fish. It is almost circular in outline and, like other members of its family, is left-eyed. (In the illustration, the dorsal fin is to the lower left.) However, as with all flatfishes, a few individuals are found with the eyes on the 'wrong' side. Its brown left (upper) side is scaleless but has large bony tubercles. The pale right (lower) side has no tubercles except in the Black Sea subspecies, *Scophthalmus maximus maeoticus*. Hybrids occur between turbot and the brill (*S. rhombus*).

Scientific name	*Scophthalmus maximus* or *Psetta maxima*
Classification	Order Pleuronectiformes (flatfishes); Suborder Pleuronectoidei;
	Family Scophthalmidae; sometimes included in Bothidae
Size	Up to about 1m (3¼ft) long; maximum weight 25kg (55lb)
Distribution	Eastern Atlantic (Arctic to Morocco); Mediterranean; Black Sea; farmed
Habitat	Bottom-living in relatively shallow waters, to 70m (230ft); estuaries
Diet	Mainly bottom-living fish; also crustaceans, shellfish and worms
Reproduction	Spawns in spring and summer; eggs and larvae float

Common or Dover sole

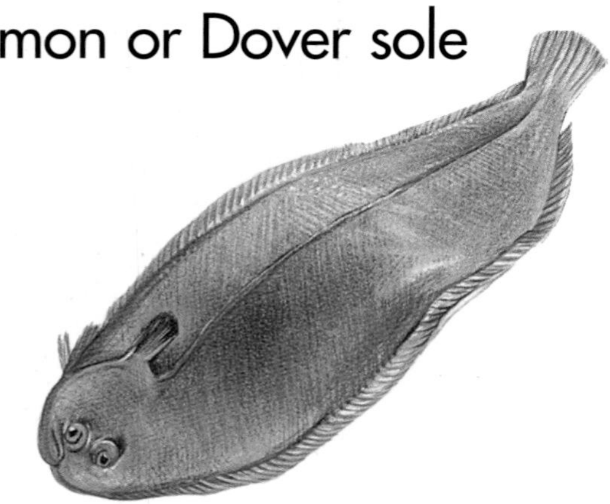

Soles form a separate suborder of flatfishes, having a small twisted mouth, small teeth and often rather small and asymmetrical pelvic and pectoral fins. Most – including members of the true sole family, Soleidae, and American soles, Achiridae – are right-eyed. The common or Dover sole is the commonest true sole in European waters, and is a highly regarded food fish. However, in North America the name Dover sole is used for a less valued flounder, *Microstomus pacificus*, also known as the slippery or slime sole. The common sole is a migratory species, wintering in deeper waters but moving to shallows in spring to spawn. It feeds mainly at night.

Scientific name	*Solea solea* or *S. vulgaris*
Classification	Order Pleuronectiformes (flatfishes); Suborder Soleoidei;
	Family Soleidae
Size	Up to about 70cm (27½in) long
Distribution	Eastern Atlantic (Norway to Senegal); Kattegat; Mediterranean
Habitat	Bottom-living, on sand or mud of continental shelf, to 150m (500ft)
Diet	Crustaceans; molluscs; worms; some small fish
Reproduction	Spawns in spring and early summer in shallow water; eggs float

Red-toothed triggerfish

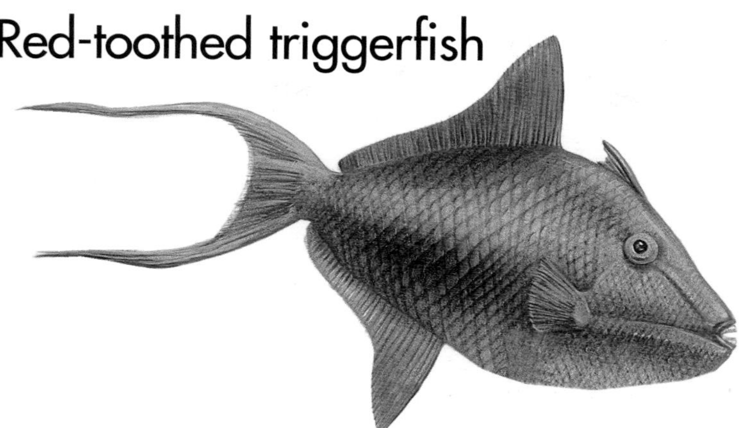

Triggerfishes get their name from the way the long front spine of their dorsal fin can be locked in position when it is raised as a defensive response to a predator. The small second spine moves forward, locking the first with a ball-and-socket mechanism; the long spine can be flattened again only by releasing this 'trigger'. Triggerfishes can also enlarge their pelvis by rotating the pelvic bone, making themselves look bigger to an attacker. By using both mechanisms, a fish can wedge itself in a rock or coral crevice and is very difficult to dislodge. The tropical red-toothed species is a popular marine aquarium fish, and is also eaten fresh or salted.

Scientific name	*Odonus niger*
Classification	Order Tetraodontiformes (triggerfishes and allies); Suborder Balistoidei; Family Balistidae
Size	Up to about 50cm (20in) long
Distribution	Indian and Pacific oceans (Africa to Japan, Polynesia and Australia)
Habitat	Mainly seaward side of coral reefs, at 5–40m (16–130ft)
Diet	Sponges; small planktonic animals
Reproduction	Spawns in sandy depression, guarded by male

Long-nosed or harlequin filefish

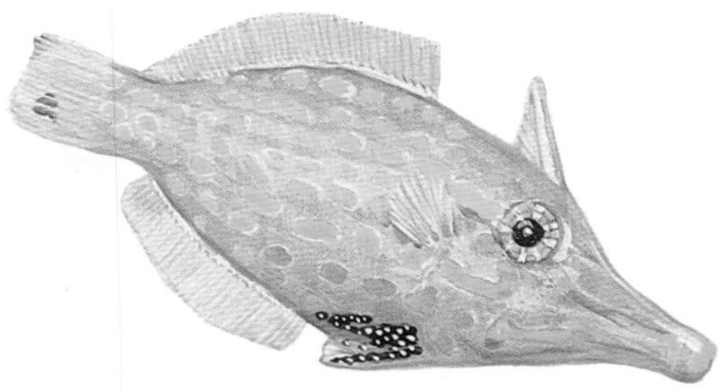

Filefishes are closely related to triggerfishes (*see p.273*), and also have a locking mechanism to keep the long first dorsal spine in position. However, they are much slimmer-bodied, and their scales have bristles that give the skin a file-like texture. Filefishes are among the few creatures that feed directly on corals, because these have powerful stinging cells. The long-nosed filefish is even more unusual in eating the polyps of only one coral genus – the branching or plate coral *Acropora*. The Red Sea long-nosed filefish, *Oxymonacanthus halli*, is very similar to the Indo-Pacific species, but is smaller and has a black bar on the tail in place of a black spot.

Scientific name	*Oxymonacanthus longirostris*
Classification	Order Tetraodontiformes (triggerfishes and allies); Suborder Balistoidei;
	Family Monacanthidae; sometimes included in Balistidae
Size	Up to about 12cm (5in) long
Distribution	Indian and Pacific oceans (East Africa to Ryukyu Is, Samoa and Australia)
Habitat	Clear lagoons and seaward side of coral reefs, to 30m (100ft)
Diet	Polyps of *Acropora* corals
Reproduction	Spawns on bottom, on site prepared by male

Long-horned cowfish

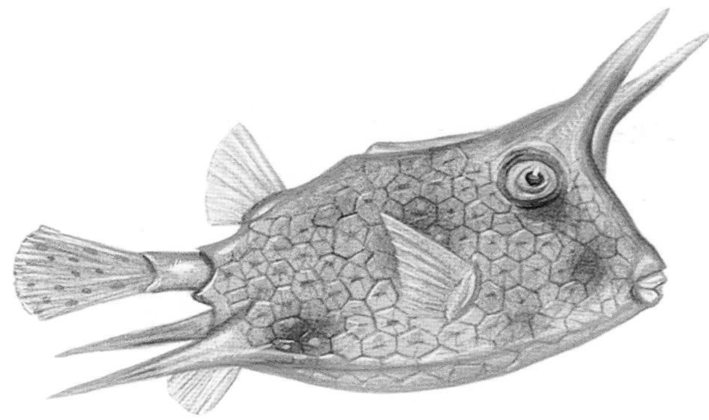

This box-like fish has such a curious appearance that it is sometimes dried to make an ornament. Like other members of its family – which includes boxfishes and trunkfishes – its body is encased in bony, mostly six-sided plates, with gaps for the eyes, small mouth, fins and other openings. The purpose of the 'horns' is not known. As if the hard shell and cryptic coloration were not enough protection from predators, most trunkfish secrete a highly toxic substance called ostracitoxin from their skin. The long-horned cowfish also has a curious method of feeding: it blows away sand from the lagoon floor with a water jet to expose small invertebrates.

Scientific name	*Lactoria cornuta* or *Ostracion cornutus*
Classification	Order Teraodontiformes (triggerfishes and allies); Suborder Balistoidei;
	Family Ostraciidae (or Ostraciontidae)
Size	Up to about 46cm (18in) long
Distribution	Indian and Pacific oceans (Red Sea and East Africa to Korea, Polynesia)
Habitat	Bottom-living on sand or gravel of shallow lagoons and coastal reefs
Diet	Bottom-living invertebrates
Reproduction	Spawns at dusk; eggs float

Long-spined porcupine fish

Porcupine fishes, like their less spiny relatives the puffer fishes of the family Tetraodontidae, are able when threatened to rapidly take large amounts of water into their stomach and puff themselves up like a ball. Few predators are big or brave enough to swallow such a large, spiny object. Many species of both families also have highly toxic skin, flesh or internal organs. (Puffers include the fugu [*Takifugu* species], whose flesh is highly prized by the Japanese despite the organs containing deadly poisons.) The long-spined porcupine fish is not toxic, but the similar and closely related common or spotted porcupine fish (*Diodon histrix*) is.

Scientific name	*Diodon holocanthus*
Classification	Order Tetraodontiformes (triggerfishes and allies); Suborder Tetraodontoidei; Family Diodontidae
Size	Up to about 50cm (20in) long
Distribution	Almost worldwide in tropical and subtropical waters
Habitat	Shallow reefs, lagoons and open sandy sea-bottoms, to 100m (330ft)
Diet	Shellfish; sea urchins; crabs; hermit crabs. Feeds at night
Reproduction	Spawns on bottom, in nest

Ocean sunfish

One of the most curious-looking of all fishes, the ocean sunfish looks as if the rear part of its body has been cut off, for it stops immediately after the tall, narrow dorsal and anal fins, and it has virtually no tail. The size and bulk of what 'remains' is shown by the fact that it is the heaviest of all bony fishes (that is, excluding sharks and rays). Despite its size and ungainly appearance, it can swim at a good speed, but it also often drifts or swims slowly at the surface, its dorsal fin breaking out of the water. Its mouth is small, with beak-like teeth; it feeds mainly on soft-bodied invertebrates. Another record it holds is for the number of eggs it produces: over 300 million.

Scientific name	*Mola mola*
Classification	Order Tetraodontiformes (triggerfishes and allies); Suborder
	Tetraodontoidei; Family Molidae
Size	Up to 3.3m (11ft) long; maximum weight 2 tonnes or more
Distribution	Worldwide in warm and temperate waters
Habitat	Open sea, often near surface, but sometimes to 300m (1000ft)
Diet	Small squid; fish; starfish; jellyfish and other invertebrates; also plants
Reproduction	Mature female may produce more than 300 million floating eggs

Leatherback turtle

The leatherback is the biggest turtle, weighing up to 910kg (2000lb), but averages less than half this weight. Its carapace (shell) has no horny external plates but is like hard rubber, with seven ridges; unlike in other turtles, it is not joined to the spine or ribs. Leatherbacks go ashore only to lay eggs, which take up to four months to hatch, depending on temperature. The hatchlings are about 65mm (2½in) long, and must dig themselves free and scramble to the sea. Adults swim long distances – even into subpolar regions – with flippers spanning up to 2.7m (9ft). They have soft jaws and eat mainly jellyfish, but may die if they mistake plastic debris for food.

Scientific name	*Dermochelys coriacea*
Classification	Order Chelonia; suborder Cryptodira (hidden-necked turtles)
	Family Dermochelyidae
Size	1.5–2m (5–6½ft) long
Distribution	Worldwide but rare
Habitat	Mainly warm oceans; breeds on tropical and subtropical beaches
Diet	Jellyfish; sea squirts
Reproduction	Buries several clutches of 80–100 eggs in sand, at 10-day intervals

Green turtle

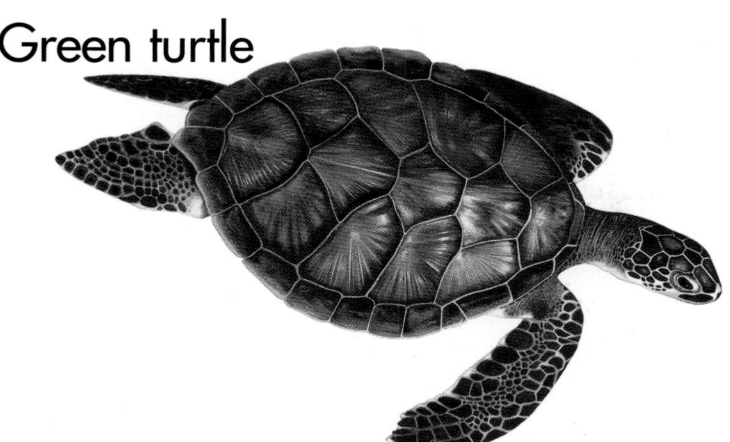

Once widely hunted for their carapace (shell) and meat, and used to make turtle soup, green turtles are now an endangered species. They are the largest hard-shelled turtles, and have extraordinary migratory habits. They always return to breed on the beach where they were born, often travelling 1300km (800 miles) or more from their shallow, warm-water feeding grounds. There are only a relatively few breeding beaches, where hundreds of turtles go each year. Important breeding sites include Ascension Island in the Atlantic, the Galápagos Islands, and certain islands and beaches in Hawaii, south-east Asia, the West Indies, Mexico and Florida.

Scientific name	*Chelonia mydas*
Classification	Order Chelonia; suborder Cryptodira (hidden-necked turtles)
	Family Cheloniidae
Size	1–1.2m (3¼–4ft) long
Distribution	Worldwide in tropics and subtropics
Habitat	Seas no colder than 20°C (68°F); breeds on beaches
Diet	Mainly seaweed and other sea plants; some crustaceans and jellyfish
Reproduction	Buries one or more clutches of about 100 eggs in sand of beach of birth

Salt-water or estuarine crocodile

The biggest of all crocodiles – and the most dangerous to humans – the salt-water or estuarine crocodile is slightly misnamed. Although it does live in salt or brackish (weakly salty) water near coasts and in estuaries and mangrove swamps, it is also seen in freshwater swamps and rivers – where it breeds. Breeding coincides with the wet season. A female scrapes together a mound of vegetation on land, in which she lays her eggs and which she defends. Decaying vegetation keeps the eggs warm, but in hot weather she may cool them with water. Salt-water crocodiles feed in and out of the water, sometimes leaping into the air or rushing onto land for prey.

Scientific name	*Crocodylus porosus*
Classification	Order Crocodilia (crocodiles and alligators)
	Family Crocodylidae; subfamily Crocodylinae
Size	Up to 7.5m (about 25ft) long or even more; usually 4–5m (13–16½ft)
Distribution	Southern India, through south-east Asia to northern Australia and Fiji
Habitat	Brackish estuaries, swamps and coastal waters; breeds near fresh water
Diet	All kinds of aquatic and land (waterside) animals – including humans
Reproduction	Buries 50 or more eggs in mound of vegetation beside river or swamp

Marine iguana

With the appearance of prehistoric monsters, marine iguanas are unique in several ways. They live only on the Galápagos Islands of the Pacific and are the world's only truly marine lizards. They are usually dark grey or blackish, but on some islands are blotched red and greenish, as shown. They live and breed close to rocky shores, and brave waves and spray to get the seaweed that is their main food, which grows between high- and low-water levels. They also swim and dive – large adults as deep as 15m (50ft) – for food. When they haul themselves out on a rock, water sprays from their nostrils, excreting excess salt from a special nasal gland.

Scientific name	*Amblyrhynchus cristatus*
Classification	Order Squamata; sub-order Lacertilia or Sauria (lizards)
	Family Iguanidae
Size	Up to 1.2–1.5m (4–5ft) long
Distribution	Galápagos Islands
Habitat	Shoreline; splash and intertidal zone; inshore waters
Diet	Mainly seaweed; sometimes small invertebrates
Reproduction	Up to six eggs, laid in burrow dug in sand or volcanic ash near shore

Sea-krait, or common sea snake

Unlike most sea snakes (such as the banded species; *opposite*), the sea-krait is not fully adapted to life in the water. Both it and its close and somewhat bigger relative the yellow-lipped sea-krait (*Laticauda semifasciata*) come ashore to lay their eggs. Using the wide scales on their belly – which are more like those of a land snake than of a true sea snake – for grip, they clamber over rocks and even climb low cliffs to find a suitable cave or rock crevice. For this reason, herpetologists (reptile experts) regard them as intermediate types between land and true aquatic snakes. Like all sea snakes, however, they have powerful venom with which they very quickly immobilize their prey.

Scientific name	*Laticauda laticaudata*
Classification	Order Squamata; suborder Ophidia or Serpentes (snakes)
	Family Elapidae (subfamily Hydrophiinae), Hydrophiidae or Laticaudidae
Size	Averages about 80cm (32in) long
Distribution	Eastern Indian Ocean to western Pacific
Habitat	Tropical inshore waters; breeds on shore
Diet	Fish
Reproduction	Lays eggs in cave or rock crevice

Banded sea snake

One of the true sea snakes, this species is so well adapted to life in water that it cannot survive if washed up on land. Unlike the sea-krait (*see opposite*), it has no wide belly scales with which to grip the ground and return itself to the sea. Adaptations to aquatic life include a laterally flattened body, a paddle-like tail with which to propel itself, and nostrils situated on the top of its head that can be closed by flaps when it dives. It does not even come ashore to breed; it is ovoviviparous – that is, the female produces eggs that are retained within her body until they hatch and are born, but unlike a mammal she does not nourish the developing young.

Scientific name	*Hydrophis cyanocinctus*
Classification	Order Squamata; suborder Ophidia or Serpentes (snakes)
	Family Elapidae (subfamily Hydrophiinae) or Hydrophiidae
Size	Up to 2m (6½ft) long
Distribution	Indian and Pacific oceans from Persian Gulf to Japanese waters
Habitat	Mostly coastal waters
Diet	Fish
Reproduction	Ovoviviparous; gives birth to 2–6 live young

Polar bear

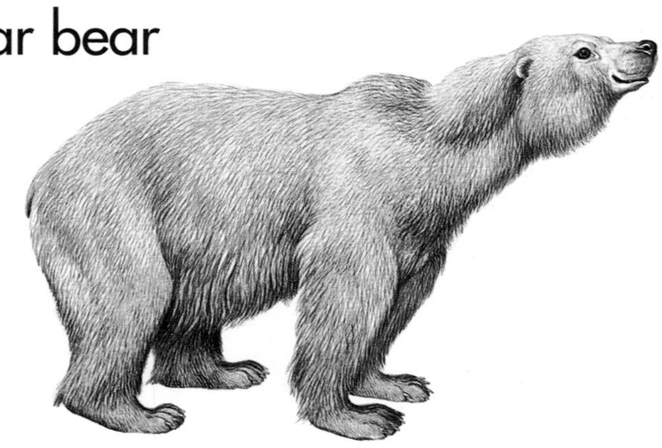

One of the biggest of all bears, the polar bear is the only truly semi-aquatic species, equally at home on the tundra, pack-ice and ice floes, and swimming in the ice-cold Arctic seas. Its thick oily coat is impermeable to water and gives good insulation. Even the soles of its feet are fur-covered for good grip on the ice and snow and to retain warmth. A membrane between the toes helps swimming. Except during the mating season, adult polar bears are mostly solitary animals. Pregnant females spend much of the winter sleeping in a den dug under the snow, where they give birth, but others travel in the winter, moving over the ice in search of prey.

Scientific name	*Ursa maritimus*
Classification	Order Carnivora; suborder Fissipedia (terrestrial carnivores)
	Family Ursidae
Size	Up to 2.5m (8¼ft) long, sometimes more, including 10cm (4in) tail
Distribution	Arctic
Habitat	Coasts, ice floes and pack-ice
Diet	Seals; fish; seabirds; hares; reindeer; musk-oxen; plant matter in summer
Reproduction	One to four cubs, born in winter after about 9-month gestation

Sea otter

Sea otters – the most fully marine otters – are loved for their playfulness and their skill in diving for food, then floating on their back and cracking open an abalone shell by hitting it on a stone balanced on their chest. They sleep in the same way, entwined in a frond of kelp (a large seaweed) as an anchor. Sea otters have thick double-layered fur – among the finest of any animal – that keeps them warm by trapping air near the skin. They were widely hunted until protected internationally in 1911. Only about 2000 remain in California, but they are recovering elsewhere. Among their greatest dangers are oil spills, which ruin their fur's water-resistance.

Scientific name	*Enhydra lutris*
Classification	Order Carnivora; suborder Fissipedia (terrestrial carnivores)
	Family Mustelidae; subfamily Lutrinae
Size	Up to 1.4m (4½ft) long, excluding tail
Distribution	Pacific coasts of Russia, Alaska and parts of US West Coast
Habitat	Shallow inshore waters, especially where kelp grows
Diet	Mainly shellfish such as abalones; sea urchins; crabs; octopuses; fish
Reproduction	Single pup may be born in any season, after 4–5 month gestation

South American fur seal

Fur seals and sealions are distinguished from true seals (*see pp.291–297*) by their external ears and long hind flippers, which they can use to help to propel themselves on land. They probably evolved from bear-like animals. Various species of fur seals of the genus *Arctocephalus* live in many seas and coasts in the Southern Hemisphere and as far north as California. South American (or southern) fur seals have long been hunted for their fur, leather and oil, but are now protected in all countries. Males defend territories during the breeding season. Females give birth soon after coming ashore, and then mate with the male in whose territory they are.

Scientific name	*Arctocephalus australis*
Classification	Order Carnivora; suborder Pinnipedia (marine carnivores)
	Family Otariidae; subfamily Arctocephalinae
Size	Varies over range; males up to 2m (6½ft) long; females up to 1.5m (5ft)
Distribution	Southern Atlantic and Pacific coasts, southern Brazil to Peru; Falkland Is
Habitat	Inshore and offshore seas; breeds on rocky coasts
Diet	Fish such as anchovies, sardines ; crustaceans; mussels; squid; penguins
Reproduction	Polygynous. Single pup, born in spring after 11–12 month gestation

Northern fur seal

Northern fur seals, like other related species, have long been hunted for their fur, but since 1985 they have been hunted only by the native peoples of the Aleutian and other islands where they breed. Almost three-quarters of the million or so northern fur seals breed on the Pribilof Islands of the southern Bering Sea, but other breeding colonies (called rookeries) are scattered from California to the Kuril Islands, north of Japan. Mature males arrive in late spring, and establish breeding territories. Females arrive, give birth within two days, and then mate with a male – who may have a harem of up to 100 females. All return to the sea by early winter.

Scientific name	*Callorhinus ursinus*
Classification	Order Carnivora; suborder Pinnipedia (marine carnivores)
	Family Otariidae; subfamily Arctocephalinae
Size	Male up to 2.1m (7ft) long; female up to 1.4–1.5m (4–5ft)
Distribution	Northern Pacific Ocean, from Japan to Alaska and California
Habitat	Cold seas, to 160km (100 miles) offshore; breeds on rocky islands
Diet	Mainly fish and squid
Reproduction	Polygynous. Single pup, born in summer after 11–12 month gestation

California sealion

Named for their noisy, roaring bark, sealions are closely related to fur seals (*see pp.286–287*) and are similarly able to use both front and hind flippers to manoeuvre on land. In fact, most trained 'performing seals' in zoos and marine parks are California sealions. Very closely related animals – which may form a subspecies of the California sealion or a separate species, *Zalophus wollebaeki* – live in the Galápagos Islands. Another, now extinct group used to live in the Sea of Japan. Like fur seals, male California sealions keep a breeding harem of females – usually about 15-strong. They set up a territory on a beach or rocky coast and mate with the females soon after these give birth.

Scientific name	*Zalophus californianus*
Classification	Order Carnivora; suborder Pinnipedia (marine carnivores)
	Family Otariidae; subfamily Otariinae
Size	Male up to 2.5m (8¼ft) long; female about 1.8m (6ft)
Distribution	Southern British Columbia to Mexico; *see also above*
Habitat	Inshore seas; breeds on rocky, gravel or sandy islands and coasts
Diet	Fish; squid; octopuses; crabs; lobsters; shellfish
Reproduction	Polygynous. Single pup born early summer after 11–12 month gestation

Steller's or northern sealion

This species is the biggest of the sealions, although females reach only about a third of the weight of males (which can weigh as much as 1 tonne). It sometimes kills other, smaller seals. It is an endangered species, numbers having dropped severely – in Alaska especially – since the 1970s, and is protected in most areas. A major reason for its decline is thought to be the impact of commerical fishing. Pollack, salmon and other commercially caught fish form an important part of its diet, and these have been caught in huge numbers in the Bering Sea and Gulf of Alaska. Like other species, females give birth and then mate with males, who defend their territory and mate with many females.

Scientific name	*Eumetopias jubatus*
Classification	Order Carnivora; suborder Pinnipedia (marine carnivores)
	Family Otariidae; subfamily Otariinae
Size	Male up to 3.3m (11ft) long; female up to 2m (6½ft)
Distribution	North Pacific rim, from Japan, Russia and Alaska to California
Habitat	Shallow coastal and offshore waters; breeds on rocky sloping beaches
Diet	Fish; squid; octopuses
Reproduction	Polygynous. Single pup born early summer after 11–12 month gestation

Walrus

Unmistakable with their huge tusks in both sexes, walruses are otherwise rather like very large sealions (*see pp.288–289*). There are two subspecies, in separate populations in the northern Atlantic, from Canada to northern Russia (the Atlantic walrus), and in the Bering and Chukchi seas (the larger and much more numerous Pacific walrus). A third population, in the Laptev Sea north of Siberia, may be a third subspecies or a form of Pacific walrus. Walruses spend most of their life at sea in groups, diving to forage for food on the bottom. They haul themselves out on ice floes, or sometimes shores, mainly to breed in winter and spring, but mate at sea.

Scientific name	*Odobenus rosmarus*
Classification	Order Carnivora; suborder Pinnipedia (marine carnivores)
	Family Odobenidae
Size	Male up to 3.6m (12ft) long; female up to 2.6m (8½ft)
Distribution	Far North Atlantic, North Pacific and Arctic
Habitat	Cold shallow seas; ice floes; shores
Diet	Bottom-living molluscs (mainly clams); crustaceans; other invertebrates
Reproduction	Single calf, born on pack-ice in spring after 15–16 month gestation

Mediterranean monk seal

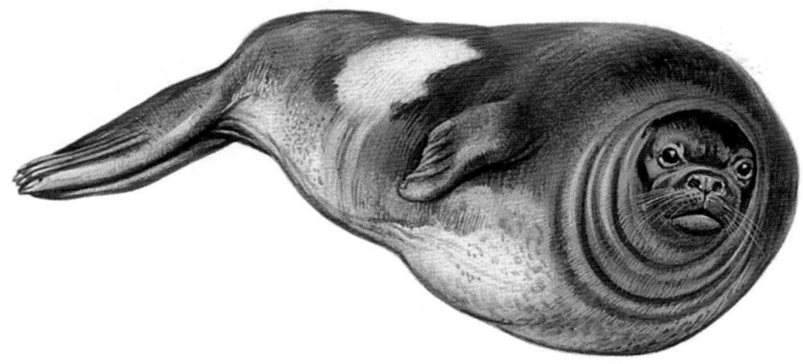

This species – once found widely on the Mediterranean, Black Sea and African Atlantic coasts – is the most critically endangered of all seals, with fewer than 500 survivors. The closely related Hawaiian monk seal (*Monachus schauinslandi*) is also rare, and the Caribbean species (*M. tropicalis*) became extinct in the 1950s. The name comes from their dark coat, said to be like a monk's robes. Mediterranean monk seals often have a pale patch – especially marked in young animals, and variable in shape – on their underparts. They used to live on beaches, but tourism, building, fishing and the use of motor boats has driven them to isolated caves.

Scientific name	*Monachus monachus*
Classification	Order Carnivora; suborder Pinnipedia (marine carnivores)
	Family Phocidae; subfamily Monachinae
Size	Male about 2.4m (8ft) long; female slightly smaller
Distribution	Small areas of Mediterranean and north-west African Atlantic coast
Habitat	Rocky coasts, sea-caves and shallow coastal waters
Diet	Wide variety of fish; squid; octopuses
Reproduction	Single pup, born most often in autumn after 10–11 month gestation

Leopard seal

With their spotted coat, large head and mouth, relatively slim body and long front flippers, leopard seals are distinctive and aptly named. The name also fits their hunting habits. In the Antarctic summer – December to February – they kill many young of other seal species, especially crab-eaters (*Lobodon carcinophagus*), and also small penguins. These are caught mainly in the water, where leopard seals' long flippers give them great speed and manoeuvrability. As with other seals, males and females mate (in the water in this case) soon after the young are born, but the fertilized embryo is believed not to start growing until several months later.

Scientific name	*Hydrurga leptonyx*
Classification	Order Carnivora; suborder Pinnipedia (marine carnivores)
	Family Phocidae; subfamily Lobodontinae
Size	Male 2.4–3.2m (8–10½ft) long; female slightly larger
Distribution	Around Antarctica; strays north to Australasia, South America, Africa
Habitat	Cold Antarctic waters; edges of ice shelf; pack-ice; ice floes; islands
Diet	Squid; fish; other seals and penguins in summer; krill in winter
Reproduction	Single pup, born on ice floe in summer after 11–12-month gestation

Southern elephant seal

Male elephant seals are highly territorial and aggressive in the breeding season, engaging in fierce – though rarely fatal – head-swinging battles with rival males to control patches of beach. This lets them collect a harem of up to 100 females, with which they will mate soon after the females give birth. Because of this competition, the males have evolved to a huge size; most are smaller than the maximum figures below, but males average four times the weight of females – the biggest difference among all mammals. The main breeding colonies are on South Georgia and other subantarctic islands, and in southern Argentina. The rest of the year is spent at sea.

Scientific name	*Mirounga leonina*
Classification	Order Carnivora; suborder Pinnipedia (marine carnivores)
	Family Phocidae; subfamily Cystophorinae
Size	Male up to 6.2m (20½ft) long and 4 tonnes; female up to 3.7m (12ft)
Distribution	South polar, subpolar regions; South Atlantic; southern South America
Habitat	Cold seas; beaches
Diet	Squid and fish
Reproduction	Polygynous. Single cub, born in spring after 11–12-month gestation

Hooded seal

Male hooded seals have an inflatable crest, or hood, on their forehead. They breed on drifting ice floes, out of the reach of predatory polar bears. When a female leaves the water to give birth in spring, a male accompanies and guards her, waiting for the chance to mate. He wards off rivals by inflating his hood. His septum – the red membrane separating the nostrils – is also inflatable, making a balloon the size of a football, and he uses this both to court the female and to threaten rivals. As soon as the pup is weaned and abandoned by its mother – only a few days after birth, the shortest time of any mammal – the male and female mate in the water.

Scientific name	*Cystophora cristata*
Classification	Order Carnivora; suborder Pinnipedia (marine carnivores)
	Family Phocidae; subfamily Cystophorinae
Size	Male about 2.6m (8½ft) long; female about 2m (6½ft)
Distribution	Far North Atlantic Ocean; parts of Arctic Ocean
Habitat	Deep waters; ice floes; edge of pack-ice
Diet	Fish; squid and other invertebrates
Reproduction	Single pup, born in spring after 12-month gestation

Ringed seal

Named for the markings on its coat, the ringed seal is the smallest of all seals and is the most common and widespread Arctic species. Isolated groups live in the Baltic and in Lakes Ladoga and Saimaa, in Russia and Finland. Ringed seals breed and live much of their life on the pack-ice, making and keeping open holes in the ice through which they dive for food. As the ice breaks up in summer, they move north to follow it. Baltic and lake populations frequently land on shore in summer, when the ice has melted. Like all true seals – which evolved from otter-like animals – their short flippers are little use on land or ice except to haul themselves clumsily along.

Scientific name	*Phoca* (or *Pusa*) *hispida*
Classification	Order Carnivora; suborder Pinnipedia (marine carnivores)
	Family Phocidae; subfamily Phocinae
Size	Varies over range; 1.1–1.75m (3½–5¾ft) long; male longer than female
Distribution	Arctic Ocean; Bering Sea; Sea of Okhotsk; Baltic Sea; subarctic lakes
Habitat	Pack-ice; cold seas (including under ice)
Diet	Fish; crustaceans; other invertebrates
Reproduction	Single pup, born in den on ice in spring, after 11-month gestation

Ribbon seal

It is difficult to understand why the ribbon seal evolved its distinctive coat pattern, but it may be a form of cryptic coloration that helps to disguise it against the broken pack-ice where it spends the winter and spring, and where it breeds. Apart from the four yellowish to white 'ribbons', each 10–12cm (4–5in) wide, around the neck, fore-flippers and hind part of the body, adult males are almost black. Females have the same pattern, but it is less distinct against their lighter brown coat. The pattern takes about four years to develop; pups are born silvery-white, but this coat is shed after about a month, and young seals are blue-black with silvery underparts.

Scientific name	*Phoca* (or *Histriophoca*) *fasciata*
Classification	Order Carnivora; suborder Pinnipedia (marine carnivores)
	Family Phocidae; subfamily Phocinae
Size	About 1.6m (5¼ft) long, sometimes up to 1.9m (6¼ft)
Distribution	North Pacific, from Sea of Okhotsk to Bering and Chukchi seas
Habitat	Edge of pack-ice in winter and spring; open sea when ice melts
Diet	Mainly fish; also squid, shrimps and crabs
Reproduction	Single pup, born on ice in spring after about 12-month gestation

Common or harbour seal

Known in North America as the harbour seal, the common seal is not, in fact, as common in many areas (including the British Isles) as its cousin the grey seal (*Halichoerus grypus*). But it is certainly the most widespread species, found in the north of both Eastern and Western hemispheres. As might be expected from such a wide range, it varies considerably in size and colouring, and at least five separate subspecies are recognized. Common seals rarely venture very far from coasts, and haul themselves out of the water to breed, moult and rest in favourite sheltered spots, forming colonies of 1000 or more. Their breeding season varies with location.

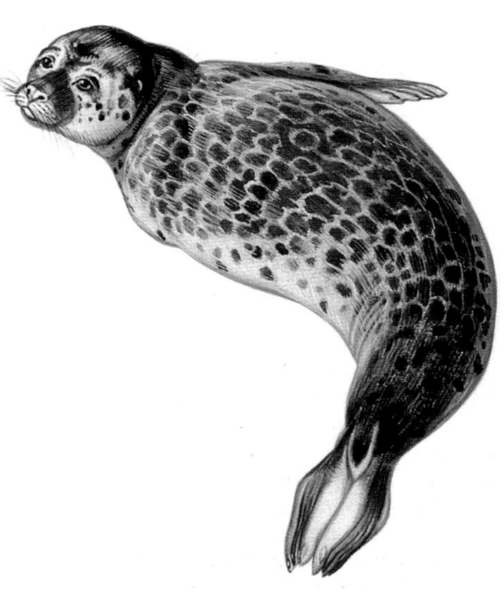

Scientific name	*Phoca vitulina*
Classification	Order Carnivora; suborder Pinnipedia (marine carnivores)
	Family Phocidae; subfamily Phocinae
Size	Male 1.4–1.8m (4½–6ft) long (largest in northern Pacific); female smaller
Distribution	Eastern and western North Atlantic and North Pacific oceans
Habitat	Temperate and subpolar coastal areas
Diet	Variety of fish, crustaceans and molluscs
Reproduction	Single pup, born in spring or early summer after 11-month gestation

Common or harbour porpoise

Porpoises are sociable marine mammals that travel in schools of 12 to 16 or more, migrating with the seasons between colder and warmer waters. They have acute hearing, and communicate by means of clicks and squeaks. They are distinguished from dolphins by their rounded head (without a beak) and short, triangular dorsal fin. When swimming, they break the surface but, unlike dolphins, rarely leap. They feed mainly on fish and crabs, consuming about 50 mackerel or herring-sized fish each day. They dive for several minutes at a time, using echo-location to find their prey. Pairs mate in late summer after long courtship rituals swimming side by side.

Scientific name	*Phocoena* (or *Phocaena*) *phocoena*
Classification	Order Cetacea; suborder Odontoceti (toothed whales)
	Family Phocoenidae
Size	About 1.5–2m (5–6½ft) long
Distribution	North Atlantic and Pacific oceans; Mediterranean; Black Sea
Habitat	Mainly estuaries and other shallow waters
Diet	Mainly fish; some crabs and other invertebrates
Reproduction	Single calf, born in summer after 10–11 month gestation

Common dolphin

The beauty and playfulness of dolphins has endeared them to artists and others for thousands of years. They travel in large schools, often of several hundred and sometimes a thousand or more animals, that leap and splash noisily; they often swim beside or just ahead of a ship's bows. They have intricate but very variable markings, with a yellowish or tan patch on each side. A number of geographical forms have been identified, divided into two basic types: the long-beaked and short-beaked forms. Common dolphins can dive to depths of nearly 300m (1000ft) as they hunt for fish, guided by echo-location. Many are caught in fishing nets and drown.

Scientific name	*Delphinus delphis*
Classification	Order Cetacea; suborder Odontoceti (toothed whales)
	Family Delphinidae
Size	Up to about 2.5m (8¼ft) long
Distribution	Worldwide in tropical and warm temperate waters
Habitat	Open ocean and shallow coastal seas
Diet	Mainly fish and squid
Reproduction	Single calf, born in summer after 10–11 month gestation

Bottlenose dolphin

Growing much bigger than common dolphins (*see p.299*), bottlenose dolphins are highly intelligent mammals that are often kept in captivity in zoos and marine parks, and taught to perform tricks to entertain visitors. They are just as playful (and longer-lived) in the wild, sometimes swimming alongside boats and swimmers, surfing and lobtailing (slapping their tail against the water). They travel in small schools, and often leap out of the water, sometimes as high as 3m (10ft). Bottlenose dolphins show many geographical variations of colour and shape, but the two main forms are the smaller inshore and more robust offshore types.

Scientific name	*Tursiops truncatus*
Classification	Order Cetacea; suborder Odontoceti (toothed whales)
	Family Delphinidae
Size	Up to about 3.6m (12ft) long
Distribution	Worldwide in tropical and temperate waters
Habitat	Open ocean (especially in tropics), shallow coastal waters and estuaries
Diet	Mainly deep-swimming fish inshore; other fish; cuttlefish; crustaceans
Reproduction	Single calf, born in summer after 12–13 month gestation

Orca, or killer whale

Despite their name, size and fierce appearance, killer whales are intelligent and playful, and tame in captivity. But in the wild they prey on almost anything that swims, from fish, penguins and seals up to sharks and even large whales; they have been known to attack boats. They are bulky, distinctively patterned whales with a dorsal fin up to 1.8m (6ft) tall in males. Despite their size they can swim at almost 55km/h (35mph) and can leap clear of the water. They sometimes 'skyhop' – raise their head vertically from the water – to scan the horizon for prey. They travel in coordinated pods (family groups) in search of food, but do not migrate regularly.

Scientific name	*Orcinus orca*
Classification	Order Cetacea; suborder Odontoceti (toothed whales)
	Family Delphinidae
Size	Male about 7–10m (23–33ft), female about 4.5–6m (15–20ft), long
Distribution	Worldwide, especially in colder waters
Habitat	Deep and shallow waters, usually within 800km (500 miles) of land
Diet	Very varied: fish; squid; birds; turtles; seals; dolphins; other whales
Reproduction	Single calf born after about 12-month gestation

Long-finned pilot whale

There are two distinct populations of the long-finned pilot whale: one in the northern North Atlantic, the other around the globe in the Southern Ocean and southern parts of the Atlantic, Indian and Pacific oceans. They may, in fact, form separate species – just as the pilot whale itself was only in the 1970s realized to consist of very similar but separate long-finned and short-finned species (the latter, *Globicephala macrorhynchus*, living in warmer waters). Both have a markedly bulbous forehead, which is largest in older males. The long-finned species has a strong blow, more than 1m (3¼ft) high, and can dive to at least 600m (2000ft).

Scientific name	*Globicephala melas* or *G. malaena*
Classification	Order Cetacea; suborder Odontoceti (toothed whales)
	Family Delphinidae
Size	Male may exceed 6m (20ft) long; female slightly smaller
Distribution	Cold temperate waters of all oceans except North Pacific
Habitat	Mainly deep offshore waters; often feeds in coastal and shallow waters
Diet	Mainly squid; also fish
Reproduction	Single calf, usually born in late summer after 12–16 month gestation

Narwhal

Mature male narwhals have a single long tusk – very rarely two – protruding from the upper lip; it is usually about 2m (6½ft) long but may grow to 3m (10ft). It is in fact an elongated tooth. Narwhals are born with only two teeth, both in the upper jaw. Usually, neither erupt (enlarge and grow from the gum) in females, and only one in males; it penetrates the lip and grows in a 'barley-sugar' twist. Some females also grow a tusk, but it is much shorter than the male's. The tusk's purpose is uncertain, but it is probably a sexual characteristic; male narwhals have been seen jousting with their tusks, and the winner can probably mate with more females.

Scientific name	*Monodon monoceros*
Classification	Order Cetacea; suborder Odontoceti (toothed whales)
	Family Monodontidae
Size	Up to about 6m (20ft) long, including male's tusk; female 4.5m (12ft)
Distribution	Far northern North Atlantic and Arctic oceans
Habitat	Cold Arctic waters, near pack-ice
Diet	Fish; squid; crustaceans
Reproduction	Single calf, born in summer after 15-month gestation

White whale, or beluga

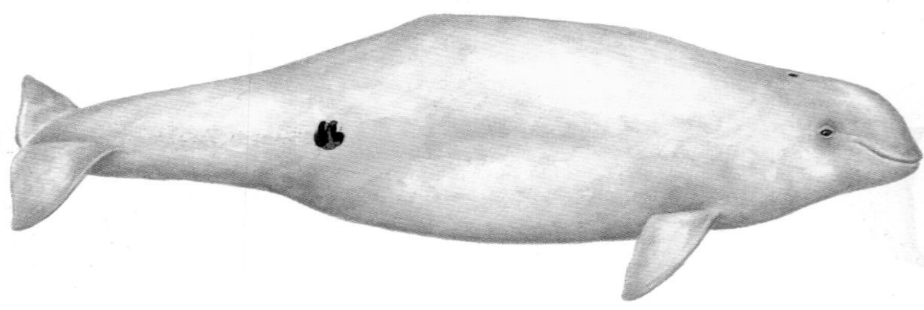

The white whale is aptly named, although it is dark brownish-grey at birth and only gradually becomes paler up to the age of about six years. Like the related narwhal (*see p.303*), it has no dorsal fin, but it does have a ridge on its back. It is sociable, usually swimming slowly in groups ranging from 10 or 20 up to many hundreds in estuaries when food is plentiful in summer. White whales, or belugas, are among the most vocal of all whales, making a wide variety of clicks, squeaks, trills and lowing sounds; whalers used to call them 'sea canaries'. They manoeuvre well in shallow water and among ice floes, but are often attacked by polar bears.

Scientific name	*Delphinapterus leucas*
Classification	Order Cetacea; suborder Odontoceti (toothed whales)
	Family Monodontidae
Size	Up to about 4–5m (13–16½ft) long; sometimes up to 6m (20ft)
Distribution	Arctic and northern oceans, to Japan, southern Alaska and Nova Scotia
Habitat	Offshore waters; coasts; bays; rivers; not open ocean
Diet	Mainly crustaceans; some fish
Reproduction	Single calf, born in summer after 14-month gestation

Northern bottlenose whale

The bottlenosed whales – the southern species (*Hyperoodon planifrons*) lives south of 30°S – belong to the beaked-whale family, so called because of their beak-like snout. They have a bulbous forehead and usually only two teeth, both in the lower jaw. All members of the family dive deeply, but the northern bottlenose is believed to be one of the deepest and longest-diving of all whales. It often dives for more than an hour, and may remain submerged for as long as two hours. It swims in small groups of up to ten individuals. It is attracted by the sound of ships, and many thousands were killed by whalers until the species was given protection in 1977.

Scientific name	*Hyperoodon ampullatus*
Classification	Order Cetacea; suborder Odontoceti (toothed whales)
	Family Ziphiidae
Size	Up to about 7–10m (23–33ft) long
Distribution	North Atlantic and Arctic oceans, north of about 30°N to pack-ice
Habitat	Mainly in ocean waters deeper than about 1000m (3300ft)
Diet	Mainly squid
Reproduction	Single calf, born in spring or summer after 12-month gestation

Sperm whale

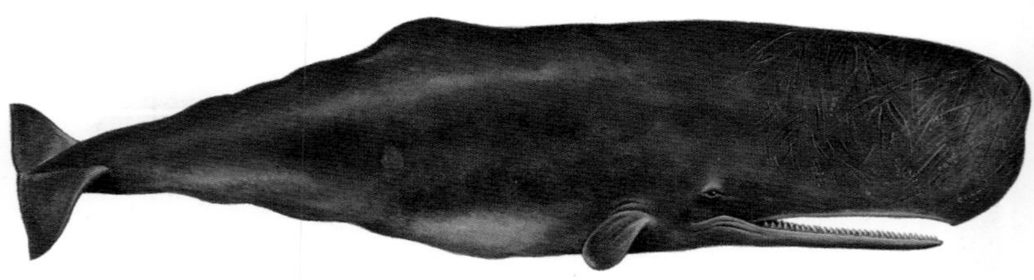

Unjustly immortalized in Herman Melville's book *Moby Dick* as an aggressive killer, the sperm whale was for centuries hunted for its spermaceti, long used as a fine lubricating oil; for ambergris, a fatty substance from its intestines used as a 'fixative' in perfume making; for its fatty blubber; and for its 20cm (8in) teeth, a kind of ivory. It is now largely protected, but long-term hunting of large males reduced numbers greatly. Spermaceti is found in cavities in the whale's head, and may aid buoyancy during deep dives to 1000m (3300ft) or more; it may also help to focus echo-location sounds. Adult males are solitary but breeding females live in groups.

Scientific name	*Physeter macrocephalus* or *P. catodon*
Classification	Order Cetacea; suborder Odontoceti (toothed whales)
	Family Physeteridae
Size	Male up to about 18m (about 60ft) long; female much smaller
Distribution	Worldwide except coldest polar regions
Habitat	Open ocean and offshore waters in water more than 200m (650ft) deep
Diet	Giant deepwater squid; fish; other squid and octopuses
Reproduction	Usually single calf, born after 14–16 month gestation

Grey whale

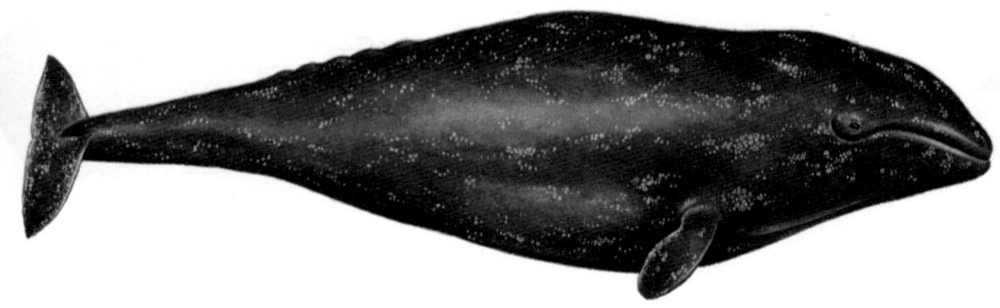

Sometimes called the California grey whale because it is often seen off the coasts of that state, where it winters, this species is a filter-feeding baleen whale. It has no teeth, but up to 180 fringed, horny plates of baleen, or whalebone, hang from the roof of its mouth. It feeds on the bottom, sucking in sediments; small food organisms trapped by the baleen are retrieved by the whale's tongue. Atlantic grey whales were hunted to extinction. A few may survive in the western Pacific, wintering off Korea and migrating to the Sea of Okhotsk in summer. California grey whales migrate farther than any other mammal, 10 000km (6000 miles) to the Bering Sea.

Scientific name	*Eschrichtius robustus*
Classification	Order Cetacea; suborder Mysticeti (baleen whales)
	Family Eschrichtidae
Size	Up to about 14m (46ft) long; male slightly smaller than female
Distribution	Summer in northern North Pacific; winters farther south (*see above*)
Habitat	Coastal waters; farther offshore in summer
Diet	Small crustaceans, worms and other bottom-living invertebrates
Reproduction	Single calf, born in winter after 12-month gestation

Blue whale

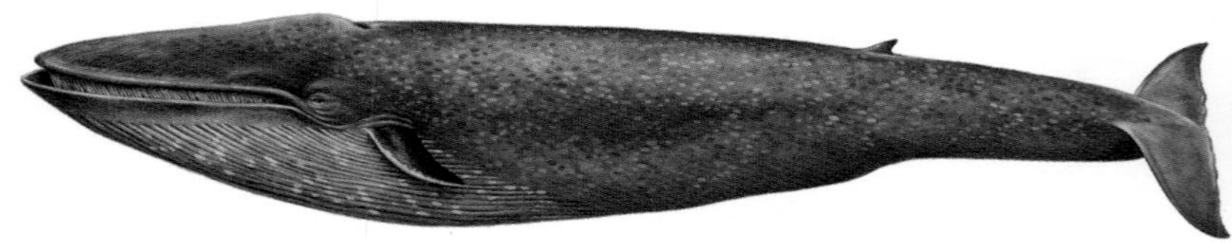

The blue whale is the biggest animal on Earth – heavier, if not longer, than the biggest dinosaur. (The species name *musculus* – Latin for 'mouse' – is a joke.) Its average of 24m (80ft) and 100 tonnes is, however, much less than the record size (*see below*). Blue whales can swim at up to 50km/h (almost 30mph), and were safe from whalers until steam power and exploding harpoons enabled large-scale killing. Despite protection since 1966, only about 5000 blue whales survive. They feed only in summer, in cold regions, on krill (*see p.133*). Their baleen plates (*see p.307*) are up to 1m (3¼ft) long, and sieve up to 3.5 tonnes of food – 40 million krill – each day.

Scientific name	*Balaenoptera musculus*
Classification	Order Cetacea; suborder Mysticeti (baleen whales)
	Family Balaenopteridae
Size	Up to 33m (110ft) long, weighing 190 tonnes; usually smaller
Distribution	Worldwide, but biggest population in Southern Hemisphere
Habitat	Open ocean, mainly in cold waters in summer, warmer parts in winter
Diet	Krill – small planktonic cold-water crustaceans
Reproduction	Single calf, born in winter in warm waters after 12-month gestation

Minke whale or lesser rorqual

The minke is the smallest and most plentiful of the rorquals (members of the family Balaenopteridae), and was hunted on a large scale only after larger, more profitable whales were given protection in the 1970s. Since 1986, there has been a voluntary restriction on killing it, and only a few countries still do so, but it is still regarded as a threatened species. Like other baleen whales, it has a series of pleats or grooves – up to 70 in this species – in its throat. These allow the throat to expand as it takes in huge mouthfuls of water and floating food; the whale then expels the water through the baleen plates (*see p.307*), which filter it and trap food organisms.

Scientific name	*Balaenoptera acutorostrata*
Classification	Order Cetacea; suborder Mysticeti (baleen whales)
	Family Balaenopteridae
Size	Up to about 10m (33ft) long
Distribution	Virtually worldwide
Habitat	Deep, cool water, nearer Equator in winter; sometimes inshore
Diet	Planktonic krill; small fish; small squid
Reproduction	Single calf, born in winter in warm waters after 10-month gestation

Humpback whale

The hump of this whale is not very noticeable, but it has a stocky body, numerous rounded knobs on the head, lower jaw and flippers, and often many attached barnacles (*see p.125*). The flippers are long and black in Pacific humpbacks, mostly white in Atlantic animals. They are slow swimmers and often move inshore, so they were easy prey to whalers until they were given protection in 1966. They number 15 to 20 thousand, only one-fifth their original population. Humpbacks often isolate a school of fish with a ring-'net' of bubbles from their blow-hole before feeding. Males perform complex 'songs', up to 20 minutes long, as part of their mating ritual.

Scientific name	*Megaptera novaeangliae*
Classification	Order Cetacea; suborder Mysticeti (baleen whales)
	Family Balaenopteridae
Size	Up to about 15m (50ft) long; female slightly larger than male
Distribution	Worldwide; migrates
Habitat	Winters in tropical waters; spends summer in temperate and polar areas
Diet	Planktonic krill; small fish
Reproduction	Single calf, born in winter in warm waters after 12-month gestation

Bowhead or Greenland right whale

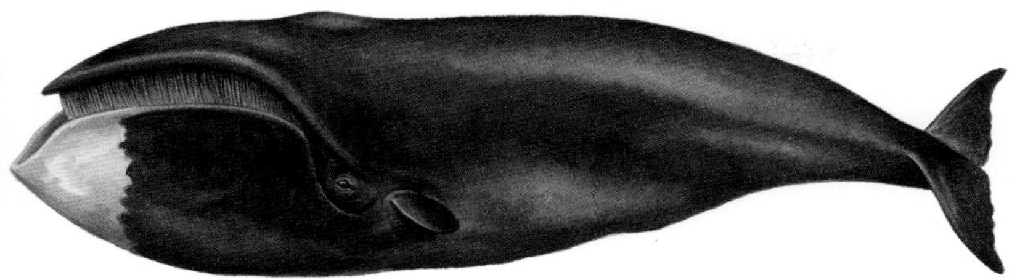

One of the most endangered whale species – with perhaps fewer than 10 000 remaining – the bowhead whale was long killed for its blubber and baleen. The blubber is up to 70cm (28in) thick, and yielded large quantities of oil. The baleen, or whalebone, is the long, thin, horny plates in the whale's mouth that filter tiny food organisms from seawater. The bowhead has longer baleen – up to 4.5m (14½ft) – than any other whale; it is springy and was widely used until the early 20th century for women's corsets, umbrella ribs, fishing rods and many other things. Today only native Arctic peoples are allowed to kill a few bowhead whales, a traditional food.

Scientific name	*Balaena mysticetus*
Classification	Order Cetacea; suborder Mysticeti (baleen whales)
	Family Balaenidae
Size	Up to 18–20m (60–65ft) long
Distribution	Arctic Ocean and adjacent seas and bays
Habitat	Mostly fairly shallow cold seas
Diet	Very small planktonic krill, copepods and similar creatures
Reproduction	Single calf, born in spring or early summer after 12-month gestation

North American manatee

The sea cows are also known as sirenians because they are said to be the origin of the legend of sirens, or mermaids, that lured seafarers to their death. They do not look much like the popular image of a mermaid, but females are said to help their new-born young to rise out of the water to breathe rather like a human mother holding her baby. The manatee is the bigger of the two best-known species (*see also opposite*), weighing up to 600kg (1300lb). It uses its flippers to gather food, and plays an important part in keeping waterways from becoming choked with weed. When not grazing, manatees rest under water, rising every few minutes to breathe.

Scientific name	*Trichecus manatus*
Classification	Order Sirenia (sea cows)
	Family Trichechidae
Size	Up to about 3–4m (10–13ft) long
Distribution	Atlantic and Caribbean from Florida and Gulf coast to Guyana
Habitat	Coastal waters, lagoons and river mouths with water at least 20°C (68°F)
Diet	Wide range of aquatic plants; some invertebrates
Reproduction	Single young, born after about 12-month gestation

Dugong

Dugongs are slightly smaller than manatees and have more streamlined flippers and a divided tail rather like a whale's or dolphin's; this enables them to swim at more than 20km/h (12mph). Males have two short tusks that are usually almost hidden by the upper lips. Dugongs live in several separate areas of tropical and subtropical waters – along the coast of eastern Africa and Madagascar, around Sri Lanka and southern India, from southern China to the Philippines, and off northern Australia and New Guinea. They live in family groups, browsing on sea plants – each eating about 40kg (90lb) a day – and only coming to the surface to breathe.

Scientific name	*Dugong dugon*
Classification	Order Sirenia (sea cows)
	Family Dugongidae
Size	Up to about 3m (10ft) long
Distribution	Parts of Indian Ocean, western Pacific Ocean and adjacent seas
Habitat	Shallow coastal waters
Diet	Seaweeds and other aquatic plants
Reproduction	Single young, born after about 12-month gestation

Glossary

Adaptation Changes in characteristics or behaviour that help a creature to survive and thrive in a particular environment.
Adipose fin Small, fleshy fin without *rays*.
Amphibious Describes a creature that can live parts of its life permanently in both water and air.
Antarctic Zone around the South Pole with cold water where surface ice exists for at least part of the year.
Aquatic Living in or related to water.
Arctic Zone around the North Pole with cold water where surface ice exists for at least part of the year.
Baleen Whalebone; the hard but flexible horn-like material found in plates in the mouth of certain whales, used for *filter-feeding*.
Barbel Long, slender sense organ on the head of some fish.
Benthic Bottom-living.
Blow Expulsion of air, water and vapour by a whale from the nostrils on the top of its head.
Blubber Thick layer of fat below the skin of a whale or other marine creature.
Brackish Describes water that is less salty than normal seawater, as in a river estuary or swamp.
Capsule, egg Tough case enclosing an egg, notably of many sharks and related fishes.
Carapace A protective shell or membrane encasing much of the body of a crustacean.
Caudal On or related to the tail; *see p.11*.
Chelipeds The adapted first walking legs of crustaceans, armed with pincers.
Chordate Animal that, at some time in its life history, has a stiffening rod (notochord) in its body; includes *vertebrates* and some others (*see pp.172–313*).
Cnidarian Group of *invertebrates* with a hollow body cavity; includes jellyfish and corals (*see pp.18–27*).
Commensal Living within or on another creature (its host), but not feeding on or damaging the host.
Compressed (of fish) Narrow, or flattened from side to side.
Continental shelf Relatively shallow and flat area of sea-bed extending from the coast around a continent.
Convergent evolution Occurs when two quite different fish or other creatures evolve into a similar form because they live in similar environments.
Crustacean Group of *invertebrates* with a body in segments, jointed limbs and a hard, horny outer skeleton; includes crabs, lobsters and prawns (*see pp.122–149*).
Cryptic colouring Confusing pattern that gives camouflage.
Detritus Broken sandy or gravelly material containing small food organisms or particles.
Dimorphism Having two distinctly different appearances, generally as between male and female.
Dorsal On or related to the back or upper side; *see p.11*.
Echinoderm Group of *invertebrates* with a skeleton of chalky material just below the skin and often with spines; includes sea urchins and starfishes (*see pp.152–171*).
Echo-location Detecting objects and other creatures by sending out sounds and detecting the echoes; highly developed in many whales, dolphins and porpoises.
Ecological niche A particular set of environmental and other conditions.
Endangered Existing in such small numbers that the species is in danger of becoming extinct.
Environment The physical and biological surroundings a creature inhabits.
Family *See p.12.*
Fin Usually flat structure used by fish to propel themselves; *see p.11*.
Filter-feeding Feeding by filtering small organisms (plant and/or animal) from a constant flow of water.
Fish Major group of cold-blooded *vertebrates*, almost all of which are wholly aquatic, having gills and fins, and a skeleton of either cartilage (*see pp.175–197*) or bone (*see pp.198–277*).
Genus *See p.12.*
Gestation Period of egg and embryo development within the parent's body.
Gill rakers Horny growths in some fishes' gills, used for *filter-feeding*.
Gill Respiratory organ of fish and many marine *invertebrates*, by which they obtain oxygen from the water and get rid of carbon dioxide.
Habitat A particular type of *environment*, such the water around a coral reef.
Hermaphrodite Having both

male and female reproductive organs.
Host The organism on or in which a *parasite* lives.
Ichthyologist Scientist who studies fish.
Incubation Period during which eggs develop into *larvae* or young individuals.
Invertebrate Animal without a backbone.
Kelp Type of very large *sessile* seaweed.
Larva (plural larvae) Newly hatched creature, generally retaining the egg's yolk-sac and often having a different form from the adult.
Lateral line Series of sensory receptors, able to detect sound and vibration, along a fish's body; often visible.
Mammal Major group of warm-blooded *vertebrates* that bear live young, which they feed with their mother's milk; marine mammals include seals, whales and their relatives (*see pp.284–313*).
Metabolic rate The speed at which a creature's internal processes – particularly its use of food energy – take place.
Metamorphosis Change from larval or immature into different-shaped adult form.
Mollusc Group of aquatic invertebrates having a soft body with an internal or external shell; includes snails, squids, octopuses and shellfish such as oysters and clams.
Mouth-brooder A fish in which an adult (usually the male) holds the incubating eggs (and sometimes the young larvae) in its mouth.
Nekton Any free-swimming creature of the water column.
Oceanic Describes deep waters beyond the *continental shelf.*
Order *See p.12.*
Organism Any living thing, plant or animal.
Oviparous Egg-laying.
Ovoviviparous Producing eggs that incubate within the female's body without being nourished by her; see also *viviparous*.
Parasite Creature that lives in or on another creature (the *host*) and gets nourishment from the host.
Pectoral (especially of fins) Relating to the front sides of the body; *see p.11.*
Pelagic Living in the water column.
Pelvic (especially of fins) Relating to the rear sides of the body; *see p.11.*
Photophore Light-emitting organ, as in many deep-sea creatures.
Plankton Any plant or animal (referred to as planktonic) that floats in the water, carried by currents rather than its own swimming action.
Pod School or family group of whales, dolphins or seals.
Polar *Arctic* or *Antarctic.*
Range The parts of the world a creature normally inhabits.
Ray Stiff, bony structure supporting a *fin*.
Reptile Major group of cold-blooded, air-breathing vertebrates with external scales or horny plates; includes turtles, crocodiles, lizards and snakes (*see pp.278–283*).
Scales Small bony or horny plates on the skin of many fish, reptiles and other creatures.
School Group of fish or other marine creatures that swim together.
Sessile Attached to rock or other solid material.
Shoal Same as *school.*
Species *See p.12.*
Spine (1) Backbone. (2) Sharp, thorn-like extended *ray* on a fish, or similar sharp structure on another creature, such as a sea urchin.
Subtropical Zone just outside (to north or south) of the tropics, with warm water even in winter.
Swim bladder Gas-filled organ in many fish that gives buoyancy; *see p.12.*
Temperate Zone with cool but ice-free water between the subtropical and polar zones.
Territorial Describes a creature whose individuals or pairs live and breed in their own specific area, usually defending it against others, especially of their own species.
Tropical Permanently warm zone either side of the Equator, in which the sun is directly overhead at some time(s) of the year.
Tubercle Small warty or bony protruberance.
Ventral On or related to the belly or lower side; *see p.11.*
Vertebrate Animal with a backbone.
Viviparous Giving birth to live young that have been nourished by the female during development.
Water column The main mass of water between the bottom and the surface.
Yolk sac Part of an egg containing nutritious yolk to feed the developing egg and *larva*.

Index